A DIPLOMATIC *Life*

From Canberra, the Bush Capital
to the roof of the world, the Himalayas

GRAEME LADE

PUBLISHING PRESS

Copyright © ABLE Publishing Press
First published in Australia in 2024
by ABLE Publishing Press

Text Copyright © Graeme Lade 2025

All rights reserved. No part of this book may be used or reproduced by any means, graphic, electronic, or mechanical, including photocopying, recording, taping or by any information storage retrieval system without the written permission of the copyright owner except in the case of brief quotations embodied in critical articles and reviews.

Because of the dynamic nature of the Internet, any web addresses or links contained in this book may have changed since publication and may no longer be vaild. The views expressed in this work are solely those of the author and do not necessarily reflect the views of the publisher and the publisher hereby disclaims any responsibility for them.

 A catalogue record for this work is available from the National Library of Australia

National Library of Australia Catalogue-in-Publication data:
A Diplomatic Life / Graeme Lade

ISBN:
9781763714465
(Paperback)

*To
Odette,
Alison & Stephanie*

Contents

Prologue 1

What's in a Name? 8

Reflections on the Day I was Born 12

Earliest Memories 17

Toys 23

Becoming a Diplomat 26

On the Road to Hong Kong 38

The Arcane World of China Watching 42
    Beginning Life and Work as a China Watcher 47

The Real China 51

Leaving Hong Kong 66

Changing of the Seasons – Colours of Japan 76

Lost Suitcases 91

Escaping to Thailand in Search of Better Life 98

Tackling Piracy and Other Refugee Issues 109

Memorable Times in Bangkok 117

Present for the Birth of APEC 126
    Monkey Business and Other Memorable Moments in Malaysia 133

Walking the Tightrope Under Mahathir's Malaysia 141

More Stories About Snakes and Other Nasties 150

Hello Uncle Sam 154

Canberra – Interlude 165
    South Asian Nuclear Tests 165
    Travel to Brunei and the Philippines 175
    Travel to Singapore and Malaysia 179

Mission to the Last Hindu Kingdom 182
    Arrival in Kathmandu 186
    Work begins 189
    Presentation of Credentials 195

Commencement of Official Duties 199

Working in the Shadow of the Himalayas 207
    Settling In 207
    Australian Community Forestry Project 209
    West Seti Hydropower Project 216

Cricket Diplomacy 222
    Education 226

Nepal – A Case Study on Finding a Durable Solution for Bhutanese Refugees 235

Off the Beaten Track in Nepal 254

 More Adventurous Pursuits 267

Chitwan National Park – Observing Wildlife 280

Some Memorable People 290

Given Up for Dead on Everest 302

Yeti Airline Crash in Lukla 310

Looking to the Future and Moving On 317

Impressions of Hanoi 329
    Hanoi Then 329
    How Has Hanoi Changed? 331

Motorbikes 332
Changing Fortunes 336

Reflections on Modernised Hanoi 341
Changing Behaviour 345
Food 349

A Sense of Place – Moving Back to Manila from Yangon 354

And Finally 361

Prologue

Having undertaken my high school and university studies in Canberra, I could say my formative years were spent in the bush capital of Australia. In January 1971, I commenced training to become a member of the Australian Diplomatic Service.

Prior to this I had never travelled overseas, but over the next thirty-eight years, I was to serve at Australian diplomatic posts in Hong Kong, Tokyo – twice, Bangkok, Kuala Lumpur and Washington, DC. My final assignment with the Australian Department of Foreign Affairs and Trade was as Ambassador to Kathmandu, home to much of the Himalayas, the 'Roof of the World'.

I feel privileged to have been able to serve in these countries and get to know first-hand their people, culture and history. I am also grateful for having been able to experience many memorable times during my travels, as well as to better appreciate living in these countries.

In 2018, I undertook a memoir writing course in Manila. The course was delivered by an American-based Filipino writer, Oscar Penaranda. A number of sections in what follows flow directly from elements in that course but fill in gaps in my early life and experiences. One distinction made in the course was the difference between autobiography and memoir.

My aim is not to produce an autobiography, but instead a collection of memoirs, anecdotes and observations. In so doing, I hope to provide some insight into the varied duties of an Australian diplomat overseas, impressions of life during my overseas service and some memorable experiences. Working for the government overseas also provides an opportunity to meet many interesting and influential people.

During my working life, I was conscious of the many misconceptions about the work of a diplomat. One very commonly held view was that diplomats are on a never-ending round of parties, getting stuck into champagne and caviar. Diplomatic receptions are important as opportunities to meet and interact with people of value to Australia's broader interests, but they are only a small part of the job. Generally, as I hope the following pages illustrate, a diplomat has to work hard, put in long hours and sometimes work in difficult circumstances.

In 1989, I was course director for that year's diplomatic intake. Their course provided an introduction to the role of the Department of Foreign Affairs and Trade (DFAT) and how it fitted into the Australian government structure. It also included brief introductions to international economics and foreign policy and, as a first for such courses, introductions to Australian Aboriginal spirituality, society and culture, as well as a short overview of Australian history provided by Professor Manning Clark.

In my role as course director, I provided a brief introduction to the role of a diplomat. In preparing my presentation, I had consulted several known writings on diplomatic practice, including Sir Harold Nicolson's book, *Diplomacy* and Sir Ernest Satow's, *A Guide to Diplomatic Practice*.

I also referred to two quotations on the role of a diplomat. The first was, 'An ambassador is an honest gentleman sent to lie abroad for the good of his country.' This seems to have been attributed to Sir Henry Wotton in 1604. The second was, 'A diplomat is someone who can tell you to go to hell in such a way that you look forward to the trip.' There is some uncertainty about who owned this saying or close variations of it, but the most likely source seems to have been US travel writer, Caskie Stinnett.

There are some generally agreed requirements for being a good diplomat. These include an ability to effectively represent the interests of your country to your host government, to demonstrate tact in your overseas dealings, to be adaptable and, very importantly, to be a good listener. Sometimes these skills can be severely tested.

There were some very capable and clever people in the 1989 intake. The majority entered the department full of enthusiasm and some felt, even though they were novices in diplomacy, that it was their role to change the world. For me, this led to what was not always the easiest of roles. I had to emphasise that, whether they liked it or not, when they were representing Australia overseas they had to faithfully reflect Australian government policy and not their own preferences as to what the policies should be.

There were two issues in particular that challenged me. Both were strongly held opinions among quite a number of the group. The first issue related to the handling of refugee policy. Many of the group felt that Australia was not as welcoming as it could be. We attended a briefing at the Department of Immigration and Multicultural Affairs. The officer giving the briefing was quite young, and not so experienced dealing with such a vocal group. She sought to outline Australian refugee policies in a factual way, but was, alas, regularly interrupted by the members of my group.

Even though it was an unpopular thing for me to do, I had to tell the group that the lady was trying to do her job, they should have given her a fair hearing, and that when they were overseas they had to faithfully reflect Australian positions whether or not they agreed with them.

The second issue related to Australian uranium exports. As a group, when we visited the Northern Territory, we included a visit to the Ranger Uranium Mine. This had featured in visits by earlier DFAT intake groups. Uranium exports were a significant export earner for Australia. Exports were covered by tight safeguards agreements.

My stay in Japan familiarised me with the workings of these agreements. Japan had a number of nuclear power stations which contributed considerably to meeting Japan's electric power needs. Australian uranium was essential to the running of these power stations.

As the Fukushima tragedy in 2011 illustrated, however, these power stations were not immune to natural disasters despite the rigid controls in place to try and maintain safety. Fukushima aside, the Japanese nuclear power stations were, for the most part, safely and effectively operated. I visited several power stations, including Tokai Mura on Honshu and Kyushu Electric's nuclear power plant in Sendai. One thing that struck me about these power stations was that they were generally in scenically beautiful and isolated locations.

Many in my group were strongly opposed to uranium exports and saw it as contributing to the risk of greater global nuclearisation, not just power stations but also weapons. I had to explain to the group that whether they liked it or not, uranium exports were strictly controlled and an important export earner for Australia. Just as I had experienced in Japan, this was an important factor in our bilateral relationship. I told them it was conceivable that some of them could be assigned to other countries where Australian uranium was exported. It was useful therefore for them to be aware of the trade and how it was controlled.

Overall, I found my experience working as a diplomat for Australia rewarding and fulfilling. I saw my role as one of seeking to pursue my duties in an honest and effective way. Some of my duties, such as when working with Indochinese refugees, played into what were important priorities for the government of the day. I saw my contribution, however, as part of the bigger picture and not one where I was seeking to play a major role in shaping government policy.

I enjoyed my periods of overseas service, although looking back my favourite assignments were Hong Kong, Malaysia and Nepal. I think it is quite common for people to attach importance and favourable memories to their first overseas assignment. For me, that was Hong Kong.

From 1977 to 1998, I was accompanied by my then wife, Christine, and later our two daughters, Alison and Stephanie. Following our divorce in 2001 and, some years later, from 2006 on I have been accompanied by my current partner, Odette, who is a Filipina diplomat. After completion of my assignment in Nepal in 2009, I have accompanied her on her home-based assignments in Manila, and her overseas assignments to Hanoi, Yangon and Melbourne.

Malaysia was special for me in a number of ways. We had a nice house and garden, the work was always interesting, although at times quite challenging because under Prime Minister Mahathir relations often did not run smoothly. My daughters, Alison and Stephanie, were old enough to appreciate the experience and we were able to travel extensively as a family and enjoy some of the many scenic attractions Malaysia has to offer, as well as enjoy the food and cultural experiences in different parts of the country.

Prior to taking up my assignment as ambassador to Nepal, I had determined I would make it my last overseas assignment, as I wished to retire while I was still young and fit enough to do something else. Having whetted my appetite to some extent with some of our discretionary aid program activities in Malaysia, I thought I would like to undertake work with non-government organisations. Nepal opened the way for me after retirement to do some voluntary work with the Fred Hollows Foundation in its quest to reduce avoidable blindness, and separately led me to being able to work as a volunteer board member for the Australian Cervical Cancer Foundation, in its quest to promote cervical cancer as a preventable disease and one which hopefully can be eliminated in Australia by no later than 2035.

Nepal was a wonderful place to finish my diplomatic career. It is a beautiful country. On a clear day when you can see the Himalayas, it is quite magical. At the time of my arrival in Nepal, Nepal was the last remaining Hindu kingdom in the world. Nepal was also the birthplace of Buddha. For these reasons, Nepal was culturally and historically interesting. The Nepalese people were generally friendly and hospitable and we formed many close and lasting friendships. Having completed her assignment in Canberra, Odette was able to join me for the last year of my assignment in Nepal.

2008 was a momentous year for Nepal. The long-running Maoist insurgency was more or less brought to a close with the arrival of the Maoists coming out of the jungle and into city life, especially in Kathmandu. Odette and I witnessed the protracted and difficult negotiations to bring the Maoists into the political mainstream, culminating in general elections in April 2008, and the abdication of the king a few months later.

Although the climate in Kathmandu was nominally seasonal, the cold weather time of the year was short and usually mild, and it often seemed like there were two spring seasons. This led to extended periods of flowers blooming and, for me, good weather to keep on playing tennis for most of the year. In the colder months of December, January and February, the local people burned charcoal for heating as well as for cooking. These were the worst months to visit as there was usually a layer of smog which affected visibility and kept the mountains veiled for much of the time.

With the end of the Maoist insurgency, there was a relaxation in the DFAT travel advice for Nepal and this made it easier for Odette and me to undertake some travel. We had particularly memorable visits to the Chitwan National Park – we saw plenty of rhinos, but alas no tigers – and to go trekking along the Annapurna circuit from Pokhara and enjoy fantastic mountain views, especially at breakfast time.

As a final comment on diplomatic life, the career offers you the chance to get to know countries in a deeper and more meaningful way than would be possible as a casual visitor. It did worry me that the constant need to move on, generally after three years, could be unsettling for my daughters. They had to make and break friendships, and this as well as having to adapt to new schools would have been difficult. On the other hand, I hope it broadened their outlook and acceptance and understanding of other cultures.

For the diplomat, there is the chance to meet many interesting and influential people. This too contributes to better understanding of the country of your assignment. In the following pages I have reflected on some of the notable people who I had dealings with.

I have also sought to provide some vignettes on different life experiences while living overseas. My aim is to create a sense of the varied and mostly positive nature of life as a diplomat overseas. I have also sought to portray some of the more interesting or challenging work experiences.

Overall, based on my experiences, I hope others will come to appreciate that diplomacy is an honourable but, at times, challenging profession. For me, it has been a satisfying and rewarding experience.

What's in a Name?

From what I understand, my parents had little trouble choosing a name for me when I was born. The issue was one of spelling.

My father wanted to name me in honour of his favourite cousin, Graeme Lewis. While still in his late teens, my father had been sent to England by the Royal Australian Navy to further his engineering studies. For much of the time, he lived with Graeme, his brother Ian and their parents. On my mother's Scottish side of the family, Graham was widely used, including her father, Dudley Graham Macdougal.

I became Graeme, not Graham.

Graeme Lewis was to influence the course of my life in other ways besides my name. Towards the end of World War II, Graeme Lewis enlisted in the British Royal Air Force and was selected to study Japanese. At the end of the war, he returned to Australia and joined the Australian Department of External Affairs. Given his expertise in Japanese, he served at least twice in the Australian embassy in Tokyo.

In third and fourth year at high school in Canberra, career counsellors would visit the school to help us students make up our minds about what career paths we wished to pursue after graduating from high school. Initially, I did not have much of an idea what to do other than going to university, not even knowing what course I wished to pursue.

The only profession I continued to have any interest in was architecture, but the career counsellors sought to discourage this as my hands tended to sweat and I usually smudged my work in technical drawing classes. The career counsellors were keen to push dentistry, as there was then, as now, a shortage of dentists in Australia. I could think of nothing worse than spending all day staring into someone's mouth.

One day I accompanied my parents to see Graeme Lewis at his home in Canberra. While they were busy talking, I was browsing through some of Graeme's photo albums, especially those covering his time in Japan. I was impressed with the colourful festivals, the temples and other scenic attractions he had been able to visit during his time in Japan. It was then I had my 'eureka' moment. I decided I would study Japanese and seek to join the Australian Foreign Service.

The rest, as they say, is history. I duly studied Japanese history, language and culture at the Australian National University and was accepted into the then Department of External Affairs. During my working life, I had two assignments in Japan totalling almost eight years. I had the chance to enjoy the scenic and cultural wonders of Japan, as introduced to me initially by the photo albums I had looked at while at Graeme Lewis' home.

I had two other key memories of Graeme Lewis. One day, we had gone to visit his house in Canberra, and he had a new coffee-table book on Greece sitting appropriately enough on the coffee table in his living room. Graeme encouraged us to look at the large photo in the book illustrating one of Greece's best-known landmarks, the Parthenon in Athens. We could see straight away why he wanted us to look at this photograph. There, clearly in the foreground, was Graeme himself.

Graeme said he had been browsing in a bookshop and just happened to pick up this book. When he saw the photo, he knew he had to buy a copy.

The other memory of Graeme was a sad one. From early 1974 to March 1975, Graeme served as charge d'affaires at the Australian embassy in Hanoi. He had flown to Vientiane to meet the incoming Australian ambassador. From Vientiane, he was travelling on an Air Vietnam flight to Saigon. Exactly what happened is unclear, but it seems the plane was brought down by an anti-aircraft rocket over Pleiku in the Central Highlands of Vietnam. Presumably, it was mistaken for a military aircraft by either the pro-communist forces or the pro-South Vietnam and American forces. No trace of the plane wreckage or the bodies of those onboard the flight, including Graeme Lewis, have to this date been found.

I was on duty in the Department of Foreign Affairs in Canberra at the time. Kim Jones, who was head of the staffing branch, called me into his office following the disappearance of the plane. Kim had served with Graeme in Tokyo and knew of my family connections with him. Kim had informed Graeme's immediate family, primarily Ian Lewis. Kim informed me, so I could arrange to let other family members know. I really appreciated Kim's thoughtfulness, but I should not have been surprised, I found Kim always to be someone for whom I had the utmost respect.

A few weeks later, a memorial service was held at Saint Andrew's Presbyterian Church in Canberra. I attended the service together with other members of my family, as well as Graeme's immediate family. The service was attended by Gough Whitlam who was Australian Prime Minister at the time. As family members, we were individually introduced to the prime minister.

Dr Peter Edwards noted in his inaugural lecture in honour of RG Neale, the first editor of historical documents at the Department of Foreign Affairs, that Graeme Lewis as a serving foreign affairs officer had, perhaps, been the last Australian casualty of the Vietnam War.

A plaque commemorating Graeme Lewis has been attached to a wall at the Australian embassy in Hanoi. I have been privileged to visit the plaque and pay my respects to someone who gave me much more than just my name.

In 2019 when I called on Craig Chittick, who was then Australian ambassador to Vietnam, we went out to look at the plaque. I had told Craig about my personal connection. The plaque had been moved. It was no longer affixed to the wall but set into a garden setting.

Reflections on the Day I was Born

Apart from marking my coming into the world, 19 September 1948 seems largely to have been uneventful. Only one notable person whose name meant anything to me was listed as being born on this day. That was the British actor Jeremy Irons. No notable people were listed as dying on this day and no events of earth-shaking importance were recorded.

However, in September 1948, either before or after my date of birth, a number of significant events were registered. In chronological order, those events were the abdication of Queen Wilhelmina of the Netherlands and the crowning of her daughter Juliana as the new queen; the northern half of the Korean Peninsula being formally declared as the Democratic People's Republic of Korea with Kim Il-Sung as prime minister; the death of the founder of Pakistan, Muhammad Ali Jinnah, and a day later, the Indian Army invaded the state of Hyderabad; and the Honda Motor Company was founded in Japan.

On reflection, three of these events resonate with things I subsequently experienced later in my life.

A Diplomatic Life

Beginning with the link of the establishment of the Honda Motor Company in Japan – I was based in Japan from 1975 to 1980. Honda had initially established its reputation by manufacturing high-quality motorbikes before transitioning to produce motor cars. In 1976, Honda announced it would be replicating one of its new model cars for export to Australia. Basically, there were a number of modifications that needed to be made to satisfy Australian requirements, the most significant of which was meeting Australian emission control standards.

Along with several other officers at the Australian embassy, I placed an advance order for one of the cars on the Australian export production line. In early 1977, my cobalt blue Honda Accord Hatchback was delivered to me at the embassy. This was the first brand-new car I had ever owned and, as such, it was special to me.

I was able to drive my Honda for a few more years till the end of my posting in Japan. I then shipped it back to Australia, where I continued to enjoy using it till 1982, when I was reluctantly required to sell it because I was again being transferred overseas.

There was one particular, and somewhat unusual, memory I associate with my Honda. One weekend I drove from Canberra to Sydney to visit relatives. Before returning to Canberra, my then wife and I decided to stop by the Sydney Fish Market. Although small compared to the famous Tsukiji Fish Market I had become familiar with in Tokyo, the Sydney Fish Market is nonetheless a fun place to visit, full of life and action, and of course wonderful fresh seafood.

We decided to purchase a couple of live Queensland mud crabs to take back and eat in Canberra. The claws and legs of the crabs were suitably trussed, or so we thought, and we placed the crabs in an open area of the car's luggage compartment. We wanted to ensure the crabs remained alive and fresh when we got back to Canberra some three and a half hours later. For people familiar with the Honda Accord

Hatchback, you will know there was no separation between the luggage compartment and the rear seats of the car.

We had not progressed very far along the road back to Canberra, when we heard strange noises emanating from the rear of the car. I stopped to check. I saw that one of the crabs had broken free of the truss holding its legs and was crawling at will around the back of the car, but fortunately its claw truss remained firmly in place. I also checked to see if it would be possible for the crab to crawl out of the luggage compartment area and potentially reach me in the driver's seat. I was reasonably confident it would not be able to do so. However, for the remaining several hours of the trip back to Canberra, our trip was accompanied by the strange scratching and crawling noises of the crab in the back of the car.

After sharing each other's company for several hours, by the time we reached Canberra I felt a certain affinity with the two crabs. When my then wife instructed that it was the man's job to kill the crabs in preparation for cooking; this was a task I approached with some reluctance, even dread. Nonetheless, I rose to the occasion, although somewhat nervously. To play the role of the executioner, I had to insert a sharp skewer between the eyes of the crabs and into their brains. I was assured this was a quick and – I don't know how it could be claimed with certainty – painless way to kill the crabs. It was just the same, with some trepidation, that I carried out the execution of the crabs successfully.

It almost seems sadistic to say after the affinity we had established in sharing the journey from Sydney to Canberra together, but the crabs were delicious!

The second experience that comes to mind from the events listed for September 1948 involves both the Netherlands and Muhammad Ali Jinnah.

A Diplomatic Life

By way of brief background, I took up the appointment as Australian Ambassador to Nepal in January 2006. When I arrived in Kathmandu, one long pending and unresolved issue remained; the fate of over 100,000 Bhutanese refugees being cared for by UNHCR in refugee camps in Nepal. After seventeen years, no meaningful progress had been made in finding a lasting solution for these refugees. Accordingly, it was becoming increasingly difficult to raise the money needed to support them as donor fatigue was becoming more apparent.

In the meantime, a contact group had been established in Geneva to consider the fate of the Bhutanese refugees. Participating countries were Australia, Canada, Denmark, Netherlands, New Zealand, Norway and the United States. Coinciding with Norwegian chairing of the group in Geneva, the Norwegian Ambassador had established a corresponding Group in Kathmandu. Soon after my arrival in Kathmandu, Australia assumed the chair of the Geneva contact group and, in turn, I became chair of the Kathmandu contact group.

As Canada, the Netherlands and New Zealand did not at the time have embassies in Kathmandu, I continued as chair of the Kathmandu group when one of these countries assumed the chair in Geneva. Ultimately, I chaired the Kathmandu group for about two and a half years.

I was required to visit New Delhi once or twice a year to meet with the representatives of Australian agencies accredited to Nepal from New Delhi, but without on the ground representation in Kathmandu. In my role as chair of the Kathmandu contact group, I also had to meet with the Canadian, Netherlands and New Zealand Ambassadors to advise and consult with them on the activities of the Kathmandu contact group on Bhutanese refugees.

On one of these visits – I think it was in 2007 – the Royal Netherlands Ambassador asked me to meet him at his residence.

Normally I would meet the ambassadors at their embassy chanceries or at a quiet restaurant for lunch. It turned out that the Netherlands ambassador's residence was in a smart-looking colonial style bungalow, at least sixty, and more probably eighty years old.

Before we got down to business, the ambassador took me on a tour of the public reception areas of the house. The house, I learned, had been the home of Muhammad Ali Jinnah prior to the partition of India in 1947. The ambassador also showed me a photo contained in a biography of Jinnah. The photo showed Jinnah standing in his study. Although the books on the shelves were clearly different, in other respects the study looked much the same as it appeared in the photo.

I felt honoured to have had the opportunity to witness the place where Jinnah had lived at the time of partition and, more particularly, to see the study where Jinnah likely spent many hours and to see that it remained little changed. On the other hand, it brought back the horrors of that tragic period of South Asian history which resulted in large-scale violence, in which thousands of people were killed and hundreds of thousands of people were forced to flee for their lives and become refugees.

Unfortunately, this tragedy continues to be played out today, with continuing tensions and differences between India and Pakistan and the outbreak of periodic armed clashes along their shared borders, or in the contested state of Kashmir.

Nonetheless, I was grateful to the Royal Netherlands Ambassador for sharing this experience with me.

In conclusion while 19 September 1948 was itself uneventful and basically just an ordinary day, events in the period close to that date have evoked, for me, some special and unique memories.

Earliest Memories

I do not know exactly how old I was, but my earliest memories date back to when I was about three when our family travelled by plane to Darwin, where my father had been assigned for his job.

I suspect it was not the first time I had travelled by plane, but I remember nothing of those earlier flights. However, there were two things about the flight to Darwin I distinctly remember. The first was looking out the plane window and seeing the fluffy white clouds. They looked so soft, like a big bed made out of cotton wool. The second was being fascinated by the pocket in the back of the seat in front. I don't properly remember what the fascination was. I think it was more being intrigued by the fact that you could hide or put things in the pocket, rather than being interested in the actual contents of the pocket.

As I was about six when we left Darwin, I have many vivid memories of life there, but there is a blur in what order I remember things.

I know it was soon after our arrival in Darwin that one shocking incident occurred. Our house was a typical Darwin stilt house with an open area underneath. This area included the laundry. I was sitting quietly with my mother and sister Penny on the back steps, when suddenly Penny fell between the slats of the steps and landed on the top of the laundry tub.

I ran down the stairs with my mother, finding Penny in the laundry tub. She had banged her head badly, but I do not remember if there was blood or if Penny was moving. My mother rushed Penny to Dr Hartley at the local clinic. I cannot remember what happened next, but fortunately Penny fully recovered.

I don't think I knew Dr Hartley's name at the time, but he was to become a regular feature in our lives in Darwin. There were two other incidents involving Penny and one involving me.

One incident involved Dr Hartley having prescribed gentian violet for Penny to treat some type of oral condition. When my mother tried to apply it, Penny reacted violently and spat it out. I ran into the bathroom to see what all the noise was about and saw purple stains all over Penny and the bathtub. I was surprised that one small amount of gentian violet could create such a mess.

On another occasion, Dr Hartley came to our house to treat Penny for a boil on her chest. I saw Penny being held firmly by my parents on a table in our living room and then hearing her screams as Dr Hartley lanced the boil. Penny's screams pierced me as well. When we saw each other in December 2022, Penny and I reminisced about this painful experience.

I, myself, had developed a bit of a history with bouts of tonsillitis and so it was recommended I have my tonsils removed. I was admitted to the children's ward at Darwin Hospital. I don't think I was yet five years old. Dr Hartley was the attending physician. I was strapped onto a narrow bed, which at the time, I thought it was an ironing board. I remember Dr Hartley looking down at me and saying something, but after that my mind was a blank as the anaesthetic took effect.

I think I only had two days stay in the hospital, my parents coming to visit me once, bringing me a toy clock to help me learn how to tell the time. However, there was one other experience in the hospital that was to have a lasting effect on me.

In the bed next to me was a child with Down's syndrome. His mother was staying in the hospital with him. I was impressed with how caring she was with her child. However, because I was alone, she included me in her activities with her son. I appreciated her attention towards me and her efforts to explain what was wrong with her son. One particularly memorable moment was the three of us looking together out the hospital window at the people below and the sea in the distance.

After this experience, I came to appreciate that people with Down's syndrome were human beings with real feelings. Many years later, when I was travelling home from university in Canberra by bus, I was upset when I saw some other young people making fun of a couple of Down's syndrome teenagers travelling on the same bus. Despite the way they had been teased, I was struck by how dignified and happy the Down's syndrome teenagers still seemed to be when they alighted the bus.

Some years later when I was Australian Ambassador to Nepal, I appreciated the opportunity to lend my support to a centre catering to Down's syndrome children. We provided some financial support through the embassy's small grant program, the Direct Assistance Program. Odette joined me in visiting the centre. What impressed me was that the staff and parents involved with running the centre showed the same strong caring attitude to these children that I had witnessed all those years ago in the Darwin Hospital.

I started school in Darwin, but my memories of that time are sketchy. I vaguely remember the simple readers we used to learn how to read. I recall the main characters were Dick and Jane.

Another memory that vividly remains from my school days in Darwin is walking home from school one afternoon, hand-in-hand with a girl in my class, whom my parents later told me was called Bronwen. I have no other memories of Bronwen other than holding her hand and her attendance at my birthday party. Suddenly, I tripped. My foot had become entangled in a loop of long grass. I don't know if there was something sharp on the tarred road, but my knee was bleeding badly. As it turned out, my parents had seen everything and came rushing towards us. For me, it was another trip to the clinic to get my knee cleaned and dressed in a bandage.

My parents suggested Bronwen was my first girlfriend. I know she did come to my birthday party, one of only two my father was able to attend while I was growing up. There was another girl present, Robin Chan, who was also from my class at school and whose parents my parents got to know very well while we lived in Darwin. Robin's father was Harry Chan who ran the grocery store my parents used regularly and later on Harry Chan was to become the first Chinese Lord Mayor of Darwin. When I was about sixteen, Harry Chan and his wife, accompanied by Robin, visited my parents in Canberra. I don't think I would have recognised Robin if she had not been with her parents.

I don't know if it was the same birthday, but I was given a blackboard and easel which my father set up for me to use under the house. The first time I tried to use it I got a rude shock. We disturbed a nest of young snakes. Where there are baby snakes there is probably a mother nearby. I don't know how my father got rid of the snakes, but he did and after that, I was safely able to use the blackboard.

Adjacent to the stairs leading to the door to our house stood a tall paw-paw tree. When we came home in the evening there was a frenzy of activity at the top of the tree as we disturbed the flying foxes gorging themselves on the fruit. I don't know if we ever got any fruit for ourselves.

Another memory I had of those early days in Darwin was being made aware of the damage caused by the Japanese bombing of Darwin in February 1942. When we lived in Darwin the ruins of the old post office remained just that – ruins. I remember driving past the site many times. What I had not appreciated till much later was that the postmaster, his family and the post office staff had all died in the bombing, ten persons in all. The site has now been cleaned up.

I also remember driving along the shore near Darwin and seeing the rusting hulks of ships that were sunk in the Japanese air raids. At the time, I'm sure I had little sense of the enormity of the Japanese attacks on Darwin, nor did I have any appreciation that several hundred people were killed. However, I do recall I was aware (probably because my parents had told me) that the damage had been caused during Japanese air raids in World War II.

In 2018, I read a book called *1942* by Bob Wurth which outlined in more detail the air raids on Darwin. I had not appreciated how extensive Japanese aerial and submarine activity in and around Australia had been. Darwin had been targeted more times than I envisioned, as had the towns of Broome and Wyndham, and the casualties were more than widely claimed. The Japanese submarine activity along the eastern coast of Australia was also more intensive than just the surprise raid by mini-subs into Sydney Harbour.

One of the most significant memories of Darwin was welcoming my younger brother, Neil, into the world. I don't remember him as a tiny baby, but I do remember seeing him in his cot which he often seemed to share with a gecko. Neil would have been about two years old when we left Darwin. A more abiding memory I have of him is when he was slightly older, seeing him sitting with his favourite stuffed toy. I'm not sure if it was a tiger or leopard, but it was named Tigger. I suspect Penny may have given the toy this name. Whatever, Neil and Tigger seemed inseparable.

While I have other memories of our time in Darwin, there was one other memory that had a lasting impression on me. One day, our school took us on an excursion to the botanic gardens where we witnessed the performance of a corroboree. I remain impressed with the performance of Aboriginal dancers to this day. Their mimicking of the movements of animals, especially kangaroos, is uncanny and lifelike. The rhythm and lightness of their dancing in time to the music of the didgeridoo and music sticks is mesmerising. I was fascinated. There was something about how thin most of the dancers' legs were, but I think this contributed to the apparent lightness of their movements.

I have subsequently seen corroborees shown on TV, but that first time in Darwin, where we watched the dances in an outdoor setting with trees all around, remains vividly with me.

When we left Darwin, we were travelling in a plane that was essentially doing the 'milk-run', stopping at many small airports to deliver mail. I remember the names of the places we stopped at; Tennant Creek, Katherine, Mount Isa, Longreach, Roma and finally Sydney, though I don't specifically remember anything about the airports themselves.

The plane was quite small, maybe it was a DC-3, and parts of the flight were quite turbulent. Many people, not me, were throwing up and my mother was trying to help others around where we were sitting.

Safely back in Sydney, we then moved to our apartment in Cavendish Hall at 2 Billyard Avenue, Elizabeth Bay.

Toys

Like most boys growing up in Australia in the 1950s and 60s, I had my fair share of toy cars and building blocks. My brother and I would make roads in the garden to play with our cars and I'd spend many hours using the building blocks to design new houses, especially with a fourth bedroom so I could have a room to myself, as well as a covered garage for our car. Although I spent many hours with these toys, there were two other toys with which I did not spend so much time but which were memorable for other reasons.

When I was seven, my parents took me to visit Santa Claus at the Grace Brothers Department Store in Sydney. (The building remains, but it no longer serves as a department store.) This was my first and only meeting with Santa Claus. When asked what I wanted for a Christmas present, I replied, 'a helicopter'. I wanted a real helicopter, not a toy.

Come Christmas Day when our family was sitting around opening presents, there among my collection was the gift from Santa. There it was – a toy helicopter. As far as toy helicopters went, it was smart-looking, the rotor blades turned freely and it was a decent size – from memory about 25cm long. But it was not real. Santa had clearly got things wrong. I was disappointed. The practicalities of how a seven-year-old boy could fly a helicopter never entered my head. I had had my heart set on getting a *real* helicopter.

I cannot remember exactly, however, I'm sure my parents would have noticed my disappointment and admonished me, as they invariably did by referring to the *worse off* children in the poor regions of Asia or Africa whenever my sister, brother or I complained about not having the toys we wanted, eating food we didn't like or wearing clothes that were different to those of other children.

Thinking back to this incident, I don't remember how my attraction to or fascination with helicopters came about.

I subsequently had the chance to fly on helicopters in Thailand, Malaysia and Nepal. For the most part, they were uncomfortable and incredibly noisy and certainly not my preferred way to fly.

When I was about ten years old, our family moved to the suburb of West Pymble located in Sydney's North Shore region. Living in a house opposite us was a boy named Robert, who was about the same age as me. Robert and I would, from time to time, go to the nearest movie theatre about 5 or 6km away in the suburb of Gordon. Generally, we would only go to watch a movie if there was a *Tarzan* movie screening.

I know it was certainly the case for both Robert and me, that we enjoyed watching Tarzan swing from tree-to-tree through the jungle. It looked like a lot of fun. We thought to ourselves, *Wouldn't it be great if we could have our own Tarzan-style rope system to swing through the bush?* Our house was facing directly opposite the Lane Cove National Park and Robert's house was adjacent to the park. Somehow, we persuaded Robert's father to help us attach a couple of 'Tarzan ropes' to trees near the edge of the park so we could swing from one rock ledge to another.

The ideal time to play this game was just after we had returned from watching a *Tarzan* movie. Like Tarzan, we could swing from tree to tree, and like Tarzan we could scream as we sailed through the bush. Unlike Tarzan, there were no wild animals, although undoubtedly there would have been snakes, but I never recall seeing any there. Unlike Tarzan, there was no Jane waiting to be rescued from one of our rock ledges.

However, for Robert and me, it was exhilarating pretending to be Tarzan in our own little patch of bush, even if it was not as dense as the movie jungle. It was fun to feel the breeze swish past your ears as you swung from one tree to another rock ledge. Screaming Tarzan-style as you went added to the fun. These were truly happy times, but unfortunately for me, they lasted less than two years as my family then moved to Canberra.

Becoming a Diplomat

The road from university to becoming a full-fledged diplomat remains a bit of a blur; things happened so fast.

I remember attending written tests along with many other hopefuls but cannot recall much about the details of these tests, other than I know that our ability to conceptualise and summarise written texts were tested as part of the selection process.

Another important component of the selection process was the series of personal interviews and group discussions in Canberra. This brought together aspiring diplomats from all around Australia.

I remember being concerned in the group discussions that time was rapidly drawing to a close and I had not had a chance to say anything. In one sense this was good, as our group had been dominated by a couple of very outspoken and loquacious individuals, who gave the rest of us little chance to demonstrate foot in mouth disease. However, I knew I had to say something and show I could think on my feet.

I therefore determined I would get in first and lead off on the next discussion topic, whatever it might be. The next topic sought our views on capital punishment. This was a subject I had never really thought about, but my die was cast and lead off on the topic I did. My views

A Diplomatic Life

formed as I spoke, and I remember arguing that the death penalty did not serve as an effective deterrent to serious crime. Little did I know at the time how big a factor issues relating to the death penalty would play in my subsequent career, especially in Kuala Lumpur and back on the Singapore desk in Canberra.

While in Kuala Lumpur, most staff were affected in some way by the ongoing process to try and obtain a reprieve for an Australian man sentenced to death for drug trafficking. Back on the Singapore desk, I was involved in the efforts to save a Vietnamese Australian who had been sentenced to death for drug smuggling. In both cases, our efforts were unsuccessful.

A further key element of the selection process was the cocktail party. Some of our fellow aspiring diplomats must have seen this as a chance to relax after a very taxing and tiring series of interviews. Getting a bit tipsy did not assist their chances of selection. I actually enjoyed the event as I found several of the senior departmental officers I met had served in or worked in Japan and were keen to share their impressions, as well as seek my views.

I obviously spoke persuasively and eloquently enough in the group discussion and handled the cocktail reception well enough to convince the selection panel, as I was offered a place in the next diplomatic intake.

On 13 January 1971, I joined my fellow diplomatic intake colleagues at John McEwen House in Canberra to commence our induction course. This was to provide a crash course on issues such as international law, economics and international relations for those of us who were not particularly versed in such fields. From memory, that was probably the majority of our group, as amongst our numbers were an astrophysicist, a clergyman, a medical doctor, a couple of mathematicians, several linguists and a motley crew of other specialisations.

I was pleased to see our group included Les Rowe, whom I recall had performed well in our discussion group. I continued to respect Les through our many years of joint service in the department. There was only one person in the group whom I otherwise knew. That was Bob Tyson. Bob and I were both graduates of the Australian National University and, one year, had both obtained holiday jobs during the long university vacation, at the then Department of External Affairs. However, it was only during the course of self-introductions when I learnt Bob and I shared one other thing in common – our birthday. The same day, but different years.

The months together on the induction course were not just a time for learning, but also a time for developing friendships and bonding with our fellow course members. This included, after three months, a group of junior diplomats from other countries. I enjoyed interacting with the foreign participants as most of them had already been working for a few years, and they brought insights to the course from their own experiences. However, most of all, they were engaging and interesting people.

The Tanzanian was a real live wire with a great sense of humour. He was keen to get the most out of his time in Australia and was willing to try anything. Then there was the Fijian participant who at every opportunity sought to remind us of Fiji's sugar industry. The Afghan was always smiling but never said much and had an aura of mystery about him, as he frequently failed to get back to Canberra on time after the weekends. The Singaporean was quiet, but very insightful when he spoke. It was no surprise to see him appointed to very senior positions in the Singapore government later on, including as Secretary of the Ministry of Foreign Affairs. Another person who left a lasting impression on me was the Nepalese participant who was a softly spoken person, but very kind and sincere.

Given the subsequent course of events in the countries of several of the foreign participants, I often wondered what became of them. This included the Afghan, the Vietnamese and the Iranian participants. At least with the Afghan, I was to learn many years later that he was a survivor.

The friendships we formed during those training days were in many cases short-lived, as we all ended up going different ways. Even amongst our Australian colleagues, there were many I never caught up with again, as our career paths did not cross. Of the foreign participants, I only ever met up again with the Thai during my assignment in Bangkok, the Malaysian during my assignment in Kuala Lumpur and the Nepalese during my time in Kathmandu. He was still the same quiet, kind and sincere person, although, unfortunately, his hearing had badly deteriorated, and I had to shout to maintain a conversation.

I had one other surprise encounter. One day in Kuala Lumpur, I think it was in 1994, I had arranged to meet for lunch with my former Malaysian colleague and he asked if I would mind if he brought along someone else. Much to my surprise, it was none other than our Afghan colleague. He had survived the political turmoil in his own country, probably largely by being able to spend most of his working life overseas. He was, at the time, representing the Afghan government in Malaysia. After more than twenty years, he had not changed much in appearance, but he was a much more self-confident person and no longer as quiet, but he still retained an air of mystery, especially as to how he had survived and continued to represent Afghanistan after all those years.

Back to the training course, there were lots of lectures and course assignments. We had some excellent presenters. Our presenters on economics were both excellent. One of them was Chris Richardson who I often see interviewed on TV regarding both international and domestic economic developments. The other was Don Stammer, who continues to do a lot of economic writing. We were lucky to have two such outstanding young economists as our presenters. This was in stark contrast to other economic presenters I have encountered in later training courses, who made economics seem as dull and boring as their presentations.

I recall a fascinating presentation by Sir Peter Heydon, who I think at the time was Secretary of the Department of Immigration, but he provided us with a brief history of Australia's foreign relations. For example, I was surprised to learn from him that at one time, towards the end of the Second World War, Australia had represented the United States' interests in Poland.

There were also the field trips, including extended visits to Sydney and Melbourne, as well as one trip to a part of Australia we were not familiar with and which we had to organise ourselves.

My group chose Queensland and the Great Barrier Reef. Our group comprised Les Rowe, Graham Alliband, Daniel Mayaka from Kenya, Peter Chan from Singapore and me. Obviously, the chance to enjoy snorkelling on the reef and admire the corals, the fish and the vibrant colours was an attraction. However, there was also a serious side to the trip. At the time, there was considerable concern that the crown-of-thorns starfish was intent on destroying one of Australia's great natural wonders and depriving Australia of the tourist revenue which the Barrier Reef generated. It is striking that this same issue is again causing major concern.

The trip did educate me to parts of Australia I was not familiar with. We spent a day at the Mount Morgan gold and copper mine and learnt about those industries. We spent a day in Ingham, getting a taste of the sugar industry; the industry, not the sugar! We also gained some sense of the variety of the Australian landscape, with the flat stretches north of Brisbane interrupted by the spectacular Glass House Mountains, the breathtaking views of the Whitsundays and the tropical rainforest areas around Cairns.

One of the few low points of the trip, from my perspective, was that I thought Gladstone, at that time, was the most depressing place I had ever visited. Not really a low point, but I was awestruck by the number of mosquitoes we encountered in Ingham. The ceiling of the house we stayed in was literally black with mosquitoes. I had never, even to this day, seen so many at one time.

Les and Graham shared the driving. At the time, I was too young to be allowed to drive a rental car. Les liked to push the speed limit as he felt the Bruce Highway, a much rougher road than it is today, was a breeze compared with what he'd been used to driving on in Papua New Guinea during his period of national service. Graham constantly screamed at Les to slow down.

The flooding north of Townsville presented us with a few challenges and showed us what a group of city-slickers our team was. We were about to ford one section of flooding and were asked if we had removed the fan belt from the car. Not one of us had a clue how to do that, so a very obliging local woman came and showed us how so we could ford the flood without blowing water into the engine and killing it. We were very grateful, but also very humbled.

We, of course, made it to the reef off Cairns. The colours were spectacular. The variety of fish were phenomenal. I saw a hammerhead shark in the reef below me and, was worried I might become dinner, and headed back to shore as fast as I could. Later, I learnt that perspective on the reef is very deceptive, and the shark was probably many tens of metres below, probably unaware of my presence. We also saw the desolation of reefs that had been attacked by the crown-of-thorns starfish. They were like graveyards compared to the vibrancy of the living reefs.

Then, as now, the numbers of trochus shells, the main predator of the crown-of-thorns starfish, had been badly depleted by people harvesting them as tourist souvenir items because of their attractive appearance when polished.

As it turned out, our group was the only one that managed to stay within budget, which, as I was to appreciate later, is an essential skill for any government official. We also wrote a report, based on our own observations and discussions with experts at Queensland and James Cook Universities, which foreshadowed the findings of a Commission of Inquiry report issued some months later. I took quiet satisfaction in this.

Another major and important field trip was when the entire training group went to Papua New Guinea for a couple of weeks. PNG was still an Australian territory and many of us would be required to represent PNG interests overseas, as in fact, was the case for me.

Apart from a trip to Tasmania when I was eighteen months old, this was the first time I'd travelled off the Australian mainland. It was quite an eye-opener and certainly a very useful experience given the amount of work I subsequently had to do, for and on behalf of, PNG interests. We were provided briefings on the PNG administration and development policies and had a chance to get around some parts of the country to see things for ourselves.

In Port Moresby, I was struck by the colour and variety of the open-air markets, the penchant of the local men for colourful shirts and the women for colourful dresses. We visited the Bomana Jail, much of which did not seem like a jail, with its wide-open spaces of grass and trees. Our guide relished in drawing our attention to one particular prisoner. 'That man,' he said, 'is a cannibal. You can tell by the crazed look in his eyes.' I thought the role of jails was to rehabilitate people back into society and not treat them as freaks, but as I have learnt in later years, Bomana then was probably a more tolerant place than many other jails around the world.

Another Port Moresby experience proved to be a portent of things to come after independence in PNG. A group of us decided to go to a local disco. The local band was pretty good and I enjoyed some lively dancing. We noticed some other foreigners dancing with local girls. We had been warned not to accept the invitations from the local girls as we had been told they would invite their partners to go downstairs for a coffee. Once downstairs, their boyfriends would be waiting to beat up and rob their unsuspecting newly found partners.

From Port Moresby, we flew to Lae and Goroka. Lae reminded me of what I remembered of Darwin when I was little; lush tropical vegetation and quite an impressive harbour. A short distance from Lae, we visited a ginger farm as an example of an industry that had potential to contribute to PNG export earnings. As someone who enjoys ginger, I hoped this enterprise would take off.

The flight between Lae and Goroka traversed some rugged mountainous and forested areas, and I had been told the air currents could be quite tricky. Sitting next to one of our course colleagues proved to be a bit unnerving. He seemed to get more and more nervous as the flight went on and kept looking out the plane window, saying we were going to hit the next mountain top. For me, the scenery was fantastic, and I had complete faith in our TAA and Ansett pilots.

Though one TAA flight did offer something unexpected and probably uncalled for. At one point the captain came on the intercom and said that if we looked below, we would see a farmhouse. He continued on that one of the flight attendants was getting married to the owner of the farmhouse the following Saturday. Another flight attendant, who clearly was not going to be the bridesmaid, walked down the aisle saying she had to get married as she was pregnant to him and that she had forced him to split up with his previous wife. Such cattiness! I hoped that was not typical of expatriate life in PNG but suspect it may have been.

The highlight of our visit to Goroka was going to a coffee plantation. PNG has almost ideal conditions for growing coffee, and this was seen as another export crop with considerable potential. The aroma from the roasting of the top-quality beans was tantalising. However, we were shown a large vat with lesser-quality beans. Although it was covered with a mesh net, the holes seemed to allow small leaves and the occasional insect to get caught up in the roasting of these beans. We were told that the beans in this vat were used for making Maxwell House instant coffee. This had a life-changing impact on me, as I sought thereafter to avoid drinking instant coffee, especially Maxwell House.

From Lae, we flew to Rabaul. Again, I thought this was a spectacular harbour with the dramatic backdrop of a volcano, which some years later caused major devastation to the city in a major eruption. The trip around the coast road revealed relics of the Japanese presence during the Second World War. For me, the main memory of Rabaul was a visit to the out-patients section of the local hospital, as I had developed acute laryngitis. I suspect I was given preferential treatment, but nonetheless I was happy with the treatment I was given and my throat improved in a day or two.

A small group of us flew from Rabaul to Bougainville. We had argued with our course supervisor that this should be done because of the growing voice for a separate Bougainville state, as well as allowing us to get some insight into the economic importance of the copper mine. Our supervisor had agreed.

First impressions of Bougainville as we came into Kieta, the main town, from the airport were of a beautiful coral sand and palm fringed coastline and a very rugged interior. It was said that during the Second World War, the terrain and malaria killed more men than the actual warfare. I could believe it.

Another impression was the blackness of the Bougainvillean people. This was something of which they seemed very proud. In fact, they boasted they were the blackest people on earth. We were in Kieta for ANZAC Day and the black skins against their white uniforms made quite an impact.

We, of course, visited the mine site. It was massive both in terms of the scale of the mine and the equipment being used. Because the mine tended to be shrouded in clouds much of the time, this took away some of the starkness of the site. At the time, there was no other venture on such a scale in PNG and the mine was seen as important to the PNG economy as a whole, but it was also seen by the Bougainvillean separatists as unfairly funding the development of other parts of PNG at the expense of Bougainville. They argued the mine would enable a separate Bougainville state to be economically viable.

It had been arranged for us to travel to the small town of Buin to meet some local politicians. Buin Airport was a first for me. It was a grass strip, and the airlines officer would drive out from town, bringing his own table and chair, to meet each flight. I don't think there were too many flights to keep him busy.

In Buin, we were to stay in a thatched hut attached to the local administration office. It had been arranged that a prominent local politician would meet us at the hut and we had purchased a bottle of vodka to make him feel welcome. The town electricity was powered by a generator which was turned off at 10pm. We waited and waited in the dim light of a kerosene lantern. I fell asleep and when I awoke my colleagues told me they had watched a rat walk across my chest. They assured me this was for real and that they weren't *having me on*.

Needless to say, the politician never showed. Our vodka clearly wasn't sufficient enough an enticement; perhaps he had a better offer in town joining in the ANZAC Day commemorations. We had earlier had a brief taste of that ourselves, watching an animated game of two-up being played. This was the first time I had seen this supposed Australian institution being played. The next morning, we had breakfast with a group of men who had stayed up all hours playing two-up. One man had lost thousands of dollars.

There wasn't much to do in Kieta on a Saturday night other than going to the restaurant for dinner. We observed a couple come into the restaurant, the man wearing a suit and the woman wearing a fur stole. Both were overdressed in such a hot and steamy climate. However, as they were the most dressed up people in the restaurant, a German waitress wanted to show she knew of the finer things in life and made a fuss over them.

Later, two men came in, obviously straight from the mine as they were dressed in their work overalls. As the restaurant was packed, another waitress showed them to the two empty chairs at the table of the overdressed couple. The German waitress went berserk and berated the other waitress in no uncertain terms. The whole restaurant turned to watch the spectacle. Our group concluded that behaviour, like that of the German waitress, was unlikely to be tolerated in an independent PNG.

After returning from PNG, most of the overseas participants were assigned to brief stints at Australian embassies or high commissions. A few returned directly home. The Australian participants had a few more days of training.

Once the formal training was completed, we were assigned to desk jobs within the department, awaiting our first overseas assignment. One of the key lessons from my desk job experience was that the department's writing style did not allow scope for literary flair or an academic style of writing. We had to be concise and to the point.

One other lesson was that I came to understand the importance of tact. One of my early jobs was to translate an essay written by a former Japanese ambassador on Australia's 'White Australia Policy'. The essay was part of a collection written by the former ambassador and, for the most part, his essays demonstrated his close feelings for Australia. However, in this particular essay he claimed Japanese could not migrate to Australia because, as non-whites, they were unwelcome, even though the 'White Australia Policy' formally ended in 1966. He further argued that Turks, who were also Asian and not white, could. This prompted a strong rebuttal from the Turkish Ambassador to the effect that as everyone knew *Turks were white!*

Following our training and desk experience, we were now, supposedly, fully prepared to go out and represent Australia and its interests to the world. My time at desk jobs in Canberra proved to be brief and, from memory, I was the third person in our group to go out on a posting.

On the Road to Hong Kong

One day, following the completion of our training course, all the members of our intake were called up individually by staffing branch to be advised where it had been decided to assign us for our first overseas posting. I had hopes of going to Japan, however, I was advised that I was going to Hong Kong. I was not disappointed as this was my second preference.

I had done a major essay on the 1842 Treaty of Nanking at university and had some knowledge of how Hong Kong came to be a British colony. I was soon referred to the excellent book by renowned Australian journalist, Richard 'Dick' Hughes, *Hong Kong – Borrowed Place, Borrowed Time*. However, this background knowledge of Hong Kong was peripheral to what I was going to be doing. I was to be a *China Watcher*.

At the time, Hong Kong was one of only a couple of Australian overseas posts headed by a senior trade commissioner and had a very small complement of foreign service staff. My boss in Canberra, Jeff Benson, joked I should change my name to Philby as I would be joining Burgess and McLean in Hong Kong. Jeff was of course referring to the infamous Cambridge University spies for the Soviet Union, Guy

Burgess, Donald McLean and Kim Philby. Our team in Hong Kong was John Burgess and Murray McLean.

Originally, staffing branch had told me I was scheduled to go to Hong Kong in the middle of the following year. However, in the first week of December 1971 I was told there was now an urgent need for me to arrive in Hong Kong before the end of the year. I would be able to spend Christmas with my family, but then would depart on Boxing Day via Perth, Singapore and Kuala Lumpur for Hong Kong.

As a foreign service officer, you are required to be flexible and adaptable, prepared to travel at a moment's notice. However, as I was to discover, travelling during the Christmas holiday period could lead to other complications.

Apart from books and a few records, I did not have many personal belongings. My clothing could fit into two suitcases, but I had to go out and buy the suitcases. The remainder of my goods would be sent by sea to Hong Kong.

I finished packing my suitcases on Christmas morning only to find they would not close properly unless they were locked. The problem was, the keys I had been given did not fit the suitcase locks. What was I to do, as, after all, it was Christmas Day?

I tried ringing the shop where I had bought the cases in the vain hope there might be an answering machine message with emergency contact details. I was blessed. A security guard answered the phone and, when I explained my predicament, he undertook to contact the manager of the shop. As a result, I was luckily able to obtain the correct keys. One hurdle successfully overcome.

After an uneventful flight to Sydney to connect with my BOAC flight to Kuala Lumpur, our flight to Perth was delayed for about an hour because of a small technical problem. Once airborne, the flight crew were determined to help me relax. Seeing it was Boxing Day, how about a 'brandy cruster' ... and what about another one!

More problems were to face us in Perth. A passenger who had checked in failed to board and we had to wait for his luggage to be located and removed from the cargo hold. This was a further delay of another two hours.

In those days, it was departmental practice for officers to travel first class. With me in first class was a family with a couple of young children. En route to Singapore, one of the children complained of feeling unwell and it turned out he had also developed a rash all over his body. The parents told the flight crew the child had been playing with some children who had chicken pox, but he had also eaten a lot of chocolate on Christmas Day, so perhaps it was hives.

The flight crew said that, regardless, a doctor would have to come onboard in Singapore and check the child before any passengers could disembark. The doctor duly came onboard and announced that, if it was chicken pox, we would all have to go into quarantine in Singapore. After examining the child, the doctor declared, 'Let's call it hives.' I was relieved I would be able to continue my journey to Kuala Lumpur. Yet another hurdle overcome, but the flight was delayed by a further hour or so.

Finally, I arrived many hours late in Kuala Lumpur. Bob Bowker, who was the second in our year to go out on his overseas posting, was at the airport to meet me. It was welcome to see a familiar friendly face.

Putting aside Papua New Guinea, which at the time was still an Australian territory, Malaysia was the first foreign country I had visited. Its capital, Kuala Lumpur, was and still is one of the most attractive cities in Southeast Asia, dotted as it is with lakes formed from the pits of old tin mines, hilly areas within the city, as well as surrounding it, and plenty of still largely virgin jungle. I was impressed with the outwardly modern looking parliament buildings, the Moorish-inspired

Abdul Samad and railway buildings in the centre of the city and the modern central mosque, although plain and austere compared with much other Islamic architecture, it had a certain grandeur.

Kuala Lumpur was also a smorgasbord of sights, sounds, colours and tantalising food smells. Bob and I had a beer on the top floor bar of the Hilton Hotel which afforded views over the racecourse (now the site of the Petronas Twin Towers), the old part of the city and the surrounding hills.

Back at street level, we wandered through some of the local markets and, wishing also to wear some Malaysian colour, I bought a batik shirt which served me well for many years for casual dinner dress. I cannot remember what else we ate, but I do remember trying some satay, for which Kuala Lumpur is justifiably well renowned.

One evening Bob and I visited my father's cousin, Harvey Lade, who was, at the time, working for Butterfield and Swire in Kuala Lumpur. His home was in a hilly suburb surrounded by thick jungle. It was dusk as we approached his home and dozens of monkeys emerged from the jungle, presumably in search of a quick and easy meal. I instantly connected with Kuala Lumpur and was taken that there were other capital cities, like Canberra, surrounded by bush and home to abundant wildlife.

I wished one day to come back to Malaysia, but now it was time to move on to Hong Kong.

The Arcane World of China Watching

I was met on arrival in Hong Kong at the old Kai Tak Airport by Murray McLean, whom I was replacing so he could undertake full-time Chinese language studies.

There were two approaches to landing at Kai Tak. One was coming in over the water. The other more dramatic way was coming in over the built-up areas of Kowloon. As you approached the runway the multi-storey buildings seemed to loom up directly in front of you and then suddenly the plane dipped, and you were taxiing down the runway. I remember meeting pilots who told me they loved the 'coming over land' approach to Kai Tak as it was one of the more challenging international airport landings and they really had to stay on full alert.

Settling into Hong Kong was a bit of a challenge also. For my first three months I stayed first in the Mandarin Hotel, and later in the Hilton Hotel. Unless I was going out with work colleagues or had official functions, meals at the hotel were included in my settling-in allowance. This got tiresome fairly quickly. I could order room service, but this meant eating alone in my room. Most nights I went to one of the hotel restaurants, but it meant I could not be casually dressed. It also meant I could not have something simple to eat like baked beans and sausages which I did occasionally in Canberra.

I looked at quite a few options before finding an apartment I liked and which came within my rental allowance. Like several other staff in the office, I found an apartment in the as yet unfinished Realty Gardens development on 41 Conduit Road in the mid-levels. My apartment was 17B Paris Court and had wonderful views over Victoria Harbour. Even after I moved in, it took a while to feel fully settled as I had to wait for my complement of furniture to be made and delivered. In those days nearly everything was made from scratch, including carpets.

I had arrived in Hong Kong just before the Western New Year and then the Chinese New Year. There were many banquets leading up to both New Years. I learned very quickly to become proficient in using chopsticks as otherwise I would go hungry. It was also a good way to be introduced to new Chinese food dishes.

The Hong Kong I arrived into could not have been a greater contrast to quiet, neat and orderly Canberra. Hong Kong offered an overload to the senses. There were masses of people in the streets; walking, going out for dinner and enjoying themselves. Walking through Causeway Bay on a Sunday was one of my early memorable experiences. The place was seething with people and walking far or fast proved a challenge. Hong Kong may be a small place, but I marvelled at some of the surrounding rugged, forested spectacular scenery.

I also needed to adjust to the noise – the traffic noises and the clanging bells of the trams, the street hawkers seeking to draw in customers and the loud staccato and machine-gun-like sound of the Cantonese language.

I was able to enjoy the wonderful tastes of Hong Kong cuisine and was introduced to foods I had never eaten in Australia, up to that time, including squid, eel and the decadent and rich Peking duck. I also took pleasure in walking past bakeries when they had just taken a batch of egg tarts out of the oven. The aroma was so tempting, and I often succumbed.

Sitting on the veranda of my seventeenth-floor apartment overlooking Victoria Harbour, I never tired of watching the boats, ships and the sea-craft criss-crossing the harbour. At night-time, I'd admire the reflections of the neon lights of Kowloon on the water.

And when I made the short and peaceful trip across the harbour on the Star Ferry between Central and Tsim Tsa Tsui, the smell of the salty harbour water beckoned me back to those trips to the beach in Australia, swimming in the salty sea along Australia's east coast.

At the end of 1971, Hong Kong was something of a paradox.

On the one hand, there was the British Hong Kong. As a British Crown Colony, a British Governor was the Queen's representative in Hong Kong. The departmental secretaries and senior government officials were predominantly British expatriates. The senior ranks of the Hong Kong Police Force were mostly filled by British expatriates. British expatriates continued to dominate the senior management of the successor companies to the original trading companies or 'hongs' that helped Hong Kong to develop into the successful entrepot port that it was. Such companies included Jardine Matheson, the Swire Group of companies and Hutchisons and they remained influential in Hong Kong business. The central district of Hong Kong preserved much colonial architecture from the days of early British settlement. Even the double-decker buses helped set a British tone.

Then there was the modern entrepreneurial Hong Kong. It was not just the old 'hongs' who continued to thrive in Hong Kong, but large numbers of local businessmen prospered, and many major international companies were lured by the prospect of using Hong Kong as a gateway for doing business with the People's Republic of China behind the Bamboo Curtain. The Hong Kong skyline continued to rise with the addition of new and grander skyscrapers. Hong Kong Harbour and Port witnessed frenetic activity almost twenty-four hours a day. Hong Kong was a mecca for shopping tourists who came to take advantage of its duty-free status and the chance to buy the latest brand-name electronic goods, cameras and fashions.

Third, there was the Chinese Hong Kong. Refugees continued to arrive in large numbers from the mainland. Squatter settlements continued to grow, often on steep hillsides, and many of these would come down in landslides following heavy rain. The government had trouble keeping pace in providing low-cost housing for all the people in need, despite the growing number of high-rise housing estates.

There were many traditional aspects of Chinese culture, such as the temples and the Kowloon Walled City and streets like Hollywood Road, Caine Road and Ladder Street crowded with old-style shops, restaurants and the occasional historic building. There were the Chinese markets which sold all manner of live animals and seafood, fruit and vegetables, household goods, clothing and just about anything else you might need for daily life. The one I was most familiar with was the Wanchai Market. It was always teeming with people whatever hour of the day. Hong Kong was also probably the best place in the world at the time to sample any variety of Chinese cuisine.

Finally, there was the Communist Chinese presence in Hong Kong. There was the formal presence represented by the Bank of China in its stark and severe headquarters near the Hilton Hotel and the Hong Kong and Shanghai Bank. Subsequently a tall and striking modern building went up in its place as the new home for the Bank of China. There were the representatives of the New China News Agency and China Travel Service. There were also the large Chinese product emporiums that provided a window into the range of Chinese manufactured produce available, such as textiles, footwear, furniture, china and glassware, artefacts and other decorative items.

In addition, there were the less obvious links. These included Hong Kong Chinese businessmen involved in facilitating trade links with China. There were the many Hong Kong families who continued to visit remaining family in China and take luxury items in with them, while returning with foodstuffs, clothing and other Chinese bric-a-brac. These people also helped provide insights into what was happening inside China.

Despite all these disparate faces, Hong Kong acted as a melting pot bringing them all together in a vibrant and fascinating symphony. All of this against Hong Kong's splendid natural setting. Victoria Peak stands imposingly behind the frill of skyscrapers that line the shore of Hong Kong Harbour, overlooking one of the world's most spectacular harbours. Dotted around the main island of Hong Kong are other scenic, but less populated islands, such as Lantau, Lamma, Cheng Chau and a host of other mostly smaller outlying islands.

In 1971, Tsim Sha Tsui on the Kowloon Peninsula was a bustling and confusing network of shops, hotels and restaurants, as well as being a major tourist centre, as it was more convenient to the airport. In those days, the only link with Hong Kong Island was by passenger or car ferry, as the Cross Harbour tunnel had not yet been built. However, as you proceeded from Kowloon to the New Territories, little modern development was apparent. Today, Shatin and Taipo Market are thriving modern centres with high-rise buildings. In 1971, they were more like rural towns and the surrounding countryside was dominated by rugged hills or farming and fishing villages.

A Diplomatic Life

Beginning Life and Work as a China Watcher

This was the Hong Kong that provided the backdrop to the work I would be doing.

In the office, I was quickly introduced to the tools of trade. Our daily fare comprised the New China News Agency print-outs, the *South China Morning Post* and *Hong Kong Standard,* and the media transcripts provided by the BBC and the Foreign Broadcast Information Service. In addition, there were other publications such as *China Reconstructs* and the *China News Analysis* produced by a Jesuit, Father Laszlo Ladany, who had been forced to leave China following the communist takeover. My main focus initially was to be Chinese foreign policy, but in time I would come also to do more work on internal Chinese politics.

The art of China Watching required us to closely monitor all such coverage and, literally, we had to try and read between the lines for hints as to changes in Chinese policy positions or changes in leadership. Omission of a name could indicate someone had fallen out of favour or been moved to another job, addition of a name could indicate someone had been promoted into the leadership hierarchy or had been rehabilitated. A change in the order of leadership lists could indicate promotions or demotions. We were also required to analyse what any changes might mean.

On foreign policy, there were clear gradations in the language used to demonstrate the strength of China's bilateral relationship with a particular country. It didn't get any closer than 'lips and teeth' as used to describe China's relationship with North Korea and especially, its then leader, Kim Il Sung. Outside of Asia, Albania had 'strong fraternal links' and for the Chinese, its leader, Enver Hoxha, stood on a pedestal compared with most other world leaders. The rest of the world was probably more likely to ask, *Enver who?*

At the bottom of the spectrum were the 'US imperialists' and their 'running dogs' or 'lackeys'. Prior to Australian recognition of the People's Republic of China, Australia often fell into this category.

Occasionally there were opportunities to gain insights into another even more closed society which, like China, had its own unique terminology. This was driven home to me when I had the opportunity to meet two British businessmen who had just returned from a visit to North Korea. Apart from their interesting insights into the politics and economy of the DPRK, the thing that had really struck them was the way that the DPRK was infused with R&B. Surely this could not be rhythm and blues as it was just so alien to my impression of DPRK society and culture. Sure enough, it wasn't. R&B referred to 'respected and beloved', a much-hackneyed term used in the DPRK in any reference to their 'dear and great' leader.

However, China was very much our main focus. There was more to China Watching than just staying in the office scouring all these written words. It was important to get out and compare notes with people from other foreign missions in Hong Kong doing similar work, media specialists working on China, academics and foreigners who had been fortunate enough to go in behind the Bamboo Curtain.

The job was not, in fact, as drab and dreary as it might sound. China Watchers were a smart bunch of people. They knew that you were far more productive if you could combine business with pleasure. And in Hong Kong what better pleasure was there than to enjoy a top-quality Chinese meal.

There was one formalised group that met regularly, and it was known as the *Washington Post* Lunch Group. This was started by an energetic former correspondent of the *Washington Post*, Stanley Karnow, when he was based in Hong Kong. Participants in the Lunch Group were a select group of journalists and diplomats. In my time in Hong Kong, the group had several favourite restaurants, one specialising in Peking, another in Shanghai and a third in Chiu Chao cuisine.

We enjoyed some wonderful food. It was through these gatherings I was introduced to such delicacies as Shanghai-style braised eel, Peking duck, and Shanghai-style prawns in chilli sauce. Coming to Hong Kong where my knowledge of Chinese food had been based on the occasional takeaway meals from the local Australianised Chinese restaurants that offered basic fare of short or long soup, sweet and sour pork, chop suey and chicken chow mein, the China Watcher lunches introduced me to real high-quality Chinese cuisine and ingredients that I would have considered truly exotic in Australia, such as eel and squid. The lunches whetted my appetite for more great food as well, of course, for more interesting and informative discussion.

There was another formalised mechanism that enabled foreign diplomats and businessmen involved in China Watching or doing business with China to meet once a month with communist Chinese officials based in Hong Kong. This was the Marco Polo Club established by Percy Chen, a citizen of Trinidad, whose father had been Foreign Minister for a time in the Nationalist Chinese Government. As with the *Washington Post* Group, this was an invitation only affair.

The evenings began with Percy Chen reciting a poem he had written or imparting some other personal wisdom. Because China's official representatives in Hong Kong were well-versed in Chinese Government policy, these gatherings provided a good opportunity to get first-hand accounts of these policies. On several occasions they also were useful in conveying messages about Australian wheat sales or other business deals.

It interested me that the venue for the Marco Polo Club gatherings was the Mandarin Hotel, one of the leading five-star hotels in Hong Kong at the time and certainly a place that you would associate more with capitalism than communism. However, perhaps because of its location, the Marco Polo Club proved a very convivial and productive meeting place.

However, from all these Hong Kong-based China Watching activities, I know I developed a very distorted view of China. The photos in China reconstructs portrayed lots of well-fed, happy and hardworking people. The New China News Agency reports suggested that everyone was working hard, diligently and enthusiastically to learn from Tachai in agriculture and Taching in industry and meet or over-fulfil production targets.

Of course, we knew that all was not well and there were continuing political tussles and divisions going on inside China. We knew that the Great Leap Forward and the Great Proletarian Cultural Revolution had impeded economic progress and driven families apart and, in many cases, turned children against their parents. However, the picture China portrayed to the outside world suggested China was in transition towards a more prosperous era and poverty, starvation and disease were rapidly being eradicated.

Perhaps I was being too harsh, but at times my impression was that, in China, people were being pushed beyond normal limits and there was no time for enjoyment or relaxation. In January 1973 I had my first opportunity to visit and get a taste of the 'real' China.

The Real China

Following its election in late 1972, the Whitlam government moved quickly to honour an election promise and recognise the People's Republic of China. They moved equally quickly to establish an Australian embassy in Beijing. Our office in Hong Kong became heavily involved in providing support for this. It also provided an early opportunity for me to go to Beijing to assist the embassy opening team.

This proved to be a voyage of discovery in more ways than one, and my image of China was to undergo major transformation. This visit, as well as subsequent visits, provided many adventures.

The first visit began dramatically at Lo Wu, the last railway station on the Hong Kong side of the Chinese bridge. My travelling companion, Peter Nurse, and I were escorting over sixty bags of diplomatic mail, containing many essentials including equipment and files for the embassy to be able to function effectively. As diplomatic safe-hand mail, it was important it be escorted by an Australian official at all times.

At Lo Wu, all our safe-hand mail was loaded onto a large trolley. I went to the end of the platform with the trolley while Peter went inside to clear HK immigration. When Peter came out, the plan was I would go in to do my immigration formalities.

A Hong Kong policeman had other ideas. He asked me what I was doing, and I explained I had to stay with the diplomatic mail until my colleague had completed his immigration formalities, and then I would go inside. The policeman told me *I had to go inside*. I repeated what I'd told him. The policeman spoke some English, but I don't think he fully understood, as he started to pull his pistol from its holster and threatened that I had to go into immigration *or else*. I tried to explain yet again, but the policeman took the pistol a little further out of its holster and threatened me even more strongly.

I'm afraid I was not going to become a martyr for the sake of Sino-Australian relations, and I reluctantly went in to do my immigration processing. Peter could see what was going on and came running out of the immigration hall. I proceeded very quickly through immigration and joined Peter on the platform. I asked the same policeman what had happened to our diplomatic mail. At first, he pretended not to understand, but then acknowledged the mail had been taken across the bridge at Lo Wu into China. (As a footnote, we subsequently lodged a formal complaint with the HK police about this incident, but never had a response from them.)

Peter and I ran as fast as we could. I'm sure we must have been the first people to run into China. It's likely the Chinese railway and security officials were surprised to see these two foreigners so desperate to enter China, that they were running as fast as they could go. The distance was not great. From memory, maybe 30-40m. Of course, when we crossed onto the Chinese side's platform, there was the trolley with our bags waiting sedately for us.

After this first traumatic experience, we were determined, one way or another, the bags would not be parted from us again. This determination was soon tested. The Chinese railway officials said we had to go up to the second floor of the station building to complete immigration and customs formalities. We explained that at least one of us had to stay with the bags. They told us there was a goods lift, and we could put the bags in that.

Sure enough, there was a goods lift. Length and width-wise it was quite spacious and could accommodate all our bags. There was only one problem. It was about 120cm high. Peter, being quite a bit shorter than me, volunteered to go in the lift and squat down with the bags. The Chinese must have thought, *These crazy foreigners*. Peter came down in the lift with the bags when we had finished our entry formalities.

When it was time to board our train, some Chinese porters helped us load the bags onto the train for us. We had to stop briefly in Guangzhou and checked in at the Dongfang (East Wind) Hotel, where we took turns to alternately guard the bags and go to the restaurant to eat dinner.

After dinner, we proceeded to the station to board the overnight Guangzhou to Beijing train. Once we had settled into the four-berth cabin (two for our bags, two for us), we noticed there was a service button in the cabin. Peter was keen to have a coffee and decided to try out the button. Soon after, a cabin attendant knocked at the door. We said, 'Coffee please.' Shortly after, he came back with our coffee, however, Peter wanted milk for his coffee.

I had only just started Mandarin Chinese lessons and did not yet know the word for *milk*. Our attendant did not understand the English word, so we tried making the gesture of milking a cow. No, that didn't work. We tried making 'moo' noises. That didn't work either. We repeated our attempts until finally something must have clicked, and the attendant backed out of our cabin and came charging in with his hands held like horns at the side of his head. We nodded our heads and said *yes*. And so, we got our milk.

At the end of day one in China, there were no signs of the Maoist automatons I had half-expected. People were generally kind and helpful. In the restaurant in Guangzhou, I had been surprised that it was hard to attract the attention of the waiting staff, as they were busy talking to each other. Rather than getting annoyed, I took that as a positive thing; they were real, normal people.

The train trip from Guangzhou to Beijing was normally thirty-six hours, so there was ample opportunity to observe life from the train window as we sped by. People were working industriously in the fields, but they also stopped for lunch breaks and 'health' breaks for a cigarette. I also observed workers just leaning on their tools and chatting. I think production quotas were probably the furthest thing from their mind, but undoubtedly were a consideration for each village administrative committee. However, my impression was that life was pretty normal.

Every time we came into a station, we would be treated to a burst of music and then a series of voice announcements. In the whole thirty-six hours on the train, we did not manage to locate the volume switch, and our volume was set high. The music was quite a lively tune and I christened it 'coming into station music'. Back in Hong Kong, I later heard it being played in a store and asked the shop attendants what the music was. It was indeed a catchy number with a catchy title, 'Spur the grain carts on'. I'm sure it was much more exciting than an award-winning film I'd read about in the Chinese English language press, namely, *The dialectics of growing peanuts*.

We were met at Beijing Station by staff from our new embassy and taken to the Beijing Hotel where we were to stay the next couple of days. It was not a beautiful building, and I guess in true Stalinist architectural style, all you could say was that *everything was big*. My bedroom was enormous. Apart from the bed and a large writing desk, there was still enough room to swing a family of cats. The attached bathroom

A Diplomatic Life

was also unfashionably large, and the bathtub almost seemed lonely on one side of the room. The hotel's corridors were long and wide. They seemed to go on forever, perhaps even 100m long and about 10m wide. We also ate every breakfast in the massive dining room.

We helped our embassy team unpack and sort all that we'd brought them, but there was still time left over to get some feel for Beijing.

It was almost obligatory for visitors in those days to attend a cultural performance. We were to attend a choral performance by an official Chinese troupe. This concert was the first sign since arriving in China that lived up to some of my preconceived notions about the country.

The singers were all over made-up. Their mouths when they sang were all unnaturally wide open. Their hands were rigidly clasped in front of their waists. Body movements were all in unison. It was almost like looking at the mechanical clowns at the Royal Easter Show in Sydney where you could win prizes by throwing balls in their mouths. The concert suggested, that perhaps, there possibly were some automatons in China.

There was no doubt that some of the songs were quite stirring, and there were some powerful voices in the choir. However, if this is what Mao's wife, Jiang Qing, and her colleagues were seeking to depict as Chinese culture, it was sadly lacking, and also not entertaining. Perhaps to overcome reactions such as mine, the encore was written into the program with several designated songs. Perhaps they knew that spontaneous appreciation was unlikely.

As we were leaving the theatre, a short Chinese-looking lady trod on my foot. She apologised and I recognised who she was immediately. I can't remember if there had been an announcement before the start of the concert, although that was quite likely, but the lady was Dr Han Suyin. I replied something to the effect, 'No worries, Dr Han.' Dr Han was the daughter of a Chinese railway engineer and Belgian mother and had been welcomed by the People's Republic as a famous 'foreigner' and sympathiser of modern China. At university, we had been encouraged to read her autobiographical books about the development of China from the start of the twentieth century to the communist rise to power. I had read most of her books, most of which also carried her photo.

On the Saturday, we took a taxi of vintage Polish-make to the Great Wall. Our route was lined with lots of people waving flags and cheering. It seemed that rent-a-crowd was out in force, but it seemed they were not exactly sure what they were watching out for. I didn't mind and maybe our Polish taxi needed some encouragement to make it up to the Great Wall. I later learnt we had been mistaken for an Albanian cycling team. I just hope rent-a-crowd had not spent all their energy on cheering our small Australian contingent and had left something in store for the Albanians.

Anyone could not help but be impressed with the Great Wall. Even though we were only visiting one stage of the wall, we could still appreciate its enormity and what an incredible architectural and engineering feat it was. Even though some sections of the wall were crumbling, much of the wall was still in excellent condition. As former US President Richard Nixon was later to declare, 'It sure is a GREAT wall!' I have wondered if former Chinese Premier Deng Xiaoping returned the compliment when he subsequently visited the United States saying, 'It sure is a GRAND canyon!'

On Sunday, we joined hundreds of thousands of Beijing residents in visiting the main shopping street of Wangfujing. I invested in some thick woollen socks and a rabbit fur-lined hat, as both my ears and feet were freezing after coming from the much warmer climes of Hong Kong. The socks didn't last well as my maid in Hong Kong obviously washed them in hot water and when they emerged, they were the size

A Diplomatic Life

of baby booties. I still have the hat and have, on rare extremely cold occasions, worn it again.

For the Chinese, a stroll down Wangfujing was a chance to relax and enjoy themselves, although in those days it was not really a shopper's paradise. At one stage inside a department store, our party of four ended up being split in two. My companion and I decided it was best to wait at the foot of some stairs as our colleagues would have to come that way. As it turned out, they had no trouble finding us. Foreigners, and especially Westerners, were still an uncommon sight, and in those days, my hair was quite blond.

We had one important chore to complete before we departed Beijing. We had brought a couple of bicycles in knock-down kit form for staff at our embassy and we needed to assemble them and ensure all parts were present, and the bicycles rode fine. At about two in the morning, we finished assembling both bicycles. As bicycles had to be registered before they could be ridden on the road, we had to find a suitable alternative. The long and wide corridors of the Beijing Hotel looked ideal. Of course, the bicycles rode just fine, but we attracted some attention from hotel staff. A few watched on with bemused looks, but a couple actually clapped.

Maybe one of the key advantages of registration was that it enabled people to identify their correct bike. I remember seeing several locations where thousands of similar-looking bikes were parked and wondering how people could know which was theirs.

Our departure from Beijing was, in its way, almost as dramatic as our arrival in China from Hong Kong. The day loomed with snow falling steadily outside. We were flying back to Guangzhou and some of the embassy staff were anxious the snow would make the trip to the airport much slower than normal. They were urging us to leave quickly. The charge d'affaires had other ideas as he wished to complete a couple of jobs for us to take back to Hong Kong with us, and he was confident we still had plenty of time. As it turned out, he was right, but if the weather had been fine, we would certainly have missed our flight.

At the airport, we checked in and asked when our flight would be leaving and received the cryptic response, 'When it is ready.' That continued be the response for a number of hours. We watched as planes were wheeled out from under the protection of hangars and snow built up on their wings. Teams of sweepers then set to work sweeping the snow off the wings. It didn't seem to be a productive use of their labour, but perhaps this was one way of guaranteeing that production targets were met.

Eventually the plane was ready, and we took off for Guangzhou. How times have changed. I remember on that first flight in China the stewardess came up to my seat, tapped me gently on the shoulder and asked me in a soft, confidential voice in slightly accented English, 'Excuse me, sir. Would you like a pear?' I selected a nice juicy pear from the basket she was carrying. Modern airlines have lost the art of such gentle personalised service. Regrettably, the next time I flew in China, the commercial influences of the West had left their mark, and service was more in line with what you would expect on almost any airline – quite mechanical and impersonal.

I made several subsequent visits to China which helped reinforce my initial impressions, as well as provide new insights. I was also lucky enough to witness some important Chinese history in the making.

Five months after my first visit, I went to Beijing again for work reasons. Our embassy by this stage had moved into its first stand-alone building, courtesy of the Chinese Diplomatic Service Bureau. It was located in an area the Chinese were trying to develop as a diplomatic enclave. My travel on this occasion was linked to helping the embassy get itself established in these new premises.

Again, I stayed at the Beijing Hotel. In those days, at the table in the dining room, you were required to always sit in the space staff had designated for you. Seating was carefully orchestrated. You were generally seated at tables with like-minded countries. Fraternal Eastern Europeans all sat at one table, Japanese at another and Australians and other like-minded Westerners at another.

In the early seventies, a rush of countries recognised the People's Republic of China. One such country was Malta. The Maltese Prime Minister, Dom Mintoff, had selected as his first Ambassador to China a former classmate of his, Joe Forace. Joe was one of many Maltese who had migrated to Australia and done well. In Joe's case, it was as a successful real estate manager. Joe had taken out Australian citizenship and I believe had to renounce it to take up appointment as Ambassador to China, and also concurrently, High Commissioner to Australia.

Accordingly, Joe sat at our table in the Beijing Hotel. He was quite an engaging character, but one morning he managed to surprise me. It was the practice then for all dining tables to have a couple of bottles of beer and soft drinks placed in the centre of the table. You could drink them if you wanted, but you were not obliged to do so.

As we sat down for breakfast, Joe cheerfully suggested, 'Let's have a beer for breakfast, just like we do in Australia!' I think Joe was being serious and not just trying to break the ice as it were. I declined as did my colleagues as we were not used to drinking beer for breakfast. However, it left me wondering what other quaint practices the Maltese migrants had picked up in Australia. Beer or no beer, we nonetheless enjoyed Joe's company.

I can't recall if it was the same morning or another morning, however, we had been up early to do some work and went into breakfast a bit later than usual. A few minutes after we sat down, the lights went out. The staff apologised and said they would be back to serve us after they had finished their English language lesson.

They returned within the hour and the lights came back on. I asked the waitress who was serving us how her lesson had gone. She said 'good' and I asked if I could see her textbook. A few minutes later she returned with her textbook. I recall that it was a bit short on practical dialogues. For example, one I specifically recall was that one friend asked the other, 'What did you do last spring festival?' The friend replied, 'I went to Beihai Park and read the thoughts of Chairman Mao.'

Annapurnas-Hiunchuli and marigolds.

On my way out of China, I had to spend the night in Guangzhou and, as was the practice then, was met and escorted by a guide from China Travel Service. My guide mentioned there was a cultural performance that evening by the Heilongjiang Song and Dance troupe, and she strongly encouraged me to go. In reality, I think she was keen to go. She had dispensed with her official blue jacket and, by the standards of the times, was wearing quite a smart checked shirt. When we got to the theatre, she went to pains to introduce me to all her guide friends. It was almost as if she thought we were on a date. I certainly didn't see it that way.

There was a screen to the side of the stage which flashed a rough translation of the songs for the benefit of foreigners in the audience. At one stage, the Chinese audience started laughing. I asked my guide what was funny. She replied that they were singing in Mongolian, and they couldn't understand it. So much for the idea of promoting a greater China in which all the different ethnic communities tolerated each other and lived in harmony.

In late 1973, the Australian Prime Minister Gough Whitlam and his wife Margaret made an official visit to China. We provided some logistical support to the visit from Hong Kong. Our staff in Beijing would make regular visits to Hong Kong to stock up on essentials and go for medical and dental appointments. One of the staff who visited Hong Kong after the Whitlam visit gave me a rather poignant photo.

The photo was of Chinese Premier, Zhou Enlai, standing and waiting on the tarmac of Beijing Airport for the Whitlams to arrive. It was obviously a cold and grey day and Zhou was standing desolate and alone, wearing a long trench coat. Zhou was supposedly the second most important man in the world's most populous country, but the photo seemed to say that life at the top was lonely. Perhaps it also reflected the manner of Chinese politics, given the many turbulent years since the communist revolution, and showed that to survive you had to rely on your own wits. I still have the photo somewhere in my stored goods in Canberra.

Although my official China Watching days were over, during my assignment to Tokyo we had a small dinner group that met about once a month to discuss things Chinese. Our venue, of course, was a Chinese restaurant. I, therefore, informally remained a China Watcher.

Graeme Lade

As my official trips to China had been confined to Beijing and Guangzhou and they allowed little time for seeing the sights, in October 1976, I decided to take some leave and visit China. I was to stay in Beijing with my old friend and colleague from Hong Kong days, Ross Maddock, and his wife Lynne. I could not have foreseen, however, what this visit had in store for me.

Ross greeted me on arrival at Beijing Airport and said a little welcoming party had been arranged for me at Tiananmen Square. Ross, of course, showed a flair for understatement. I had arrived on a day of historic importance for modern China. It was the day the 'Down with the Gang of Four' movement commenced. The Gang of Four comprised Mao's wife Jiang Jing and her close colleagues from Shanghai, Zhang Chunqiao, Yao Wenyuan and Wang Hongwen.

1976 had proved to be a year of turmoil and change in China. First, Zhou Enlai died in January. There were then clashes between people wishing to mourn publicly over Zhou's death and the supporters of the Gang of Four, and for a time, the Gang of Four seemed to prevail, blaming First Vice Premier Deng Xiaoping for these disturbances. This led to Chairman Mao Zedong's decision to remove Deng from his official position. Perhaps as a portent of things to come, in July there was the massive Tangshan earthquake in which over 200,000 people lost their lives. And, in September, Chairman Mao died.

Barely a month after Mao's death, with new Chairman and Premier Hua Kuofeng at the helm, moves commenced to curtail the influence of the Gang of Four. Their demise was welcomed by the people, as a chance to put an end, once and for all, to the more repressive policies of the cultural revolution. The denunciation of the Gang of Four proved to be a time of great celebration and this was what I had walked into.

Ross and I headed straight from the airport to Tiananmen. This is a massive square believed to be capable of accommodating over a million

A Diplomatic Life

people. When we arrived, there were easily more than a hundred thousand people there, but the square still seemed empty. People were singing and dancing, beating drums and, later on, letting off fireworks. The mood was joyous and, perhaps, unlike the launch of other political movements in modern China, our presence as foreign observers was welcomed by the crowds.

Sunday was to be the day of the mass parade, and over a million people were expected to take part. Although this was an historic day, it was also a day when you would be completely overwhelmed, if not trampled by the crowds. In any case, Ross had planned for us to join Hans Chey, the husband of Jocelyn, the Cultural Attache at the embassy, for a spot of fishing at one of the lakes near the Ming Tombs, just outside Beijing.

Hans ensured we were well prepared. We had fancy rods, lures, flies and weights, as well as some specially prepared tasty bait. In theory, it was actually a very peaceful and relaxing way to spend the day. The only disruption was the loudspeakers broadcasting the proceedings in Tiananmen Square. I don't think though, that was the reason the lake fish did not take to our special bait, nor seem impressed by our fancy fishing gear. Close by, there was a group of Chinese fishing with simple cane rods and live bait, and they managed to catch a good quantity of fish. It was definitely a case of the old triumphing over the new.

In Tiananmen, it was a different story. The new Chairman was triumphing over the old guard. Repeatedly during the afternoon, the calm was punctuated by loud shouts of, 'Da dao!' (down with). I still recall the shouts of a million or so voices coming over our nearby loudspeakers, 'Da dao, Jiang Qing! Da dao, Zhang Chunqiao! Da dao, Yao Wenyuan! Da dao, Wang Hongwen!'

As with any political movement in China, big red character posters appeared almost overnight to add to the denunciation of the Gang of

Four. I am not sure if it was quite so typical, but cartoon posters also began appearing.

One thing I did on this trip was to visit a model farm. Obviously, the farm was carefully chosen as one that demonstrated the best practice and one that had clearly taken the advice of 'in agriculture learn from Tachai'. The farm was neat and well-managed. However, I noticed many of the buildings were decorated with nicely painted scenes of Chinese life. I met the artist, who told me he had to suppress his love of painting during the cultural revolution, but he was glad he had been able to decorate buildings in this way.

Another thing I did brought back memories of assembling bicycles in the Beijing Hotel. On separate occasions, once with one of Ross' colleagues from the embassy, Brent Jones, and then with the Australian Broadcasting Commission's representative in Beijing, Warren Duncan, I joined them in going cycling in Beijing. I quickly learnt that there was a special camaraderie amongst cyclists. It didn't matter if you were a local or a foreigner, you were just part of the milling mass of cyclists.

It was a good way to see the city. We were able to see aspects of Beijing life that I would have missed travelling by car, and it was easy to stop whenever we wanted.

Warren was also a keen photographer, and he travelled everywhere with a swag of cameras around his neck. I learnt from him that if you took more photos, you were bound to get more good ones. Very logical really. Up to then I had been solicitous with my use of film, trying to carefully frame each photo. Following Warren's example, I ended up with some photos of daily life in Beijing of which I was proud. However, I was not in Warren's league. He used film like it was going out of style. After he left China, he published a selection of his China photos.

I had originally hoped to be able to visit Shanghai on this trip, but unfortunately Shanghai was off limits because it was the centre of the main power base for the Gang of Four. Yet again, my travel to China was restricted to Beijing and Guangzhou. However, Guangzhou had an almost a carnival atmosphere about it and there were even more cartoon posters. It seemed even more creative than those in Beijing.

I was also treated to the instant flowering of new Chinese culture, coinciding with the Down with the Gang of Four movement. The cultural performance on offer was a collection of some quite surreal and avant-garde dances. The one I particularly recall was set under the sea and had female dancers emerging from large clam shells. It was not just the themes that were a striking contrast to the past, but also the costumes where many of the female dancers exposed bare mid-riffs. It certainly wasn't what I had expected post-Jiang Qing.

My short interlude in China had proved very memorable and eventful. I felt privileged to have been able to witness these historic events in China. The Down with the Gang of Four movement was the opening act in events leading to the re-emergence of Deng Xiaoping as principal leader and the driving force behind China's subsequent economic modernisation. Deng used an aphorism to encourage a more pragmatic approach to economic development – 'It doesn't matter if the cat is black or white, so long as it catches mice.'

Leaving Hong Kong

My two years in Hong Kong seemed to pass quickly. I would have liked to have stayed longer, but in those days, Hong Kong was regarded as a hardship post, and two years was the norm.

I believe the perception of Hong Kong as a *hardship post* was linked to perceptions that you were confined to a small territory and that maybe, as Australians, we needed room to move. Apart from the crowds, I never found Hong Kong constricting. Rather, I found it a vibrant and dynamic place and just about every day was a new and exciting adventure.

I did acknowledge, however, that compared with the first post experiences most of my colleagues were getting, Hong Kong did not expose me to as wide a range of duties or skills. I had very little interaction with the local government authorities. I didn't have to make representations on behalf of the Australian Government. My range of local contacts was quite select and specialised.

Nonetheless, although I had originally wanted to go to Japan, I enjoyed Hong Kong very much as my first overseas assignment.

I had arrived in Hong Kong with very little in the way of personal possessions but was returning to Australia with a considerable bounty.

Hong Kong proved to be the ideal place to stock-up on household needs such as crockery, cutlery, glassware and cooking utensils, stereo equipment and tailor-made suits. I also left Hong Kong with a much deeper appreciation of Chinese cuisine and culture.

Although I did not experience a major typhoon during my assignment in Hong Kong, I experienced torrential rains and witnessed major landslides, and this was probably every bit as scary, or it should have been.

One Sunday morning I'd received a phone call that there was an urgent cable requiring attention. I rang the communications officer, Margaret Anderson, and, as it was pouring with rain, she came by to collect me in her Triumph convertible – with the roof up, of course. Although we both lived in Conduit Road in the mid-levels area of Hong Kong, the rain was so heavy, the road was under 30-40cm of water. The drainage downhill just could not keep pace.

By the time we had finished attending to the cable, it was already mid-afternoon, so we headed to the Hong Kong Yacht Club for a late lunch. We stayed on at the club for much of the afternoon and then Margaret drove me back to my apartment. The rain was still pouring down, but as it was now dark, it was harder to see how deep the water levels were.

After a light dinner, I headed to bed, but had trouble sleeping as all night there was the non-stop sound of sirens. At the time, I didn't give the sirens a second thought, but they were incessant.

In the morning the rains had eased, and I looked out at the view from my balcony, something I normally enjoyed doing. As I was seventeen floors up, I had great views over Hong Kong Harbour. This morning, however, I was greeted with a different view.

A twelve-storey building in Kotewall Road had collapsed as the result of the impact of a landslide, that had started with the collapse of a large old building, adjacent to Realty Gardens, the compound where I lived. The old building had concertina-ed down to demolish two other buildings on the way. Below me, were numerous fire engines, ambulances and police cars. I watched as bodies or injured people were brought out from the rubble. I had been in total ignorance of the drama unfolding below my building.

That day in the office, we had to monitor the situation closely, as there were suggestions that the residents of Realty Gardens may have to be evacuated if the ground underneath was assessed to be unstable. There were four of us in the office who lived there; fortunately, we didn't have to evacuate.

While our building remained safe, it took some months for the mess to be cleaned up from the landslide. And then massive engineering works were undertaken to try and secure the slopes in the event of future heavy rains.

From memory, about 110 people died in the landslide, although there was one heroic story of an expatriate lawyer being dug out alive, some ten or eleven days after the event. Landslides and resultant deaths were fairly common in the hills, where squatter huts had been built in Hong Kong, but this landslide was the biggest natural disaster to affect a more affluent, settled area of Hong Kong.

Some years later, I read James Clavell's novel *Noble House*, and in one chapter, he depicted a massive landslide which was obviously modelled on the Conduit and Kotewall Roads disasters. It brought back to me my memories of the event.

One of the perks of representing Australia overseas is that you are often given privileged access to events featuring prominent Australians.

During my time in Hong Kong, there was a tennis tournament in which one of Australia's greatest players, Rod Laver, was participating. The spectator stands only allowed for a few hundred people and

A Diplomatic Life

everyone was probably within 20m or so of the court. Watching Rod Laver play, I was bedazzled by his cross-court coverage and his range of strokes. I know the modern game uses different sorts of racquets which give more power, but for me, the artistry, athleticism and entertainment value of Rod Laver put him in a class of his own. I felt privileged to be able to see him play in person.

Along with several other Australian staff from the office, I also went to see the Bee Gees perform on an outdoor stage set up within the Happy Valley racecourse. I regarded it as a privilege to be able to see them perform. We, of course, all had to pay for our tickets.

I had many wonderful memories of my time in in Hong Kong. As I departed, memories of two particular individuals stood out. They were Francis James and Richard Hughes.

I first became familiar with the name Francis James while I was still a student. He had become embroiled in the trial of a group of Sydney University students who were charged with producing an obscene publication. When the students had been unable to find a publisher for their liberal and trail-blazing magazine, *Oz*, Francis James had come to their rescue. At the time, he was publishing the Church of England paper, *The Anglican*.

In 1969, Francis James had been visiting the regular Canton Trade Fair and was arrested and charged with espionage. This was supposedly linked to an article that James had earlier published, claiming he had secretly visited the Chinese nuclear installations at the remote location of Lop Nor.

In early 1973, shortly after the new government of Prime Minister, Gough Whitlam, had recognised the People's Republic of China, we received a discreet message that Francis James would be released from China through Hong Kong. Interestingly, Gough Whitlam and Francis James had been classmates for a while at the Canberra Boys Grammar

School and, apparently, got on quite well together.

I recall there was at least one false start prior to Francis James's actual release, but this allowed our office time to fine tune the contingency plan to meet him when he was released. Matters were complicated, as we had been informed that the family lawyers for Francis James had signed an agreement with the *Age* newspaper granting them exclusive rights to his story.

Because of the strict instructions we had received from Canberra about respecting the family lawyer's exclusivity deal, and the expected high level of media interest in his story, our plan resorted to some subterfuge, including a decoy ambulance intended to try and put the media off-scent.

In those days, the main entry and exit point for China was through the rail border crossing at Lo Wu. While they went to Lo Wu, my bosses left me to man the office and, as it turned out, to handle a number of the media enquiries.

One particularly persistent journalist came to the office itself and asked to see an Australian member of staff. I was the main person left in the office. He told me he was representing the Australian Broadcasting Commission and insisted that, as the ABC was also a government entity, I should be providing him with the details of Francis James' release. I may have been a junior officer, but I was not gullible. I was not impressed with this journalist's disingenuous, not to mention aggressive and abusive tactics, and held my ground.

Generally, however, with one or two exceptions, my experience with ABC foreign correspondents was a positive one and they seemed professional in the way they went about their job. More about this later. However, I again digress.

Francis James went on to keep all of us at the Australian Commission busy for a couple of weeks. Perhaps the most dramatic event involved my immediate boss, Egils Burtmanis. As Egils told it to me, he had been with Francis James in his room at the Matilda Hospital on Hong Kong's Peak and had ducked out to buy some cigarettes. On the way, he met a former Departmental colleague and at that time journalist for *The Australian,* Gregory Clark.

Egils said that Greg had said to him *I know why you are here* and Egils had replied to the effect that he was sorry, but Greg could not accompany him. Greg, however, continued to do so and Egils said it would have required physical force to prevent Greg entering when they reached Francis James' hospital room. Obviously, Egils could not physically restrain Greg. When Francis James saw Greg at the door, he recognised him and welcomed him to come in.

As I later learned, Francis James was not one who could be kept quiet. According to Egils, Francis James spoke at some length about his experiences and then realised he had said too much. He apparently told Greg he should not publish anything he'd said, but rather he would give him three key messages for publication.

This included advice that the Chinese should learn to play cricket. In seeing the Francis James sense of humour in action myself a few days later, I believe this was intended to encourage a sense of British fair play in the Chinese. Another piece of advice was that the Chinese needed to change their dye. This was, I believe, a play on the fact that Chinese politics were red and the majority of people were dressed in a boring dark blue. I cannot recall what the third piece of advice was, but I am sure it was something equally tongue-in-cheek.

Not surprisingly, the *Age* sued *The Australian* for having published details of Francis James' story before they had been able to do so.

One particular task that was left to me was to contact the Hong Kong Flying Club. We had been advised by Canberra that Francis James had a private pilot's licence, although they were not clear on its currency. James had been an Air Force officer in World War II and was therefore an accomplished pilot. He had earlier indicated to my bosses that he wished to go back immediately to China to clear his name and prove he had not been involved in espionage. The initial impression was that he would probably seek to go overland.

However, not wishing to take any chances, I was tasked to discreetly advise the HK Flying Club that if James approached them to lease a plane, they should be aware of the possibility he might seek to fly it across the border. I never found out whether James did actually approach them or, in fact, whether he had a physical opportunity to do so. However, he certainly did not fly back into China.

I, myself, only had one substantive direct meeting with Francis James. Not long before Francis James was medically cleared for return to Australia, I joined him, my boss Egils Burtmanis and Hong Kong-based Australian journalist Jack Spackman and his wife, Margaret, at a dinner at the Foreign Correspondent's Club. I understand Jack had known Francis James for many years.

It proved an entertaining evening. Francis James was in full flow and the rest of us basically sat back and listened for the best part of four hours. Francis James proved quite a raconteur, and certainly an entertainer. He had humorous story after humorous story and the occasional adventure thrown in for good measure. He talked a bit about his China experience. I also recall him talking with pride, about how he had managed to travel from Ireland to England without passing through British Immigration.

I tended to think this story was probably true, as I had seen one of his passports: It was marked 'valid for travel to Israel only'. Yet, as I flicked through the pages, I noticed stamps for a large number of Eastern European countries. It seemed one of his eccentricities was to try and flaunt authority or challenge established norms.

A Diplomatic Life

Overall, however, my impression was that Francis James was something of a Walter Mitty-like character. From my observation, it seemed he couldn't tell the difference between fact and fiction and seriously believed everything he was telling us was true. However, to me, a number of his stories just sounded too good to be true, or I found them simply implausible. Nonetheless, he was certainly an interesting and unforgettable character.

One other memorable character from my time in Hong Kong was the veteran Australian journalist, Richard 'Dick' Hughes. Dick Hughes was one of those larger-than-life characters, not just physically, but in the way he could keep his audience spellbound with his stories.

Dick had lived and worked in Asia, especially Japan and Hong Kong, for many years. In 1968, he had written what many people regarded as the definitive work on the prospects for Hong Kong in the lead-up to 1997 when it was due to revert to China – 'Hong Kong – Borrowed Place, Borrowed Time'. I was pleasantly surprised to see it was still on sale in Swindon Bookshop in Kowloon when I visited Hong Kong in December 2018.

Because of his long experience living in the region and the wide range of his contacts, Dick always had interesting and insightful views on regional developments. And more often than not, there was a humorous perspective.

I had the pleasure of joining Dick a number of times at his lunch table at the Hong Kong Foreign Correspondents Club. Several times this was because his goddaughter, Shelley Warner, who was a colleague of mine working in our first embassy team in Beijing, was visiting Hong Kong. Shelley was the daughter of well-known and respected Australian journalist, Denis Warner.

It seemed to me that Dick Hughes was the model for the character Craw in the John Le Carre novel, *The Honourable Schoolboy*. Some of the scenes depicting Craw reminded me very strongly of Dick Hughes and his mannerisms as I had observed them. There is one scene in the book that refers to the fantastic harbour view from the window of the men's toilet at the FCC. I can attest to the accuracy of that scene, as there was nowhere else in the club where you could get such a good view.

Being a big man and having an imposing presence, Dick would sit at the head of the table and basically pontificate or dominate proceedings. His words seemed more or less to be accepted as gospel. There was no doubt his long presence in the region gave him an air of authority few could match. At these gatherings, one common practice was to circulate a post-card for those present to write a few words on to honour an absent friend.

Now, reverting to my comments on ABC journalists, it was not long after the Francis James episode that the ABC decided to establish a correspondent post in Hong Kong. The first person assigned to this position was John Pennlington, who was well-known because of his role with the ABC program, *Four Corners*. I spent some time with John advising him of our conditions of service provisions as a possible model for the ABC. In all my dealings with John, I found him to be very professional, as well as a true gentleman.

There was one particular incident where I had cause to be grateful for John's assistance. Dr Stephen FitzGerald passed through Hong Kong en route to taking up his position as Australia's first Ambassador to China. There was considerable press interest in Stephen FitzGerald and what he hoped to achieve in China. Accordingly, our office arranged a press conference at the Mandarin Hotel. The press conference was well-attended by local journalists, as well as a number of Australian journalists.

Much to my horror, the Mandarin Hotel had told a very drunk

A Diplomatic Life

Australian that Australia's new Ambassador to China was, at that time, giving a press conference in the hotel. This man barged into the room and shouted for Dr Fitzgerald to listen to him and not to the assembled media. He claimed he had something to say about trade prospects. I think Dr Fitzgerald was perhaps a bit nonplussed, as was I, not knowing how we could control the man's drunken ranting.

It was here John Pennlington came to our rescue. I saw John approach the man and persuade him to go outside with him.

Later, John told me the story. John said he had recognised the man, as years before *Four Corners* had done a story on the launch of a new brand of pet food. My memory of the details is a bit hazy, but I think it was that they had introduced an American-style advertising blitz to promote the new pet food, an approach which at the time was not familiar to Australians. John had told the man that it sounded like he had a story to tell and, as he was an ABC correspondent, he was happy to hear the man's case.

We heard nothing more from the man. The rest of the press conference proceeded smoothly. For my part, I was extremely grateful to John for his good memory and diplomatic skills in resolving the problem.

Changing of the Seasons – Colours of Japan

Autumn.
>Autumn leaves falling.
>A tapestry of colours.
>Time to wear my coat.

I began my first assignment in Japan in early autumn, although when I arrived there were still some hot and humid days, reflecting the final throes of summer. As I settled into life in Tokyo, I appreciated the changing of the colour in the small garden I passed coming up from Gotanda Station to my apartment.

My first apartment in Tokyo had some features I considered to be distinctly Japanese. I had to bend down to get through the front door. The first room reached, after taking off my shoes at the raised entry level, was a toilet. There was a wash basin in the dining area, the kitchen lights were way too low and I kept banging my head. The cupboards in the two bedrooms were designed for storing futons, but not really suited to hanging clothing.

Having studied Japanese history and language at the Australian

National University, I had been keen to get a posting to Tokyo and appreciated this opportunity. However, I soon found the Japanese I had learnt at the ANU was more academic in its approach, rather than familiarising you with colloquial everyday spoken Japanese. Initially, I found I did not have the correct language to provide instructions to taxi drivers or to the barber to get my hair cut. I realised I had a lot of learning still to do.

An early purchase was a television, to help expose me to more colloquial Japanese. One expression I picked up early from TV advertising was 'shin-hatsubai' (new product). There seemed to be lots of them. Some of the TV advertising seemed to have lodged in my brain. I am still reminded of the slogan for Japanese tea – 'Yamamotoyama – ue kara yonde mo, shita kara yonde mo – Yamamotoyama.' (Whether you read it from the top or whether you read it from the bottom, it is always Yamamotoyama.)

Late September and October was a good time to be in Tokyo. Daytime was generally mild, although the nights were starting to get cooler. It was therefore ideal weather for exploring the sights of Tokyo and nearby places. Early on, I visited Asakusa, Ueno Zoo and Kamakura, all of which afforded much better chances to appreciate the variety of autumn colours than the area around my apartment.

The Australian embassy itself had a magnificent garden with a history dating back to the Tokugawa Shogunate. I began playing tennis regularly and the path to the tennis court traversed some shady and attractive areas of the garden.

Three years previously, I had visited Japan for a few weeks as part of my annual leave. On that occasion, I linked up with one of my departmental colleagues. Don Dobinson, who sadly died some years ago, at a young age. Don had been sent to Japan to learn Japanese and, as part of the course, was encouraged to travel within Japan and practice speaking Japanese.

Don had met me at Haneda Airport in his dark blue Alfa Romeo and we set out immediately to drive down the coast of Honshu, the main island, across to the island of Shikoku and then back up Honshu to Tokyo. En route out of Tokyo, we stopped at a roadside restaurant. This was my first experience of such places. I thought it was a self-serve place and quickly distinguished myself by trying to take one of the realistic plastic meal models. I didn't make that mistake ever again, although some of the models are so realistic, they do seem good enough to eat.

As we drove down through Shikoku, we traversed some magnificent scenery with deep valleys, mountains and forests. I cannot remember the place exactly, but I remember somewhere along this route coming to the most spectacular autumn colours I ever encountered in Japan.

Winter.

Light cover of snow.

Pretty at first, turns muddy.

Traffic congestion.

In Canberra, I had been used to cold frosty mornings and the dreaded task of cleaning ice off the car windscreen. Snowfalls in Canberra were not common and usually did not settle on the ground, other than very briefly.

Tokyo winters were cold, but never as cold as those Canberra mornings. However, while snowfalls were not so common, they were probably more common than in Canberra. It was, in fact, in Tokyo where I first experienced driving in snow. Our Embassy Trade Office had arranged an order from the Australian Wine and Brandy Corporation. The order was delivered to the home of the Senior Trade Commissioner, and I had to go there to collect my order of a few cartons of wine.

On the day I had arranged to go, it started snowing. It was not heavy snow, but it was enough to provide a coat of a couple of centimetres. The snow accumulated a bit more where the road curved down to the gutter. As I sought to back away from collecting the wine, I found the car started to skid towards the gutter and the fence. I was slightly alarmed. I tried to straighten the car and apply a bit more throttle. I skidded again. However, after two or three attempts, I was able to drive away and take my wine purchase safely home.

When I first arrived in Tokyo, the Embassy Social Club would arrange occasional excursions for embassy staff. One of these excursions was to Sapporo, the main city on the island of Hokkaido. Much of Hokkaido was a winter wonderland, although in the city streets, the snow tended to be a bit slushy and dirty.

Our main purpose in going to Sapporo was to ski. I had never before tried skiing, but I was assured by the excursion organisers there would be ski instructors on hand to help. There were indeed ski instructors, but they were all men, and they seemed more interested in teaching the females in our group. My instruction was very rudimentary – go to the top of a small slope and then use your stocks to propel yourself downhill. If there were any instructions on how to stop, they did not register with me. When I saw myself veering towards a tree, the only way to stop was to fall over.

I persevered with my self-instruction and practice for several hours. I did become marginally more proficient. However, what I found was that it was hard work falling over and then raising yourself back into a standing position. I ended up getting hot and sweaty.

The location where we were skiing was an attractive-looking place, with its healthy cover of white snow. For me, however, I didn't fully appreciate the beauty of the place, as I was more preoccupied with falling over and getting up. I do remember that evening enjoying sitting in front of a warm fire in our chalet and having a well-earned drink of beer in the company of our fellow travellers.

Another memory of our wintry visit to Sapporo, and apparently a must-do in winter, is our visit to a crab restaurant. It was the season for king crabs. These are seriously big crabs. I think the restaurants were so used to serving them, they produced nut-crackers and long forks that enabled you to access the crab meat more easily. Perhaps because it was easier to get the meat, I enjoyed these crabs more than most other crab meals I have eaten, but maybe being caught in cold waters also rendered the crab meat sweeter and tastier.

As an aside, while it is a completely different experience, I have also greatly enjoyed chili crabs in one of the open-air restaurants along Singapore's east coast. This is inevitably a messy eating experience, but also very enjoyable.

Annapurnas-Macchupuchre with marigolds.

In my second year in Tokyo, I was enrolled in the United States Foreign Service Japanese Language Institute in Yokohama to polish my Japanese and qualify for basic interpreter level proficiency. Although it was a lot of hard work, it was a fun year, and I had many happy memories of my time at the school in Yokohama.

A Diplomatic Life

One particular memory was the day it started snowing. I was in a Japanese reading class, together with my fellow Australian Embassy colleague Richard Rigby, New Zealand colleague, Hillary Brick, and Canadian colleague, Bob Mason. I cannot remember the name of our teacher, but she was the youngest teacher at the school and had spent some time teaching in Australia.

Midway through our class, our teacher started giggling and pointed out through the windows that it had started snowing. Her giggling increased. I think she was not so used to seeing snow. From memory, Richard was the first to be infected by her giggling, but it wasn't long before all of us were laughing uncontrollably. This demonstrated to me how mass hysteria could develop rapidly from seemingly minor beginnings. There was only one solution. We had to break early for lunch. This gave us a chance to go into the school gardens to look at the snow. A few snowballs were also thrown.

Winter in Japan, of course, is not all about snow. In the almost eight years I spent there, over two separate assignments in Japan, I came to associate winter with New Year. Most years, we would go to Meiji Jingu (Meiji Shrine), usually in daytime, but several times at night. There were certain rituals that became part of our routine. Each year, we would return our wooden arrow and *ema* (a small wooden plaque decorated with that year's Chinese zodiac animal).

New Year's Day itself saw many women come to the shrine in their finest kimono as it was a good day to get blessings, as well as to be seen. Usually, the women were only too happy to pose for photographs.

Another great day to see young women in the most impressive kimonos, was the second Monday in January for Seijin no Hi (Coming of Age Day). This was when the girls turning twenty would parade in public at the Meiji Shrine and other temples. They too were keen to pose for photos.

One New Year's Eve, I went with some friends from the embassy to welcome in the New Year at the Takayama Prince Hotel. (After the Meiji Restoration, Japan adopted the Gregorian Calendar and celebrated New Year's Day on the first of January.) This night was the only time I can remember physically helping to make *mochi*. This is the traditional Japanese sticky rice cake eaten at New Year, but also on other ceremonial occasions. The sticky rice is placed in a large wooden vat and people take turns beating it with a wooden hammer. Because the hammer tends to stick a bit to the rice, it is actually more hard work than it looks. However, by participating in hammering the rice, you are supposed to accrue good luck.

Seated at the next table to ours was Agnes Lum and her chaperones, minders or hangers-on. Agnes was the number one pin-up girl in Japan at the time. She was from Hawaii, and I think, predominantly, ethnically Chinese. She was incredibly popular in Japan and was often in the weekly magazines, calendars or making TV appearances, even though she did not speak Japanese. Usually, she was shown in bikinis and was the ideal that many Japanese women aspired to. And, for Japanese men, because she looked Asian, she was the sort of girlfriend they unrealistically aspired to have.

I glanced a number of times at her table, and it seemed Agnes was having a very gloomy time. I thought when the dance music came on again, I should go and ask her to dance and hopefully help relieve her boredom. However, when the music resumed, she and her party all stood up and left. Just my luck!

Another popular New Year's tradition in Japan was NHK's Kohaku Uta Gassen (The Red and White Singing Contest). Not every year, but several times we caught the end of the contest between the popular female (dressed in red) and male (dressed in white) singers.

One year there was particular interest because, it seemed, one of the most popular female duos would not be able to compete. This was the duo known as Pink Lady, comprising Mii and Kei. We had got caught up in some of the Pink Lady phenomenon and had one of their records.

About a week before the contest, Kei was rushed to hospital for an emergency appendectomy. I don't think the option of laparoscopic surgery was available at that time and so normally Kei could have been expected to spend a few days in hospital and avoid rigorous activity for a few weeks. The expectation had been that Pink Lady would be withdrawn from the Red and White Singing Contest. However, much to everyone's surprise Kei competed. All the more surprising as Pink Lady's repertoire included basic dance moves to accompany all their songs.

Spring.

Cherry blossom time.

Hanami, sake, sushi.

A time to party.

Spring brings with it cherry blossoms. Maps are posted in Japan showing the blooming of the blossoms from south to north as the weather gradually warms up, starting first in Kyushu and ending a month or so later in Hokkaido. There are people who seek to follow the blossoms on their journey northwards.

Every flowering cherry tree provides an excuse for celebration. I saw people trying to squeeze into the small space, barely 3m square, under the sole cherry tree in the little garden I used to pass on my way up from Gotanda Station. It didn't seem to matter where the trees were. When we lived in Aoyama, we would see lots of people crowding into Aoyama Cemetery, where there were many spectacular blossom trees. The Japanese did not seem to be at all superstitious about partying in the cemetery – imbibing the spirits they were carrying, usually sake, in the company of the resident spirits.

Living in Japan, I too got into the cherry blossom party mood. Perhaps my first experience was when I was at Japanese Language School in Yokohama. Apparently, it was a school tradition that the Canadian students would host a *hanami* or flower viewing party. The year I joined in, we went to Sankeien, an impressive garden in Yokohama. Teachers and students all participated. Laden with mats, sake and sushi, we found a good clump of cherry trees to sit under and celebrate the blossoms in traditional Japanese style. It was quite common when groups were partying in large expansive gardens to play some games. We found an open space and played softball.

Another tradition was the Imperial Spring Garden Party hosted by the emperor at the Akasaka Imperial Gardens in April to admire the cherry blossoms. Another Imperial Autumn Garden Party was usually held each November to admire the chrysanthemums. In addition to invitations extended to Japanese political leaders and other prominent people, a small number of invitations were extended to each embassy. The Australian Embassy sought to hand around the invitations so each Australian officer would experience the chance to attend at least once during their posting to Tokyo.

I remember attending one such Garden Party hosted by Emperor Hirohito. Perhaps given his age, Crown Prince Akihito and Crown Princess Michiko assumed the role of walking around the gardens and stopping to speak briefly to the assembled guests. They stopped briefly where I was standing, although I cannot recall if I actually spoke with them.

One other tradition associated with these garden parties was that you were encouraged to keep the small cypress wooden cups in which you were served sake. The cups were marked with the Imperial crest. The cypress wood helped infuse a special, but pleasant taste in the sake. Small cakes were served on white saucers decorated with the Imperial chrysanthemum emblem. I am not sure if we were encouraged in the same way to keep these as souvenirs, but I did end up with a couple of saucers.

I also had the chance in 1976 to attend a Cherry Blossom Garden Party at Shinjuku Gyoen, hosted by the prime minister of the time, The Honourable Takeo Miki. Shinjuku Gyoen is a large national park that straddles an area between Shinjuku and Shibuya. It's an impressive and well landscaped park, with over a thousand cherry blossom trees.

One thing that surprised me was that much of the food served was Kentucky Fried Chicken. If it was good enough for the prime minister to serve, I figured it would be good enough for others to serve at their functions. However, I never did follow Prime Minister Miki's example, because as far as possible, I was keen to serve Australian meat to my guests.

On another occasion, I accompanied my friend the embassy science counsellor, Bert Anderson, to visit gardens at Tokyo University. This had been arranged by one of Bert's scientific contacts. It was an excuse for some *hanami* in a quieter setting as it was not open to large crowds. We brought picnic foods, some sake and some mats. I recall the weather was almost perfect and we enjoyed our picnic lunch under some large old cherry blossom trees.

Another memorable cherry blossom experience was when I visited Kumamoto in Kyushu. Kumamoto was a place in Japan I had wanted to visit since studying Japanese history at university. My honours thesis had looked at the Shinpuren (Divine Wind Association) or Keishinto (Respect the Gods Party) Uprising, a samurai uprising that occurred in Kumamoto in 1876. There is a detailed account of the uprising in the novel *Runaway Horses* by Yukio Mishima.

Following the Meiji Restoration in 1868, there were pockets of samurai resistance within Japan which objected to the increasing

Westernisation of Japan and the undermining of the former privileged status of samurai with the formation of a conscript army, banning the carrying of swords and requiring samurai to cut off their topknots. One focus of the Shinpuren Uprising was Kumamoto Castle.

When I was attending Japanese Language School in Yokohama, we were required as part of the course to visit different places in Japan, both to get to know Japan better and to practice Japanese in places where little English was spoken. This was my chance to visit Kumamoto, including the castle. We had eight days for travel, so I arranged an itinerary which included two other places of historic interest – Shimabara and Nagasaki. Much time was spent sitting in trains to get from one place to the other.

My visit to Kumamoto coincided with cherry blossom time. The avenue leading up to the castle was lined on both sides with cherry trees. The trees were in full bloom. It was a spectacular sight, particularly against the background of the mainly black painted castle. In those days, I had a Zeiss Praktika camera. It had served me well, but it was getting old and I had to manually adjust the light settings. Nonetheless, it still took good photos. However, maybe being old, it might have looked a bit like a museum piece. This perhaps also helps to explain what happened next.

I had reached the foreground, before proceeding to the Castle itself, when I was approached by two American Mormon missionaries. In typical Mormon style, they were neatly dressed with dark trousers and pressed white shirts. They each had a name tag attached to their shirts. And they both had very short haircuts.

They greeted me and said they were pleased to see me as I was the first foreigner they had seen for several weeks. They then commented on my camera noting that it was an unusual-looking camera. Would I mind letting then have a closer look? I showed them the camera and

A Diplomatic Life

they asked a number of questions. I think perhaps they wanted to draw me into a discussion about their religion or maybe they just wanted to talk English for a while. Whatever, I excused myself, saying my time in Kumamoto was limited and there was still much I wanted to see and do. I didn't say so, but my first priority was to visit the castle. So, at that point we parted ways.

I think Kumamoto Castle was one of the few castles in Japan I was lucky enough to visit when the cherry blossoms were in full bloom. To be able to visit the castle at such a time and see a place I had written about at university and put it in a better historical perspective, was a memorable experience.

Summer.

Hot and humid months.

Wiping the sweat from my brow.

Thoughts of a cold beer.

Summer is probably my least favourite season in Japan. The weather is characterised by hot temperatures and high humidity, or what the Japanese describe as 'mushiatsui' (muggy). It is not a pleasant season to spend extended periods outdoors. You just hope you have access to good air-conditioning. The summer months are also when the heaviest rainfall tends to happen. The rain only provided a brief respite from the hot and humid weather.

The Australian Embassy had a couple of beach cottages in Shimoda at the southern tip of the Izu Peninsula. These were allocated to staff on a rostered basis. Shimoda is a small city by Japanese standards and is located in a scenically attractive part of Japan with some nice beaches. It is also a historically important place, as this is the port opened to the Americans as a result of the Treaty of Kanagawa signed by Commodore Perry in 1854, paving the way for commerce between Japan and the United States.

It is a mostly attractive drive to Shimoda of two and a half to three hours, usually from Tokyo and, part of the way, if the clouds are behaving, you can get some good views of Mount Fuji. For much of the route, you are skirting the coast, however, in summer, Shimoda is a magnet for Japanese holiday makers and becomes very crowded.

On one occasion, I was rostered for one of the cottages in the week of Obon. Obon week falls in mid-August and is when Japanese pay respects to their ancestors. It has also become a popular time for taking holidays in Japan and abroad. This particular weekend, the traffic was so heavy, it took me eight hours to get there. To make matters worse, the air-conditioning was not working in my old Nissan car – I had not yet taken delivery of my new Honda Accord. When the traffic moved at reasonable pace, there was some cooling breeze, but for much of the trip it was stop and start driving and it was like sitting in an oven.

When I eventually got to Shimoda, I couldn't wait to go for a swim. However, the beach was much more crowded than I had previously experienced, and it was not such a relaxing experience.

One problem with really hot weekends during summer is that there is a mass exodus of people heading to the beaches. After such weekends, you would often see in the newspapers that a hundred or more people had drowned. I think there were two reasons for this. One, is that the majority of Japanese people do not know how to swim properly and go out into deeper water, unable to cope, or they get into treacherous water. The other reason, which I witnessed myself, is that so many people cram into the water, there is no room to move freely, and people are essentially trampled upon.

When I lived in Japan, the practice of deploying properly trained lifeguards was virtually non-existent. Maybe things have improved today, as I understand Japanese have been trained as lifeguards in Australia or other countries. I therefore expect, at the more popular beaches, there would now be lifeguards on duty.

One final summer experience I wish to mention is an occasion when I accompanied one of my embassy colleagues, Graham Wilson, returning to Tokyo from Shimoda. He had been introduced to a special place which he wanted me to see. 'Rotemburo' or open-air bathing places are quite popular tourist attractions, as they are usually in scenic locations.

I cannot remember the name of the place, but we took the inland route from Shimoda, not the coastal route. We travelled for an hour or so before climbing to the top of a hill and could see a river in the valley below. This was the place. There was an entrance to a cave. Near the entrance, there were male and female changing areas. There were a few frogs in the male changing area. Perhaps they were waiting for a beautiful princess to appear!

There were no beautiful princesses awaiting us in the bathing area. Rather, there was a small group of elderly ladies, average age seventy plus. However, we only saw them when we entered the bathing area and followed its U-shape to its end. I think the ladies were somewhat surprised at the arrival of two much younger foreign men. They had a good giggle. We exchanged a few pleasantries.

However, the main attraction opened up before us. There was an opening in the cave, and we were looking through a waterfall down the valley to the river below. It was an unusual but beautiful sight. It had been well worth the visit.

Summing up my experiences in Japan, I came to appreciate the sensitivity of Japanese life and culture to nature around them. It permeated so much of Japanese life. Particular flowers and trees were associated with each of the seasons, and these were reflected in flower arrangements – 'ikebana' and the lay-out of Japanese gardens. The seasons were associated with particular foods and, when served, these foods were also garnished in such a way, for example, with a leaf or a flower to illustrate the season. Japanese literature, especially poetry, placed strong emphasis on nature. Often the seasons were not referred to directly, but through allusion to insects or birds or other symbols associated with particular seasons.

Lost Suitcases

Being in a line of work where you have to do a lot of travel, inevitably from time to time, things do not always go smoothly or to plan. Missed or delayed flights are inconvenient, but lost or delayed luggage is not only an inconvenience, but sometimes can have other interesting consequences.

My first two memorable experiences involving lost luggage both relate to luggage sent from Japan.

In the first instance, we had travelled from Japan to enjoy a family holiday with my parents in Tasmania. We had to collect our luggage in Melbourne and clear customs there. However, there was no sign of our luggage. We were encouraged to take our connecting flight to Hobart and the airlines undertook to forward our luggage when, with confidence, they said it had been located. I told them we could not come back to Melbourne to collect it. The reply was 'no worries', it would be delivered to Hobart.

Sure enough, a day later we received a phone call advising our luggage had arrived in Hobart. I asked if I had to go and collect it from the airport. No, they would deliver it to where we were staying. I guess this was the reward, as we didn't have to line up in long customs queues.

In the second instance, at the end of our posting to Japan, we arranged to send some unaccompanied luggage ahead of us. I cannot remember how many cases were involved, but all but one of the cases turned up safely. After some months passed, we thought we had lost the other case permanently. One day out of the blue, we received advice that the missing case had turned up. I had to go to the customs office to collect it.

When I recovered the suitcase, I found it had a number of different baggage tags attached. From what I could make out, our suitcase had first ended up in Argentina. I surmised that maybe at the Tokyo baggage handling area, there were areas adjacent to each other for luggage to Australia and luggage to Argentina and this one suitcase had ended up in the Argentina area.

Although we had survived without the suitcase for some months, it was a relief to get it back in the end.

Twice I experienced luggage not making it on to the plane because of late plane departures, meaning the time in transit was much reduced.

The first time, I was travelling from Kathmandu to Melbourne via Bangkok. When I got to Melbourne, standing at the baggage carousel waiting for my luggage, I was approached by some Thai Airways ground-staff asking if I was Graeme Lade. I confirmed I was, and they explained that my luggage had not been transferred in Bangkok. However, their computer records showed it would be transported on the same flight the following day. I was impressed that, thanks to computerisation, they could track the location of my luggage.

As Melbourne's Tullamarine Airport is quite a distance from the city, I was concerned I would have to come back the next day to collect my suitcase. They replied they would arrange delivery to my hotel. Fortunately, I had packed extra shirt, socks and underpants in my carry-on luggage. This was just as well, as I was due the next day to begin my mid-term consultations in Melbourne.

The second time I was traveling from Hobart to Canberra via Melbourne. When my luggage didn't show up, I asked the customer service desk whether they knew what had happened. Their computer tracking showed there had been insufficient time to transfer my luggage to my flight, but it would be on a later flight from Melbourne. I could either depart the airport or wait about ninety minutes. I chose to wait. I was not the only person whose luggage hadn't showed up. Some others chose to wait too. Qantas provided us each with a meal voucher, which I appreciated, but it meant I had to go back through security checks, as all the places serving food were inside the restricted area of the airport.

Another luggage incident occurred when I travelled to Sharm El-Sheik in Egypt to meet up with Odette, who had been attending an international conference there. I had travelled on Qatar Airways from Manila to Cairo. I had to collect my luggage and go through customs before boarding my Egypt Air flight to Sharm El-Sheik. It was a new suitcase and was in good condition when I'd checked in for the domestic flight to Sharm El-Sheik.

Odette had come to the airport to meet me on arrival in Sharm El-Sheik. Waiting at the baggage carousel for my luggage, initially there was no sign of it, and then, the last bag to come out was a mangled mess. That was my new suitcase. It looked as if it had been run over by a truck – I expect that it was. Some of the contents were showing, but fortunately because of the internal lining of the suitcase, I was not aware of losing any of its contents.

By this time, most of the airport ground staff had disappeared. After some searching, I found someone who I could report to about my damaged suitcase. Although the contents seemed to be intact, I could not carry the suitcase as it was, without things falling out. I explained to an airport staffer that it was a brand-new suitcase and how I also needed a bag, or something I could transfer my case contents into.

From memory, the staffer was a woman who was quite sympathetic to my plight. I had, of course, to fill out some forms. She assured me they would arrange to get me a replacement case. Eventually the woman returned with a new suitcase. It was the same colour and material as my damaged suitcase, but slightly larger. She explained they had obtained the suitcase from the duty-free shop. As such, it was probably more expensive than my suitcase, but I was assured the airline would meet the replacement cost.

It was almost two hours after landing that Odette and I were able to leave the Airport and go to our hotel. We ended up having a late dinner in an open-air restaurant in Sharm El-Sheik, but glad to have resolved the damaged luggage issue.

I have left my two most dramatic experiences to last.

As we had been advised that Tet (a festival for Lunar New Year), was not the best time to be in Vietnam as nearly everything closed down, Odette and I accordingly decided to go to Myanmar, to the cities of Yangon and Bagan. We had a very pleasant few days, but on return to Noi Bai Airport in Hanoi, there was no sign of our suitcase. It was a fairly new case and filled with clothing for both Odette and me, including some of my best trousers, as well as souvenirs from Myanmar, including a quite expensive lacquer bowl we had bought in Bagan.

Despite repeated enquiries to Vietnam Airlines, who many times told us that they had tried following up with their staff in Yangon, we continued to get the same response; namely, they had been unable to locate our suitcase. We also had travel insurance with Assist Card or Assistencia and they were trying to follow up as well. Eventually, Vietnam Airlines agreed to pay us compensation based on the assessed weight of the suitcase. This was considerably less than the value of the

A Diplomatic Life

contents.

I advised Assist Card of this, who advised they would continue to process our claim. I was encouraged to phone them initially in their Miami office, and subsequently in their Colombia office, and although they could not provide an accurate assessment of the worth of our suitcase and contents, as I did not have any receipts, things moved reasonably quickly after dealing with the Colombia office, and a payment was made to our bank account.

Even with the Vietnam Airlines and Assist Card payments together, it was still considerably less than what I had estimated the total worth to be. Replacing the trousers presented something of a problem too, as it was so hard to get anything approximating my size in Vietnam.

To this day, we do not know what happened to our suitcase. The airlines had suggested one possibility was that the baggage tag was not properly attached. Given the chaos at the airport, that was quite plausible. Another possibility was that it was routed to different destination, even though efforts were supposedly made to contact other airports, such as Nagoya and Paris, where flights were headed the same day. The third possibility was that being a fairly new-looking suitcase, it may have been stolen from the baggage carousel in Hanoi. I expect we will never know.

However, based on this experience, I now always collect my purchase receipts and put them in my hand carry-on, only disposing of them when my luggage has safely arrived.

Perhaps the most dramatic lost baggage experience was when my suitcase went missing in Colombo. I was in the early stages of a long, official overseas trip, which ultimately took me to a conference in Kiev. I had agreed, for the first time, to use one of our Division's Samsonite suitcases, a standard-size black affair.

Most of the flights into Colombo seemed to arrive after one in the morning. I was travelling with Singapore Airlines. I guess immigration clearance for foreigners was slower than for locals as by the time I got to the baggage carousel, many suitcases had been collected. Nonetheless, I still waited for quite some time for my suitcase to appear, but it did not come. However, there was still one black Samsonite suitcase on the carousel. I knew it wasn't mine, as it was quite badly scuffed.

I reported my loss to Singapore Airlines. They assumed the owner of the remaining suitcase had inadvertently taken mine. However, rather than detain me even longer at the airport, they had me fill out the required lost baggage forms and gave me about US$100 to cover purchase of emergency needs. I wasn't sure there would be much open at 3am to use this, but I guess it was to cover me if they could not locate my suitcase. They also gave me the Singapore Airlines First Class Passenger toiletry kit, and I did make use of some of its content, such as the yukata-type robe to try and sleep in. Two other items impressed me; these were the two pairs of paper underpants.

I got to my hotel about 2:30 in the morning and immediately rang the number Singapore Airlines had given me to contact them at the airport. The good news was that they had located my suitcase. The man in their office told me they had rung the local phone number on the suitcase and the woman who answered confirmed that her husband had been travelling but said he was not due back till the following day. A short time later, the man himself had come back to the airport with my suitcase and confessed he had gone to the home of his mistress. I understand he wanted his suitcase back rather urgently, as there was a gift of some sort for the mistress.

A little after 4am my suitcase was delivered to my room at the hotel. I obviously didn't get much sleep that night as I had to be showered and breakfasted by 7:30am, as my first official appointment was scheduled for 8:30am, but at least I could dress respectably in a suit as

I had my suitcase back.

As to the man who accidentally took my suitcase, I'm sure he had some serious explaining to do when he got home to his wife. I wondered, in hindsight, if his marriage survived or if the missing suitcase saga was the beginning of the end. While the man had, fortunately for me, included his phone number on the baggage tag, it was clearly not so fortunate for him. What lesson does this teach? Perhaps if you are going to take a mistress, it is a good idea not to write your home phone number on the baggage tag. Perhaps more morally, it teaches that if you try to cheat on your wife, you will be found out in the end.

For me, the moral was to never again use the Division's suitcase, but rather to have a suitcase that is clearly recognisable, either a non-standard colour or an attachment of coloured ribbons.

Escaping to Thailand in Search of Better Life

In Thailand, my duties primarily related to Indochina, covering both policy issues relating to long-term peace for Cambodia and refugees. On refugees, one of my main duties was to work closely with our immigration team and advise them on political developments in Indochina, in order to assist them in making decisions on eligibility for refugee settlement.

However, my duties also entailed seeking to understand the broader policy implications of refugee issues to evaluate their humanitarian needs, particularly in the case of the Cambodians settled in camps scattered along the Thai-Cambodian border. This, of course, meant regular travel throughout Thailand to visit the various refugee camps, observing the situation, and to sit in on interviews with refugees seeking resettlement.

A few weeks after commencing work at the embassy in Bangkok, I made the first of many visits to Aranyaprathet on the Thai-Cambodian border. Aranyaprathet had probably been something of a sleepy backwater town until the UN agencies and international non-government organisations started turning up, primarily to assist the displaced Khmer living in camps along the border.

By the time of my first visit, the town was teeming with representatives from the UN Border Relief Operation (UNBRO), World Food Program (WFP), UN High Commission for Refugees (UNHCR) and other UN agencies and numerous NGOs, including the International Committee of the Red Cross (ICRC) and Medecins Sans Frontieres (MSF), as well as the Thai military. Hotel accommodation was at a premium.

I travelled with a colleague from the embassy, and we stayed at a hotel called Amnuay Suk 1. My colleague had warned me conditions were fairly basic and that I should bring a roll of toilet paper with me. This was, he said, not for the usual purpose, but to plug all the holes in the insect screen to try and keep the mosquitoes out. It was good advice as the insect screen was indeed torn in many places.

My colleague was also right about the hotel being basic. The bed sheet had almost as many holes as the insect screen and the first time I used the wash basin, my feet were drenched as there was no down pipe to take the water away. For breakfast, we had to go to the partner hotel, Amnuay Suk 2. I soon learnt when travelling up-country in Thailand, that a standard Western-style breakfast was either unavailable or unpalatable. So, congee it was, and the congee was usually quite tasty.

I ended up staying many times at either Amnuay Suk 1 or Amnuay Suk 2. Sometimes we would go to the market for lunch or dinner, although for dinner there were a couple of more upmarket options where we could dine to the accompaniment of aspiring, mostly female, singers.

However, during the day, we were out visiting the camps – Nong Chan, Nong Samet, Ampil or Ban Sa Ngae and (after they were overrun in a Vietnamese offensive at the end of 1984 and early 1985) Site

II. These were all camps that showed allegiance to Son Sann's Khmer People's National Liberation Front (KPNLF). We also usually called on the ICRC Hospital and other facilities at Khao-I-Dang. The hospital would be familiar to people who watched the movie, *The Killing Fields*, as the final scenes of the movie were filmed in front of the Khao-I-Dang hospital.

These camps contained more people than many cities, yet the conditions they lived in were rudimentary. There was a mass of blue plastic sheeting and bamboo. From these materials basic shelters were made. Latrines were often just a hole dug in the ground. In the dry months, they were dustbowls and in the wet months, turned into great ponds of mud. Hardly ideal living conditions.

However, compared with where they'd escaped from, camp life offered a number of advantages. Some of the camps were better administered by their Khmer leaders than others, but generally, security was better than what they had left behind in Cambodia. For nearly all of them, it would have been a treacherous journey across Cambodia escaping from the ordeal of living under the Khmer Rouge, facing up to robbers and avoiding stepping on landmines. Cambodia at the time was one of the most heavily land-mined countries in the world.

Within the camps, not all was perfect on the security front. There were occasional clashes amongst the Khmers themselves and, as the Vietnamese offensive in late-1984/early-1985 showed, they could still be militarily vulnerable, even so close to the Thai border.

In other respects, the camps provided the people with regular food supplies, health care and basic education. Many of the more committed and responsible young refugees got jobs helping the international aid agencies. This helped them to develop working level skills in English, as well as some useful work experience.

I was impressed with the resilience of the children. A refugee camp is not a good place for children to grow up. They didn't have fancy toys, such as my own daughters were used to, and had to improvise. One day, I saw a couple of small boys having a great game playing with their home-made toy car. It was made from a piece of wood to form the body of the car and some tin cans that had been cut in half to form its wheels. The car was pulled by a piece of string.

Living in a refugee camp would have been no fun, especially for the children. Hygiene was clearly far from ideal, and children with runny noses or in need of a good wash were prevalent. However, there was something endearing about being greeted by these children with their big smiles and their friendly greeting of, 'Hello. Bye-bye.'

There must have been something about the Khmer living conditions and lifestyle that bred people tough. One example was when I visited one of the Khmer hospitals and saw a row of premature babies. There were, of course, no humidicribs as we would expect in our hospitals. Rather, all they had was a blanket and an ordinary desk lamp to keep the babies warm. Yet according to the hospital staff, the survival rate was almost 100%.

Another more telling example occurred when I visited Khao-I-Dang Hospital after the Vietnamese offensive against Nong Chan Camp. There was a team of Australian doctors and nurses assisting to treat the wounded. The timing coincided with upcoming federal elections in Australia. As voting is compulsory in Australia, the doctors were determined to exercise their right to vote. My visit, in part on this occasion, was to act as assistant returning officer to enable the doctors and nurses to vote.

The workload for the Australian medical team in that period was incredible and often they would work twenty-four-hour shifts. In any case, the surgery was pretty well manned twenty-four hours a day. When I arrived at the hospital, some of the doctors were in surgery, but they remained determined to vote. They asked me to come into the operating theatre. I was shown to one corner of the operating theatre.

The medical team at that time were operating on a young Khmer man of about twenty years old. He was a mess. He had lost an arm and had shrapnel wounds all over his chest and abdomen. As I watched, the doctors were pulling out his intestines and cutting out bits with large chunks of shrapnel embedded in them. To my untrained eye, there was a lot of blood, but the doctors told me the patient had already lost (almost) as much blood as was possible, without actually dying. All in all, it was not a pretty sight.

In-between a snip here and a snip there, a suture here and a suture there, each member of the team took turns to come over to the corner where I was to cast their vote. I witnessed, the hopefully rare occurrence, where Australians literally had blood on their hands as they cast their votes.

Returning to the subject of the resilience of the Khmer, I went back to Khao-I-Dang a couple of weeks later and asked how the young man, whose surgery I'd witnessed, was getting on. I, in fact, met him. He was up and about. His first reactions to me were that the sooner he could get back to the battlefield the better, as he wished to get stuck into the 'Vietnamese aggressors'. While I wasn't sure he would ever be up to fighting again, I could not help but be impressed by his indomitable spirit.

There was a section at Khao-I-Dang that was devoted to making prosthetic limbs, mostly legs, for people – men, women and children, who had lost their legs in a landmine explosion or in the course of battle. The prosthetic limbs were made of wood and bits of rubber tyres. They were pretty simple in construction, but they served the purpose. Again, it was inspiring to see the determination of the people learning to use their new prosthetic limbs.

A Diplomatic Life

Perhaps because of these observations, at Khao-I-Dang in particular, and seeing the extent of injuries caused following the Vietnamese offensive, I was easy prey for one of the Canadian nurses at the hospital. She convinced me I should donate some blood. She was ecstatic when she learnt I was O-negative and the universal blood donor. Her reaction of glee seemed almost like a vampire being let loose in the blood bank.

I cannot remember how much blood they took from me, but I know it was more than the usual extraction volume because of their pressing needs. I am sure this was why I felt a bit weak for a couple of weeks after. On one occasion back at Khao-I-Dang, I almost fainted. It was very hot and oppressive in the hospital that day and that may have also contributed to my becoming faint. For a change, the nurses ministered over me and gave me water and salt tablets. However, perhaps because of that experience I have not donated blood since.

The refugee population of followers of Prince Norodom Sihanouk and his FUNCINPEC (National United Front for an Independent, Neutral, Peaceful and Cooperative Cambodia) organisation were mostly located at Green Hill, O'Smach, Site B and Tatum. These were accessible through the Thai city of Surin, better known for its annual elephant festival, which unfortunately I never got to see.

In contrast to Aranyaprathet, Surin was a proper city. It had a long history and many grand and imposing buildings. It was better laid out and did not have the feel of haphazard and uncontrolled ramshackle growth that marked Aranyaprathet. I cannot remember the name of the hotel we stayed at in Surin, but it was a large building with normal hotel rooms.

The hotel had one feature which was not entirely uncommon in Thailand. As an annex it had a massage parlour which Chris Lamb, my immediate boss at the time, delighted in showing visitors from

Australia. You walked in the entrance and there was a large group of scantily clad girls sitting behind a large glass window. This was one-way glass – we could see the girls, but they could not see us. It was almost like looking into a large fishbowl.

To get from Surin to the FUNCINPEC camps was a bit more challenging country than that around Aranyaprathet, which was largely flat or gently rolling hills. The FUNCINPEC camps were actually nestled in the Dangrek Mountain Range and protected by tracts of forest.

While some of the KPNLF camps straddled the border with Thailand, the FUNCINPEC camps were generally all well inside Cambodia. I recall stopping at the crest of a mountain on one occasion and having a photo taken of Chris Lamb and myself shaking fists at each other over a border marker stone – one of us on the Cambodian side and the other on the Thai side. This stone was some distance from the entry to the camp.

Perhaps because of their location, being surrounded by trees, the FUNCINPEC camps did not seem as depressing as the KPNLF ones, although they were still comprised of masses of bamboo and blue plastic. Maybe it was just my impression, but I felt that entering Green Hill, where there were a couple of administrative or ceremonial buildings made of bamboo that stood out, the camp had the air of being slightly better organised.

During my time in Thailand, it was Australian government policy that we not seek to visit camps occupied by the Khmer Rouge. However, on one occasion my ambassador, Gordon Jockel, asked me to accompany his journalist friend, Peter Hastings, on a visit to the Thai-Cambodian border. Peter wanted to go to a Khmer Rouge camp. We drove to the entrance of one of their camps and I waited in the car, anxiously hoping that Peter would return safely. He did of course.

Peter had visited Phnom Penh and met with Hun Sen, who had

A Diplomatic Life

become leader following the Vietnamese withdrawal. Hun Sen had been a member of the Khmer Rouge initially but defected from their ranks. I recall Peter telling me about his meeting with Hun Sen. Hun Sen had clearly come across as a tough and determined person. Best demonstrated when Peter asked me, *Did I know that Hun Sen had a glass eye* – that was, he said, the kind eye.

As mentioned before, one aspect of my job was to assist and advise our immigration team involved in processing refugees for resettlement of the political situation in Cambodia and Vietnam and what had transpired in the past, so they could better determine whether prospective refugees were telling the truth. I think for the most part we were taking the right people, but undoubtedly a few people, who lied about their association with the Khmer Rouge, got through.

To play this role with immigration, it was useful for me to sit in on some of the refugee interviews. Sometimes they were quite moving and, sometimes, they provided a few laughs.

Most of the refugees we interviewed on trips to Aranyaprathet for resettlement were Cambodians. However, there was a small group of Vietnamese refugees who had been held inside one of the KPNLF camps in an area specifically designated to them, known as NW82. The international community had agreed that all these people would be accepted as refugees for resettlement and Australia had agreed to take its share of these people.

While discussions were continuing on the resettlement of the Vietnamese caseload at NW82, I accompanied a visiting Australian Parliamentary delegation to Nong Samet, and we met the Vietnamese refugees staying at the NW82 platform area. The platform was so named, as a special raised platform had to be built because the area designated for the Vietnamese refugees was on swampy ground. The Vietnamese refugees would have been aware, at the time of our visit, that efforts were being made to find a resettlement solution for them. However, the leader of the Australian delegation naively asked the Vietnamese refugees how many would like to be resettled in Australia. Surprise, surprise. Nearly every hand went up.

Some of the refugee interviews stood out and left lasting impressions. I remember on one occasion our immigration officer asked a Cambodian man what his occupation had been. He replied that he was a tree climber. Our Immigration officer perhaps did not understand, and so his next question was, 'And what does a tree climber do?' 'You know,' the man replied through an interpreter, 'you climb up the coconut trees and knock down the coconuts.'

On another occasion, interviewing a young and quite attractive Vietnamese woman, where subject to health checks, her acceptance for resettlement to Australia was assured, our Immigration officer asked her what she had done in Vietnam. She replied, again through an interpreter, that she had been a 'sexy clothes dancer'. I think this particular immigration officer must have been born yesterday, because his follow-up question was, 'And what does a sexy clothes dancer do?' She calmly replied, 'You listen to the music and slowly take off your clothes.' I hope she found another profession when she came to Australia.

On another occasion, I was fascinated by an interview with a Vietnamese man from NW82. His wife was a mathematics professor and he'd been an officer in the South Vietnam military. His wife had been able to work to some extent following reunification, but his life was one of constant hardship and deprivation. He had spent time in labour camps and knew he had no prospect in the foreseeable future of resuming a normal life in Vietnam. Some of his descriptions of life in the labour camp were quite harrowing.

One feature of the interviews with the Cambodians was that it was quite clear that their 'bush radio' system worked well and refugees when interviewed would report quickly back to their colleagues.

For example, on one occasion we had told a refugee that he'd been accepted for resettlement at the end of the interview. He had told us he'd worked as a bicycle repairman in Cambodia, and he must have thought this was a much sought after profession in Australia and that's why he'd been accepted. The reality was that he had been accepted because he had close family already in Australia. However, at the next four or five interviews, the men all claimed they had been bicycle repairmen.

Perhaps the most moving interview I attended involved a Cambodian man in his mid-sixties. We were his last hope. He had already been rejected by the Americans, the Canadians and the French, despite having one fairly close relative living in France. His claim for resettlement in Australia was based on a second cousin, whom he did not know, as a relative in Australia who could support him. The man had been an illiterate farmer in Cambodia. He had no surviving close family amongst the other refugees, and none in Cambodia, though he admitted to having some good friends among some of the older refugees in the camp.

After interviewing this man, the immigration officer, rightly in my view, determined he did not have the capacity to adapt to life in Australia, particularly if his second cousin did not directly support him. He assessed that he would be better off staying with his friends in the camp. The man was clearly heartbroken as he'd probably built up his expectations of getting out of the camp existence. He started sobbing uncontrollably and got down on his hands and knees, grabbing Joe (the immigration officer)'s leg.

It was clearly an emotional and upsetting decision for the man, and it was upsetting for us too knowing he's probably had raised hopes of getting away from his refugee existence. Joe waited patiently for a few minutes hoping the man would let go and leave. However, when he did not do so and, because our time to conduct the interviews was limited, Joe called in the next family for interview. Joe calmly carried out the interview, with the man still clinging to his leg and quietly sobbing. Eventually, the man let go and departed.

It was a difficult situation, but I thought Joe handled it well. I still believe it was the right decision. The man had no skills, he knew no-one in Australia. He had not sought to develop any skills in the camp. I believe he would have been overwhelmed and indeed, even unhappier, if he went to Australia and there was no guarantee that the Cambodian community would be prepared to look after him. Nonetheless, by seeing someone's hopes dashed in that way, it was hard not to get a bit emotional as well.

Tackling Piracy and Other Refugee Issues

Another aspect of my work involved Vietnamese boat people. The Australian Government made a substantial contribution to UNHCR and the Royal Thai Navy for anti-piracy operations. This took the form of money to UNHCR or provision of Nomad aircraft and training for the Royal Thai Navy for surveillance activities.

Piracy was a major problem encountered by refugees seeking to flee Vietnam by boat. A very large percentage of the boats were attacked by pirates. Some boats were just robbed. They were probably the lucky ones. Others had people thrown overboard if someone resisted the pirates' demands.

In many cases the women were raped, either onboard their own boat, or taken onto the pirate boat or a deserted island. After a woman had been used for a while, she might be dropped somewhere not far from shore, although more often than not, the women were either killed or thrown to the sharks. UNHCR applied a general rule that if a woman did not show up within three weeks, we could assume she was dead.

The Royal Thai Navy anti-piracy activities were predominantly run out of the southern Thai city of Songkhla. In order to monitor progress on the anti-piracy activities, I was required to visit Songkhla regularly. To get to Songkhla, I would fly to Haadyai (now Hat Yai) and then take a car to Songkhla.

Haadyai was a bustling city and the centre of cross-border trade with Malaysia, both legal and illegal. It had a thriving market where you could buy the latest electrical goods or cameras, although probably most of these had 'fallen off a boat'. For me, the main shopping requests I had in Haadyai were for bird's nest and cashew nuts. I did not want to touch the possibly 'hot' items. Another feature of Haadyai, was its very busy nightlife. For a city its size, it had more than enough massage parlours. It was said that many of the clients came across from Malaysia.

Haadyai also had a very good university – the Prince of Songkhla University. I visited the university a number of times and had frequent interaction with some of the faculty staff from the university who had studied in Australia, mostly under the Colombo Plan. In Bangkok, I was involved in the launch of the Thailand Australia Technical Services Centre (TATSC) which was set up by returned alumni from Australian universities to try and give back to Thailand some of the technical services and skills they had learnt in Australia. The engineering gaculty at the Prince of Songkhla University, in particular, had a very strong chapter in the TATSC.

By contrast, Songkhla was a sleepy and quite sprawling town along the coast. I always stayed at the Samila Hotel, which was located adjacent to a beach. My usual morning ritual was to go to the beach for a swim. I would often be sharing the water with Muslim women and their children, all fully clothed – I wore my regular Australian-style bathers. We always exchanged a few friendly words. After my swim, I would go to a small cafe next to the hotel called Sandy Jack's. It made the best banana pancakes I have ever tasted. They were served with a delicious pineapple jam. Then it would be down to work.

Our schedule usually involved meetings and briefing with the Royal Thai Navy and UNHCR, practical aerial and nautical surveillance activities, and a visit to the holding centre in Songkhla for newly arrived boat people.

Until Australia donated a Nomad aircraft, the main surveillance aircraft was a four-seater Cessna plane. While you could get a good view from the Cessna, it was a bit cramped for recording and taking good photos of suspicious activities. The Nomad offered more space to do this and was more comfortable, and hopefully, more effective.

I went up in the Cessna several times. However, I remember one occasion when the weather was becoming threatening, but the RTN airmen were confident they could go up and be back before the storm hit. As time was limited, and there were only two seats, the US and Italian ambassadors were given first priority. Lucky them. I was not at all envious on this occasion.

The storm did in fact come faster than expected, and so our intrepid ambassadorial fliers were forced to put down in Haadyai and come back to Songkhla by road. That evening a reception had been arranged with senior Thai Navy personnel and local government representatives at the Samila Hotel. We enjoyed a pleasant evening. Unfortunately, the two ambassadors arrived late and only had a short time to relax with the other guests.

On another occasion, shortly after the Royal Thai Navy had taken delivery of an Australian-made Nomad aircraft and their pilots had returned from training in Australia, I was prevailed upon as the sole Australian representative among the UNHCR staff and other donor country representatives, to show my faith in the plane and go up in the inaugural local flight. The flight was fine, and the plane certainly showed it had better space capability for carrying out the surveillance work, however, the landing was pretty rough.

The Navy airstrip at Songkhla was not designed specifically with crosswind landings in mind, and yet often pilots encountered crosswinds as they came in to land. The pilots who had been training in Australia said they hadn't yet experienced any crosswind landings. The plane survived the landing though, so the Thai Navy then invited other representatives to experience flying in the Nomad. I had done my bit for flag and country.

One other small thing that impressed me about the Thai Naval Air wing was the badge which one of the pilots wore, describing himself as a pirate hunter.

The same trip on which the US and Italian ambassadors had been diverted from Songkhla in their Cessna flight, also involved a trip to sea on one of the Naval patrol boats. I'd been looking forward to this as a chance to get my first real taste of how difficult the task was, and how well the Thai Navy managed, given these difficulties.

All the foreign representatives, as well as some senior Thai Navy officers who hadn't been to sea for a while, boarded the patrol boat. We set sail towards the mouth of the Songkhla River. As we neared the river mouth, the water became increasingly choppy. I was quite enjoying the thrill of going to sea, but I could see some of my colleagues were not so impressed, especially a couple of the senior Thai Navy officers and the Italian ambassador, who seemed, literally, to be turning green.

In response to their obvious discomfort, it was agreed we would turn back. I was disappointed as it didn't give us a chance to assess the potential and effectiveness of the anti-piracy surveillance operations. I guess, however, it did provide some sense of how rough the seas could get and how this compounded the difficulty of their task.

A Diplomatic Life

Usually, when we went to Songkhla, we visited the UNHCR refugee holding centre for new boat people arrivals in southern Thailand. On one such occasion, I was greeted by UNHCR personnel with the news of a two-year-old girl who had arrived a few weeks back, but without her mother. Others on the boat said that she'd been taken by pirates. They didn't know the name of the little girl but knew her mother's name and reported that the mother had spoken of having a husband, already living in Sydney. UNHCR asked if there was anything I could do to help the girl to be resettled in Australia.

I was introduced to the girl, but as a two-year-old, she obviously couldn't talk very much, and so she could not provide any further useful information. I suggested that others on the boat seek to contact their families, or the boat organiser in Vietnam, and try to find more information about the identity and whereabouts of the girl's father. I was not confident we would be successful, but it was worth a try.

Some six to eight weeks later, when I went back to Songkhla, I was greeted by the UNHCR officials with good news that they had succeeded in obtaining the details of the girl's father. I was accompanied on this visit by the head of our immigration team in Bangkok and he took over the little girl's case. Within a comparatively short time, compared with usual refugee processing times, the little girl was on her way to be reunited with her father. When the immigration head told me this news, I was so excited, and quite moved that I had played a role in helping the girl join her father in Sydney. However, I forgot to find out more details about who she and her father were.

While I think this was one of my most moving experiences during my foreign service career, in hindsight I am disappointed that I didn't know more about the girl and her father. She is now probably slightly older than my oldest daughter, Alison, and therefore would be in her early forties. I often wonder how she fared in Australia. I certainly hope she has enjoyed a successful and enjoyable life.

Unfortunately, as for her mother, UNHCR's advice was that as so long had passed from when her mother had been taken by pirates off the coast of Thailand, it could be assumed she was dead.

On another occasion, UNHCR had arranged for us to visit a court hearing in which the first prosecution in Thailand against alleged pirates was taking place. Generally, it was very difficult to secure successful prosecutions as it was hard to obtain water-tight evidence that would stand up in court and, secondly, many refugees, having been resettled abroad, wished to put the trauma behind them and not return to Thailand to appear in court.

Piracy was a complex issue. In some cases of piracy, Thai fishermen went to extend a helping hand to the refugee boats and expected some reward or payment in return. In some cases, when the refugees could not or resisted paying up, robbery and violence ensued. Other cases were motivated by the fact that the Thai fishermen eked out a very meagre existence and the fishermen saw this as a ready opportunity to profiteer but were not intent on violence. And yet other cases seemed to be premeditated opportunities for rape and pillage. However, in no cases could piracy be condoned.

In this particular case, one of the alleged pirates had been charged with murder, and there were some surviving witnesses who had agreed to appear in court. On the face of it, it seemed to have been a particularly brutal attack. However, what surprised me was the reaction of some of my colleagues, including a number who had studied law. They took one look at the key accused and said *there was no doubt he was guilty*. He probably was, but we didn't stay for the whole trial. I had always understood our western legal systems followed the practice of being innocent until proven guilty.

Although the question of Indochinese refugees was one of my work priorities in Bangkok, we did have to pay attention to other refugee issues. Although Burmese refugees were not a top priority, just the same, we had to keep abreast of their situation. On one occasion, together with my immigration colleague, Mike Bonney, we visited a Karen refugee camp near the Thai town of Tha Song Yang. This proved to be quite an adventure.

To get to the refugee camp, we had to hike about 3km through low scrub and repeatedly criss-cross the river that flowed through the lower plains. Much of the way, we had to go bare-footed, as we had not been prepared for all the river crossings. Fortunately, most of the ground was made up of fine and soft sand. Towards the finish there was a short climb. As we neared the campsite, we discovered we had been feasted on by leeches, and so several minutes were spent as we sought to remove the bloated parasites.

When we reached the camp itself, my first impression was that this must be what Shangri-La looked like. The site was beautiful, with tall mountains behind, views of the river and natural vegetation all around. Conditions in the camp itself were basic, but orderly. However, who could complain with a view like that? However, our hike to the camp did underline the difficulties for UNHCR and other aid agencies to bring in food and other relief supplies.

On our return from the camp, and not far from where our car had been parked, we were treated to a rather surreal view. We were standing on a plain and could see the U-curve of the river. On the other side of the river were some rugged cliffs and hills. We could see Burmese Army troops on the cliffs on one side of the U-curve, lined up against ethnic rebel troops on the other side of the U-curve – they would have been Karen. We could see shots occasionally being fired. Although we could see clearly what was going on, my guess was that the conditions were so rough and rugged, the opposing troops could not have seen each other.

After visiting many refugee sites in Thailand, there was one point of common ground. While conditions may vary from camp to camp, life in a refugee camp was tough and certainly not a good place for children to grow up. However, for the majority of refugees, they would have been better off in the camps than facing the dangers of remaining at home.

Memorable Times in Bangkok

Alison was a three-month-old baby when we arrived in Bangkok. This increased the imperative of quickly finding somewhere to live, but our initial few weeks were spent living in one of the embassy's vacant fifth-floor apartments. When we went to eat out at a restaurant, the waitresses jostled with each other over the honour to nurse Alison. This left our hands free to eat, and we much appreciated the attentiveness of the waitresses.

When I first arrived in Bangkok, I was lucky to be able to study the Thai language intensively for ten weeks. This was a good way to settle into the city, as it meant classes in the morning and homework in the afternoons or evenings. It gave me a chance to spend time in the afternoons looking for somewhere to live or, more importantly in terms of my Thai lessons, to practice speaking.

Ten weeks learning Thai was enough to be useful. I could bargain with taxi drivers, buy fresh fruit in the markets or bargain for cashew nuts or birds' nest when I went to Haadyai. However, it was also enough Thai to be potentially dangerous.

One occasion when I was on an official trip and travelling from Aranyaprathet, I had to get to Surin to stay overnight. For some reason, we were running late and we encountered a road block that would have prevented us going on. While much of the usual route did not take us very close to the border, there was a curfew in travelling along certain roads close to the border after a particular time of night.

I had to explain to the policeman in my limited Thai, why it was important that we keep going. It was not easy, and it seemed like an eternity. The policeman continued to be adamant that we had to turn back. I was concerned that I was escorting an official visitor, and we had a full program around Surin the next day. Indeed, we had nowhere convenient to return to. I kept trying, as best I could, to explain why we had to go on. Eventually disaster was averted, and I succeeded in persuading the policeman to let us through. We got to Surin without any further incident.

My three years in Bangkok witnessed a heavy volume of senior official visitors. As one of the emerging 'tiger' economies, and given its important role within ASEAN on Indochina, it was to be expected that Thailand would merit such attention from Australian ministers. I was closely involved in many of these visits.

One of the most significant, was the visit by Prime Minister Bob Hawke and Foreign Minister Bill Hayden. As our Deputy Head of Mission, Miles Kupa had been appointed as ambassador to Iraq and his replacement had not yet arrived; I was Acting Deputy Head of Mission and chief coordinator for the visit.

This was a politically sensitive visit, as Thailand in particular, but also other ASEAN countries, were concerned about the Indochina policy initiatives being pursued by the Hawke Government. While the visit ended up smoothly, with an improved understanding by both sides of our respective attitudes on Indochina and some level

A Diplomatic Life

of acceptance of what Australia was seeking to do, the visit did not commence auspiciously.

Prior to Mr Hawke's arrival, the Thai government officials I had been dealing with were puzzled by the detailed information required for Mr Hawke to agree to travel onboard a Thai helicopter in order to visit an Australian aid project in northern Thailand.

The Thai officials told me the helicopter they were providing was the one used by His Majesty, the King. They said I would know how deeply revered the king was and therefore suggested I could understand just how carefully this helicopter was maintained. I said I could appreciate that, but these were standard requirements to be satisfied for Australian prime ministerial visits.

As it turned out, the prime ministerial VIP aircraft was delayed leaving Darwin en route to Bangkok, as a bird had got caught up in one of the aircraft's engines. As a result, Mr Hawke's delayed arrival meant he no longer had time to take the helicopter trip to the Australian aid project. My Thai counterparts subsequently, but gently, reminded me of how concerned we had been about the safety of the Thai helicopter, yet we could not prevent problems occurring with our own prime minister's VIP aircraft.

Following Mr Hawke's arrival in Bangkok and, as we were proceeding in the motorcade from the airport to the Oriental Hotel, there was a loud bang which came from the front of the motorcade. The motorcade came to a stop. My first thought was, *Please don't tell me some lunatic has had a pot shot at Mr Hawke.*

No, thank goodness. The word came back to us that a tyre had blown in the PM's car. The PM had been transferred to the spare car at the front of the motorcade and all was well. One important lesson from this was how important it was to have a spare car in your motorcade line-up!

Not long after the party had checked into the Oriental, we held a briefing session for the PM and his party. This was quite standard practice for prime ministerial visits. However, the briefing session did not go as smoothly as such sessions should normally go.

My ambassador in Bangkok was Gordon Jockel, a very seasoned diplomat. I had never before seen him flustered. He was, however, on this occasion, though I did not blame him. Mr Hawke was asking questions and not letting Mr Jockel finish his answers, or he would start asking a question and change direction mid-sentence. It was a very puzzling performance. It left Mr Jockel confused and struggling to keep up.

I knew that Mr Hawke was a very intelligent man, and that academically he had been among the highest achievers, winning a Rhodes Scholarship. My initial reaction to the way he was conducting the briefing session was that he had not read his written briefing material *and* therefore did not understand the issues. However, after about fifteen minutes, Mr Hayden spoke up and the atmosphere of the briefing session changed, becoming more relaxed and business-like.

Afterwards, I spoke with Mr Hayden's Senior Private Secretary, Mike Costello, and commented how I was puzzled by Mr Hawke's handling of the briefing session. Mike said that it was all about asserting control and that Mr Hawke used similar techniques to control cabinet. Nonetheless, it was a somewhat nerve-wracking session, leaving me wondering what other dramas were in store.

The next anxious moment came at the official banquet, hosted by the Thai Prime Minister for PM Hawke and his party. I was seated a bit too far back to hear what was said, but I could see the PM was momentarily unsettled. Bob Hawke had got up to respond to a toast offered by the Thai PM Prem Tinsulanonda. What I observed was that he had raised his wine glass to his lips, took a sip and then giggled and blushed and put his glass straight down. Another glass was quickly brought.

I was concerned that, perhaps, one of my worst fears had been realised. We had received very firm instructions from Canberra that the PM was to be served nothing but the non-alcoholic wine that had been specially despatched from Canberra. I had explained this both orally and in writing to the Thai authorities, reinforcing it again by personally delivering the PM's special non-alcoholic wine to the relevant Thai hospitality officials.

Despite my best efforts, it seemed that things may have gone wrong. Although I was not alone in witnessing the incident, nothing more was heard or said about it subsequently, and the two prime ministers seemed to end the banquet on friendly and convivial terms.

After a hesitant start, the visit ended up going well and achieving its key objectives. It opened the way for further visits by Mr Hayden, as he sought to explore ways to bring lasting peace to Cambodia. Mr Hayden ended up visiting Thailand eight times in two years and established a very close rapport with his key Thai counterparts, especially the then Thai Foreign Minister, Siddhi Savetsila.

On one visit, sometime after the two ministers had established a close rapport, there was a memorable incident. The meeting was taking place at the Oriental Hotel in one of its function rooms. The ministers had finished the substantive part of their discussions and Siddhi said he wanted to tell Mr Hayden about a recent experience with a visit by the Soviet Vice Foreign Minister, Kapitsa.

Siddhi said that the Thais had arranged for Kapitsa to meet with His Majesty. According to the protocol for meetings with the king, visitors should not raise politically contentious issues and not talk publicly about what was discussed. Siddhi said the Thais were incensed at Kapitsa's behaviour in ignoring these protocols.

At this point, Siddhi stood up and said if Kapitsa ever came back to Thailand, he would personally give him a bloody nose, and indicated with his fist how he would do it. Just at this moment, as luck would have it, the meeting room doors were opened, and the waiting press hoards saw Siddhi throwing his punch towards Mr Hayden.

Most of the accompanying Australian press were not aware of the close rapport that had developed between Mr Hayden and his Thai counterpart and jumped to the conclusion that Australian policy in Indochina still angered the Thais. Headlines in Australian newspapers the next day, suggested stories like 'Thai Foreign Minister socks it to Hayden'. Only one journalist sought to find out what had actually happened. That was Michael Richardson, a very capable Australian journalist, based in Singapore and well-versed in Southeast Asia.

Prior to another visit, I'd been asked to deliver an urgent message to Foreign Minister Siddhi. It was a Sunday and Siddhi was at home relaxing, but the Thai Foreign Ministry confirmed I could proceed to his home to deliver the message. I arrived at his home to find he was wearing shorts and a shirt, working busily in his garden. This was obviously one way he chose to relax and find a moment's respite from international problems. I was actually touched by the informality of the moment, despite the urgency of the message.

There was another occasion when I was required to deliver an urgent message during my time in Bangkok. Former Australian prime ministers continue to receive assistance from embassies when they are travelling overseas, and former Prime Minister Gough Whitlam was transiting Bangkok, when we received a message to pass to him. I rang his hotel and spoke with Mr Whitlam and he asked me to come around straightaway. I told him it would take about twenty minutes.

On reaching his hotel, I rang his room from downstairs. *Please come on up* was the advice. I did as I was told and rang at his hotel room door, to have it opened by the former prime minister dressed in a towel wrapped around his waist. It was not exactly how I expected to meet the great man. However, duty was duty. I handed over the message and duly departed.

One other memorable incident occurred during the transit through Bangkok of the Vietnamese Foreign Minister, Nguyen Co Thach. Thach was en route home after a visit to Australia. I accompanied our then ambassador to Vietnam, Richard Broinowski, to the airport to greet Thach and offer him the facilities of the Airport's VIP waiting room.

Thach had originally been scheduled to meet with Thai Foreign Minister Siddhi during his transit through Bangkok, but the meeting was cancelled at short notice. Ostensibly, the cancelation was caused by Thach not being well, having picked up a flu-like virus in Australia. However, the Thai press reported that it was cancelled because of dissatisfaction at Thai attitudes to Vietnam and the Cambodia problem.

Richard and I were having a friendly discussion at the airport with Thach. Although he was clearly not well, it did not prevent us from talking. However, after some time, the staff at the VIP room came in and said a throng of journalists had turned up outside, assuming that Thach was there and wished to speak to him. I accompanied Thach outside to meet the journalists. Thach put his hand to his throat and made hoarse sounds to the effect that he was indeed unwell and could not talk. It was an Oscar winning performance. The press bought it and withdrew. Thach and I went back inside and rejoined our discussion with Richard as well.

I figured, afterwards, I had been given a masterclass in the art of diplomatic illness.

There is one personal memory that stays with me from my time in Thailand. I had been due to make my first visit to Haadyai and

Songkhla in connection with the UNHCR anti-piracy program. On the way to the airport, I'd been a little nervous, as we were witnessing a spectacular electrical storm with torrential rain as we were driving along. I kept hoping the storm would be finished by the time I got to the airport, and I would not be expected to fly in such weather.

However, matters were taken out of my hands. The embassy car broke down on the expressway en route to the airport. As a result, there was no way I could have got to the airport on time. This was in the days before mobile phones, so the driver had to find a phone and get another embassy car to come and rescue me and take me back to the embassy. At that time, we were still staying in one of the embassy transit apartments.

Annapurnas-mountain scenery.

When I got back to the apartment, Christine was standing outside the front door talking to Susan, the lady from the embassy staff who lived in the adjoining apartment. Christine was so surprised to see me, she inadvertently closed the apartment door. We were both worried that our young baby daughter, Alison, was alone in the apartment. There was no time to be thinking of the risks; immediate action was required. My main focus was on ensuring Alison was safe and sound.

So, I went into our neighbour's apartment and climbed from her balcony across into our apartment balcony. Susan lent me a stool to help me climb up onto the balcony railing. I then grabbed hold of the support railing between the two apartment balconies and jumped down onto our apartment balcony. I was able to enter the apartment through the back door and rescue Alison. Alison was sleeping soundly in her bassinet and was totally oblivious to the fact that no-one had been in the apartment with her.

Years later, I have wondered about my actions; what if I had slipped? The apartments were on the fifth floor of the embassy building. There wasn't much to hold on to crossing from one balcony to the other and, for someone like me who often had sweaty hands, there must have been a real chance of slipping. It was a long way to fall, had I slipped, and there was really nothing in the way to cushion a fall. I think the large tree in the Malaysian embassy yard next-door was just too far away.

The dangers never crossed my mind at the time. I acted quickly and decisively, as I wanted to ensure Alison was fine, and in the event, I had no problem crossing from one balcony to the other. I guess that night my guardian angel was with me. Jackie Chan would have been proud of me, performing such a feat without a safety net.

Present for the Birth of APEC

In 1989, I was transferred to join a newly established team to prepare for the first Asia Pacific Economic Cooperation (APEC) meeting, to be held in Canberra in November that year. The idea of APEC had germinated out of discussions in Seoul between Australian Prime Minister Bob Hawke and President Roh Tae Woo of South Korea.

The Secretary of Foreign Affairs and Trade, Richard Woolcott, had acted as Prime Minister Hawke's personal envoy and visited all the countries in the region, as well as the United States and Canada, to ensure support for the first meeting.

Knowing the background to this first meeting, I always found it amusing that many others claimed credit for the creation of APEC.

For us, on the preparatory team in Canberra, it was a very busy year and involved many weekends in the office. The first indication that all this work was paying off, came at the first senior officials meeting at the Gazebo Hotel in Sydney in September 1989. The meeting itself was businesslike and very much focused on arrangements for the first APEC ministerial meeting. The thing which marked this first meeting

A Diplomatic Life

and set it apart, however, was the night-time cruise and dinner on Sydney Harbour.

The cruise proved to be an excellent idea. The participants in the meeting were able to relax in a stunning environment, admiring the sights and lights of Sydney Harbour, by night from the water. As well, they were able to enjoy some good food and wine. The cruise wove its magic and helped promote a sense of bonding amongst the participating officials, which seemed to carry through to subsequent senior officials meetings over the next few years. From my experience observing the series of the first three APEC meetings, those officials who had been present on the cruise in Sydney, and who continued to work on APEC for some years afterwards, maintained that special bond.

Not just because it was the first meeting in what has become a regular fixture on the international calendar and one that now also includes an APEC leaders meeting, the first APEC meeting proved memorable for a number of other reasons.

The ministerial meeting took place on 6 and 7 November 1989, in the conference room at the beautiful old Hyatt Hotel in Canberra. Foreign and Trade or Economic Ministers attended from the then six ASEAN countries: Japan, Republic of Korea, New Zealand, United States, Canada – and Australia as host.

Some of the ASEAN countries, notably Indonesia and Malaysia, showed some reluctance about the APEC process at the outset, as they were concerned that it might undermine ASEAN as an institution. The meeting also coincided with the running of Australia's richest horse race, the Melbourne Cup. Both of these provided the background to some of the things that helped make the meeting memorable.

The Australian Foreign Minister, Senator Gareth Evans, chaired the meeting and was supported by the Australian Trade Minister, Michael Duffy. Michael Duffy, as it turned out, was a very keen race-goer and punter. It was said that he had been disappointed when he learnt that the APEC meeting clashed with the running of the Melbourne Cup. As a concession, it was arranged that there would be a pause in the meeting procedures, to allow a break to watch the running of the race. This also meant visiting ministers would need to be told why such a break was taking place.

Apparently, the Australian ministers did such a good job explaining the Australian Melbourne Cup tradition, that most of the visiting Ministers participated in Melbourne Cup sweeps. It was also said that some of the members of the visiting Indonesian and Malaysian delegations went one step further and placed bets at the TAB (a chain of betting shops). There was a horse running called Pacific Mirage, and these Indonesian and Malaysian delegates felt it was a good name to sum up their views, at that stage, about APEC. Fortunately, Pacific Mirage finished well back in the field and did not serve as an omen for the future development of APEC.

The other memorable event of that first APEC Ministerial Meeting occurred on the afternoon of the second day. There was one of those freak torrential storms that occasionally beset Canberra. The meeting conference room was on the lower ground floor of the Hyatt Hotel and there was flash flooding in the area in front of the hotel, with water streaming into the hotel itself. Hotel staff were frantically running around trying to stop the water flowing into the meeting room. Probably, every spare towel in the hotel was put to use for this purpose.

At the end of the meeting, we had arranged for a press conference to take place on the lawns to the side of the Hotel. Given the torrential downpour, we were glad that our arrangements had included a waterproof tent for the press conference. Senator Gareth Evans, not one to waste an opportunity, kicked off the press conference by announcing that the *just concluded first APEC Ministerial Meeting* had truly marked a 'watershed' in Asia Pacific relations!

At the second ministerial meeting in Singapore in 1990, the Singaporeans sought to do something a bit different and provided some entertainment for the end of meeting dinner attended by ministers and officials. We were all ferried to the island of Sentosa, home to an amusement park, aquarium, golf course and interesting museum, as well as other recreational activities.

As we proceeded into the dinner venue, we were greeted by a microcosm of Singapore popular attractions – there were street performers on stilts, jugglers, fortune tellers and transvestites. Then the musical fountain began to perform, changing its colours and patterns in time to tunes from each of the APEC economies. We had previously wondered why the Singaporeans had asked for the music of a representative Australian song. Hardly showing great originality, we had provided 'Waltzing Matilda'. We now knew why.

From the Third APEC Ministerial Meeting in Seoul, a couple of things stood out in my memory.

First, prior to commencement of the ministerial meeting, and while delegations were undertaking last minute preparatory consultations or bilateral meetings between ministers were taking place, we heard the air raid siren sound. At first, we didn't know what was going on, but we could see from the Hotel Silla windows that the streets were rapidly being emptied. We had not been alerted what to do in the case of an air raid siren.

Fortunately, this was only a training exercise, something which the residents of Seoul were apparently used to. Nonetheless, it showed how much concern there was about a possible attack from the ROK's northern neighbour. I'd had the opportunity some years earlier, to travel by helicopter to Panmunjom and get a sense of just how close Seoul was to the border with the DPRK.

Second, at the final dinner at the conclusion of the meeting, I remember the speech by Philippines Foreign Secretary, Raul Manglapus. He had us all laughing when he spoke of how this meeting had been dominated by the Lee's or Li's. The ROK ministerial delegation comprised two Lee's and the ROK APEC ambassador responsible for organising the meeting was also a Lee – there was a Li amongst the Chinese Ministers and there was Brigadier-General Lee from Singapore. And, finally, he said there was Alatas A-LEE (Ali) from Indonesia.

Third, I was asked by Senator Evans to carry his bag of golf clubs back to Australia, as he was heading off to Russia for an official visit. I was not in a position to say no to my boss, yet it was a task that filled me with some trepidation. *What if I accidentally damaged the clubs?* Or, *What if there was a new club or shoes in the bag that should be declared to customs?* I checked with the Australian customs representative in Tokyo, and he told me that customs would be alerted in Sydney that I was carrying this important baggage, belonging to the foreign minister, and that I therefore should not worry. As it turned out, I had no problems with customs in Sydney and the golf bag was safely returned to Senator Evans in Canberra.

Perhaps sensing he was imposing on me, when I went to collect the bag of golf clubs from Senator Evans' hotel suite, he sat me down for a few minutes while he tidied things in his bag and told me his impressions of how the meeting had gone. I was honoured to receive the briefing on his assessment of the meeting, something the senior officials in the Australian delegation had been keen to know, but unable to ascertain before Senator Evans set off on the next leg of his overseas travels to Moscow.

Between APEC ministerial meetings, there was much ongoing work at the officials' level to give substance to commitments made by ministers or to progress the agendas of the various working groups that had been established by APEC. One working group I had responsibility for in the APEC section, was the trade promotion working group. Australia had offered to hold a working group meeting for senior officials in Sydney.

I was responsible for identifying a venue. I had been asked to try and find somewhere a little more relaxed than the usual big five-star hotel. I found the ideal place in the Manly Pacific Hotel. The rooms had a relaxed feel about them and the view was certainly relaxing, overlooking Manly beach.

I was also tasked with identifying some Australian speakers. In order to ensure high level overseas participation, we wanted some prominent Australian businessmen or women as keynote speakers. I worked through a list of potentially good choices, most of whom were either Melbourne or Sydney-based. This was quite an enlightening experience, and perhaps, demonstrated the different business culture in both cities.

I found that with the Melbourne business executives, I had to communicate through their official secretaries and put everything formally in writing. With the Sydney business executives, when I explained to their offices what I was doing, I was put straight through to the business executives themselves.

In the end, I identified two Sydney-based executives who were willing to address our working group meeting. One was Ian Burgess, CEO of CSR Limited, at the time Australia's leading sugar company and one of the largest construction companies, and Rob McLean, chairman of the management consulting firm, McKinsey and Co. I was very grateful to obtain commitments from two such leading business figures. However, my subsequent dealings with Ian Burgess left me even more impressed.

Ian Burgess told me that, unlike the foreign minister, he had no staff to write speeches for him and that *he would write his own speech*. However, as he wished to ensure his speech fully met our requirements for the meeting, he asked if I would mind checking it in draft before he finalised it. In due course, I received a hand-written manuscript for comment. Overall, I thought the speech was very good, and from memory, I only made one comment suggesting a small amendment that would tie things in more directly to the objectives of the meeting.

The night before the working group meeting, I was tidying up the draft of the speech to be delivered the next morning by the Australian Trade Minister, Dr Neil Blewett, and it suddenly dawned on me – the Australian duo speaking at the meeting were Burgess and McLean. This reminded me of what my boss had said to me before I left on my first posting to Hong Kong. I would be joining Burgess (John Burgess) and McLean (Murray McLean) and my boss suggested tongue-in-cheek that perhaps I should change my name to Philby given the role of Burgess, McLean and Philby as members of the infamous espionage ring at Cambridge University.

We managed to work in a short joke about this in Dr Blewett's speech, noting no connection between our two Australian speakers and the infamous British espionage duo of the same name. Both Ian Burgess and Rob McLean delivered good speeches which were very well received by the meeting.

However, it was Ian Burgess who again made the more lasting impression on me. While Ian Burgess was a successful and well-respected business leader, my dealings with him had shown him to be a humble and unpretentious man. However, in delivering his speech, he showed another side to his character that filled me with greater admiration.

Several times during his speech, he began to stutter, and I could see him concentrating hard to keep his speech impediment demons under control. He generally did a good job in doing so. It led me to thinking that it required considerable courage to face up to such challenges in speaking publicly and yet, clearly given his prominence in business, he would be required to face these same demons again and again.

In writing about this many years after the event, I have now had the opportunity to see the movie *The King's Speech* about how King George VI overcame his speech impediment and where, in his role as King, he was often required to speak in public. I can now also better appreciate what a performance Ian Burgess gave.

Nonetheless, I felt proud that my efforts to secure the help of both Ian Burgess and Rob McLean had been vindicated, and was very grateful to both speakers.

Monkey Business and Other Memorable Moments in Malaysia

Following my initial visit to Malaysia, en route to my assignment in Hong Kong, I retained a soft spot for Malaysia and had been keen to secure a posting to Kuala Lumpur.

I was disappointed when the outcome of the posting round was announced in late 1991. I was offered Rangoon, which had not been a priority for me. As my daughters were young, aged nine and seven, the lack of adequate schools and medical facilities were of real concern. Unlike some other officers, I did not wish to put my daughters into boarding school. I believed it was important to keep the family together, at least until my daughters reached university age. I therefore declined the offer of Rangoon.

As it turned out, the person who'd been offered Kuala Lumpur was more interested in focusing on Eastern Europe and declined Kuala Lumpur. He ended up getting what he wanted, and I ended up getting what I wanted, as I immediately put my hand up for Kuala Lumpur.

This was a good outcome and my daughters both enjoyed their time at the International School of Kuala Lumpur.

We ended up living in a nice house in Jalan Tebu (tebu is sugar cane in Malay) in the Ukay Heights area in Selangor State, just outside the Federal Capital Region. Our house had a large expanse of front lawn and a few impressive large trees. It was located over the road from some virgin jungle. As we found, this had some pluses and some minuses.

One of the trees in our garden was a huge rambutan tree and when it was in fruit, monkeys would come across from the jungle and play havoc with the tree. The fruit was coloured yellow, not the usual red, but the taste was the same. Maybe better, as they were hand-picked by us. There was an equitable sharing arrangement for the rambutans, as the monkeys would go for the higher up fruit and we would go for the lower branches we could reach. I didn't really welcome the presence of the monkeys, as they could be quite aggressive if cornered on the ground.

We had a dog, Rusty, that we'd adopted from another Australian family, as we were told it was good to have a dog living in a house with such a large garden. We also had a night-watchman, or *jaga*, and the theory was that if intruders broke into the property, which they tried to do on at least one occasion of which we were aware, the dog would wake up the *jaga*, who would invariably be asleep, instead of awake and alert, and then the *jaga* would wake us up to sound the alarm.

Fortunately, Rusty did not have much to do in his guard-dog role, but he certainly became very agitated when the monkeys were in the rambutan tree. Rusty would do his best to scare the monkeys off, but his efforts proved more bluster than real threat and the monkeys continued to feast on the fruit. As it was such a large tree, standing at least some 8-9m high, the good thing was that the monkeys would take the fruit on the top branches and leave the fruit on the bottom branches

A Diplomatic Life

for us.

However, the monkeys were always too fast for Rusty.

Some friends from the High Commission who lived on the other side of the hill to us had an unforgettable experience with monkeys at their house.

Don and Ade Tatarelli had gone out one weekend afternoon and, as they usually did, had left their small bathroom window open. When they came home, Ade found all her cosmetics littered over the bathroom floor. Their initial reaction was that burglars had broken into the house. However, when they checked, they found nothing of value had been taken and the bathroom was the only room that had been broken into.

Looking at the way some of the cosmetics had been opened and smudged on the bathroom floor, mirrors and walls, they quickly deduced the intruder had been at least one monkey. The monkeys obviously did not think much of the cosmetic brands Ade used, as they did not seek to take any with them. Though a monkey wearing lipstick might have received a cool reception from its mates back in the jungle!

Our dog, Rusty, had one other distinguishing feature. He was a racist. He didn't mind Caucasians, Chinese, Malays or Indonesians, including our Indonesian maid, and he didn't even mind Punjabis. It was only Tamil people who were the target for his aggressive behaviour.

Our gardener, Raju, was Tamil. He was a hard-working and kind person and we didn't want to lose him. However, when we first took possession of Rusty, he showed his strong displeasure with Raju. It looked like we would either lose Raju or have to get rid of Rusty. Our solution was to tie up Rusty whenever Raju came. Eventually there was a grudging truce reached.

One day, I did not have to go to work and was at home when the garbage truck came by. All the workers on the truck were Tamil.

Fortunately, Rusty was contained securely within our yard, but I saw him get very agitated. For their part, the garbage workers from their position secure outside the fence, taunted Rusty and threw stones at him. I realised this was probably the cause of Rusty's antagonism towards Tamils. Nonetheless, I still could not completely understand how Rusty could distinguish so clearly between the different races.

Sometimes during official visits, as the representative of the Australian Mission, we were required to take the lead and show courage. One such occasion occurred in Malaysia during the visit of an Australian Parliamentary delegation led by the Honourable Laurie Brereton.

Our Malaysian hosts had arranged a program for our delegation, and we spent part of the weekend on official calls in Penang, while the rest of the weekend was reserved for some sight-seeing. One of the places on the itinerary was the Snake Temple in Penang.

The Snake Temple was so named because it was the home to numbers of pit vipers, normally a highly poisonous snake. It was claimed that all the burning incense in the Temple helped to dull the senses of the snakes and make them less inclined to attack. It was also claimed, but I don't know if this is true, that the snakes were not milked of their venom, and so, were potentially lethal.

In previous visits to Penang, I had chosen not to visit this temple because snakes are not exactly my cup of tea. On this occasion, I had no choice. When we got to the temple, staff greeted us by waving numerous snakes at us. The members of the parliamentary delegation, as one, retreated and pushed me to the front and, in unison, said, 'Graeme, you can represent us.' So, I found myself being garlanded with a pit viper around the neck and others draped over my arms.

Having volunteered me for this less than pleasant chore, I then had to put on a brave face while the members of the delegation all took photos of me festooned in colourful pit vipers. I guess one redeeming feature was that the colours of the pit vipers nicely matched the colours on the shirt I was wearing at the time.

One of the more interesting and unusual official trips I made during my overseas assignments was to go to a longhouse in the Kapit region of Sarawak. Under the High Commission's Direct Aid Program, we had funded a clean drinking water project for a longhouse there and James Masing, the local member of parliament and also a graduate of the Australian National University, had invited the High Commission to send someone to officiate at the *opening of the taps* at the conclusion of the project. I was selected for the task and I paid for my family to come with me. It ended up being quite an adventure.

The adventure started in Kuching, the state capital of Sarawak. We flew from Kuching to the busy river city of Sibu and from Sibu took a long and low-slung express boat two hours up the Rajang River to Kapit. Then from Kapit, we travelled by an outboard motorboat further upstream along the Baleh River to the longhouse.

I was lucky that the Iban people in the longhouse we went to were predominantly Christian. I was told that if they still practiced animist beliefs, I would have been expected to use a spear to kill a pig. Fortunately, there was no killing for me, but there were a number of other traditional and animist beliefs I had to observe. My family just had to observe me, and didn't have to participate in the rituals themselves.

The longhouse we visited contained eighteen doors – in other words, eighteen families had their homes opening onto the common area of the longhouse. What this meant for me, was that I had to greet the owner of each house and share a glass of home-made rice wine or *tuak* with each of them. Thankfully I only had to have basically a sip from each one. Some of the *tuak* was very smooth, but most of it was quite rough.

Next was the cleansing ceremony. This was derived from animist traditions. I had to wave a live chicken over a number of sacred objects. This has been my one and only experience of holding a live chicken. Fortunately, it proved a painless experience for me and, hopefully, for the chicken as well, although I suspect the chicken appeared later that evening as part of our dinner. Once the cleansing ritual was done, it meant another cup of *tuak* had to be consumed.

With the formalities out of the way, it was time to trek through the jungle to inspect the water project. First, we visited the site of the source of clean water to be piped to the longhouse, then followed the pipes back to the longhouse, where I performed a more usual ritual – ceremonially turning on the tap and declaring the project finished and operational. After this, we had an hour or so to freshen up and relax, before it was dinner and party time.

I cannot remember much about the food we ate, although I recall we had some wild boar, which was tough as boots. After chewing a piece for five minutes and not making any progress in digesting it, I discreetly spat it out. In remote longhouses, such as the one we were visiting, visitors were not common and therefore provided an excuse for all the longhouse community to get together and have a party. This meant more *tuak* to be consumed.

However, before the partying began, there were the formalities of speeches to be disposed of. James Masing acted as our interpreter. The speeches were not too long or formal. There was also some discussion about the livelihood of the people in the longhouse and their longer-term political and economic aspirations. And then the fun began.

I cannot recall the exact order of proceedings, however, a couple of the activities stand out in my memory. At one stage a couple of the women disappeared on the pretence of going to look for a lost

A Diplomatic Life

baby. They came back with something shaped like a baby wrapped in a *pua*. *Pua* are the woven fabrics produced by the Iban and the patterns usually reflect their totems or other important or sacred objects.

At first, I was glad that the women had found the baby. However, I soon discovered this was the excuse for a party game intended to make me drink some more *tuak*. Out of the *pua,* the women unwrapped a green coconut (this had been the baby's head), a fragile looking plate and a *parang* (a heavy, slightly curved knife used by the peoples in the jungles of Malaysia and Indonesia).

The blade, on this particular *parang,* was deliberately blunt. My challenge was to put the coconut on the plate and break it open with the *parang* without breaking the plate. Of course, it was a challenge that was impossible to achieve, and to much mirth and merriment, I failed and had to be punished by drinking another cup of *tuak*.

Another game which impressed me because of its sophistication was a *pantun* contest. A *pantun* is a Malay poem, and the idea of the game was for someone to start a poem and the next person had to come up with lines to continue it. Failure to do so meant – you guessed it – they had to drink a cup of *tuak*. James Masing gamely tried to keep pace with the verses and translate them for me. Some of the verses seemed very clever and, as James indicated, they were full of literary allusions and ordinary words that had secret or alternative meanings. As the contest went on, the verses also seemed to become increasingly ribald and daring. The Iban were clearly enjoying themselves immensely.

Alison and Stephanie had been shown a place to sleep at about 10 o'clock. The partying, however, went on and on. By two in the morning, tiredness and *tuak* had caught up with me and my then wife, Christine, and I was shown somewhere where we could sleep. We only managed about five hours, but most of the Iban continued to party all night. We had to get moving to get to Kapit in time to connect with our express boat back to Sibu, and the Iban had to take their boats to go to church, as it was a Sunday.

I was glad to have had the opportunity to visit the longhouse and participate in the project to bring them clean drinking water. It was an interesting insight into Iban customs and traditions. It was also a great privilege to be a beneficiary of their hospitality. It was interesting to see how the longhouse was formed and to admire the *pua* weavings hung around the walls of the long common area. There were some animal skulls hung from the pillars supporting the roof, but I understand in some other longhouses, where head-hunting was practiced up to a generation or so ago, human skulls would also be hung.

One of the things we enjoyed about life in Kuala Lumpur was the food. Often on our way home, we would stop at a local food court and buy satay or roti canai (Indian flat bread served with a usually vegetarian curry sauce). This became one of Stephanie's favourites. Just down the road from where we lived, there was a very popular seafood restaurant. The decor was quite basic, but the food was good. Some of our favourites were the butter prawns and the stuffed bean-curd.

On workdays, I would often go to the lane behind our high commission building and order freshly cooked char kway teow (a Penang-style fried noodle dish) or Hainanese chicken rice. There were two regular stores I would visit and the offerings of both were very tasty. Often, I would play squash at lunch-time and, after showering and cooling down a bit, would visit the lane to bring something back for a late lunch in my office.

Not only was the food good, but the variety of the work was interesting and, often not without a few challenges, as my comments on Dr Mahathir in the following chapter attest.

Walking the Tightrope
Under Mahathir's Malaysia

While Malaysia was a good place to live and provided many happy and unique memories, life on the work front was also never boring. My three-year assignment in Malaysia coincided with an interesting period in Australia-Malaysia bilateral relations. Prime Minister Dr Mahathir Mohamad whose negative approach to bilateral relations with Australia had a major impact on our daily work. However, my duties in Malaysia brought me into contact with a number of other interesting and important Malaysians.

The following represents my personal views and thus may differ in various ways from the official Australian views about Dr Mahathir.

Many things have been written about why Mahathir adopted such an anti-Australian stance. I won't elaborate on these various theories now, other than to say some were, undoubtedly, correct, some were misguided or exaggerated, and others were probably no more than rumours or hearsay. Living and working in Mahathir's Malaysia, there was much about him that I respected, there were also aspects where I believe he was misunderstood, but there were other aspects that I found unsavoury or puzzling.

Because he had such an important influence on my life and duties in Malaysia, I would like to offer some of my impressions of Dr Mahathir, even though I never met him in a formal bilateral-meeting context. I did, however, have the occasion to shake his hand and I attended numerous meetings and conferences where he was the guest of honour.

Rising to the top of Malaysian politics, Mahathir had not come from the standard mould of his predecessors and had, no doubt, encountered prejudices and obstacles that helped colour his approach to leadership. Perhaps this political upbringing is what made him not only an astute politician, but also a ruthless one, in terms of maintaining control and dealing with his political enemies.

Reflecting on his time as prime minister, Mahathir left behind a legacy which, for the most part, he and Malaysia could be proud of. Mahathir oversaw the development of a strong economy and laid the foundations for further economic development. During the Asian Financial Crisis of 1997, Mahathir stood his ground and refused to bow to the demands of the International Monetary Fund. In the end, he was proven correct in the approach he adopted.

Mahathir did much to promote a sense of Malaysian nationalism and pride in being Malaysian and, while jealousies continued within the Chinese and Indian communities about the preferential treatment of Malays, Mahathir was successful in keeping these under control. Some of these fissures, particularly among the Indian community, emerged in a more pronounced way following Mahathir's departure.

Mahathir was sensitive to the threat of other forms of Islam, different to the predominant Sunni Islam in Malaysia, and concerned about the risk of fundamentalist Islamic ideas taking hold, he acted decisively to try and curb such trends. Although not entirely successful, I believe there was a much greater sense of religious harmony in Mahathir's

Malaysia than became the case subsequently.

Mahathir was successful in enhancing Malaysia's standing on the world stage, showing Malaysia to be a country that was capable of punching above its weight. A principal means of doing this was to champion the cause of less fortunate developing countries. It was therefore inevitable there would be occasional clashes with Australian approaches, as Australia similarly sought to punch above its weight on the international stage but did so on the side of the developed world.

When I arrived in Malaysia, our relationship was just emerging from a period of frozen bilateral relations that had been imposed by Mahathir. Prominent Malaysian businessman and close ally of Mahathir, Ananda Krishnan was understood to have played a significant role in encouraging a thawing of the freeze in the relationship.

I was made to feel that I was walking into a field of landmines. And to be sure, there were a number of potential landmines just after the unfreezing of relations.

These included the release of the film based on the novel, *Turtle Beach*, by Blanche d'Alpuget. It referred to a number of past sensitivities in the bilateral relationship and had the potential to resurrect them as issues. Perhaps some astute diplomacy on our part, emphasising the non-government nature of the movie, and the fact that it was not a box-office success helped, defuse this potential landmine.

Another potential and unexpected landmine emerged in the form of the dramatic abduction by Terengganu Prince, Raja Bahrin, of his two children from the custody of his estranged wife, Jacqueline Gillespie. This case did assume an identity larger than a child custody dispute might normally warrant. There was much inflammatory media coverage in both countries, fanned in part by the fact that Raja Bahrin was a member of Malaysian royalty and Jacqueline Gillespie was directly linked to the Australian media and, in part, by the differing legal decisions in both countries, as to who had proper custody of the two children. However, the case came to light just as we were trying to put bilateral relations back on track after the diplomatic freeze. It demanded 'extra-careful' handling.

There were a number of other potential landmines besides these two mentioned, and the sense was that Mahathir had control over whether or not any of them would be detonated. Staff in our high commission who had experienced the ostracism during the freeze on bilateral relations, and how this had affected them personally, were particularly sensitive about potential factors that could, again, trigger Mahathir's ire.

However, I gained a different perspective during the so-called 'recalcitrant affair', when Australian Prime Minister, Paul Keating, was said to have described Mahathir as *recalcitrant* for not attending the APEC leaders' meeting in Seattle in 1993.

As mentioned before, I believe Mahathir was an astute politician and that often, there were other objectives at play when he encouraged verbal spats with Australia, as well as some other developed countries. To some extent, Mahathir seemed to enjoy taking on developed countries and nothing encouraged him more than when Australia or others responded vigorously to his comments.

That said, I do not wish to underrate the strength of grievance that Mahathir might have, rightly or wrongly, felt for Australia.

As the 'recalcitrant affair' clearly demonstrated, there was a strong domestic consideration behind Mahathir's reaction. The incident took place just after the conclusion of an UMNO (United Malays National Organisation) conference and, following which, key positions on the UMNO Council remained to be decided. Paul Keating had unwittingly provided ammunition for starting a contest for UMNO contenders to prove their loyalty to Mahathir.

A Diplomatic Life

The more the Australian-side sought to respond and defend its position, the more ammunition this provided for the battle for the UMNO council membership. One senior UMNO politician at the time confirmed as much to me, when he expressed that even though we could be assured he remained a good friend of Australia, he had to prove his loyalty if he wished to get one of the positions on the UMNO council.

One other lesson from this incident was that it showed how successful Mahathir was in motivating the Malaysian public and winning them over to his side. The most telling examples of this, from my personal experience, were when a taxi driver refused to take me to the Australian high commission during the period of the 'recalcitrant affair' and, secondly, when I was waiting in the check-in line, with my then mother-in-law for her flight back to Australia, and a Chinese-Malaysian turned around and abused me for being an Australian.

Some years later, working on the Malaysia desk in Canberra, there were some further Mahathir outbursts regarding Australian regional diplomacy. Some of these had been taken out of context or misquoted. However, I think Canberra by then had learnt its lesson about Mahathir's domestic agenda. Foreign Minister Downer's approach, by drawing on a cricket analogy of just letting Mahathir's remarks 'pass through to the keeper', was a more sensible one. It took the heat out of the issue and did not play into Mahathir's domestic agenda.

I used to puzzle about Mahathir's friendships with the likes of Robert Mugabe, former President of Zimbabwe, and Kim Jong-Il, former supreme leader of the DPRK. It seemed odd, to me, that Mahathir would make such a play of his friendships with people like these. Though purely speculation on my part, perhaps, knowing that these men were not well respected in the broader international community, Mahathir hoped it would help draw attention to issues faced by developing countries, by riling the developed world. If this was the objective, it was an odd way of going about things by supporting countries of limited value to Malaysia's broader and longer-term interests, while offending countries, such as the United States and the UK.

Reflecting on my time living and working in Malaysia, and then later working on Malaysia in Canberra, I did have a chance to watch Mahathir at reasonably close quarters. I know that Mahathir could be charming. I got some sense of this in seeing how Mahathir interacted with Malaysians, in particular, at the conferences I attended where he was the chief guest. My high commissioner, John Dauth, told me, after his introductory meeting with him, that Mahathir had been charming. Prior to that meeting, John had asked me if I could think of a suitable gift for him to take. I had suggested an Akubra hat, as I'd noticed that Mahathir was often pictured wearing different sorts of hats. John told me that Mahathir had seemed genuinely pleased with his Akubra hat.

Mahathir was said to have a good sense of humour. I remember calling on the Malaysian Trade Minister, Rafidah Aziz, on one occasion and she seemed in a particularly good mood. When asked about this, she said she had just come from a meeting with Mahathir, and he had been busy cracking jokes. Then, Rafidah turned to us and, somewhat tellingly, said that this was a side of Mahathir that *foreigners* seldom saw.

I also believe that Mahathir was, for the most part, respected and regarded with affection by many of his UMNO colleagues and the broader Malaysian public. I'm sure there was a fair amount of some party members, hoping to gain favour and perhaps secure better positions. On one occasion, I recall waiting for a senior official Australian visitor, inside the restricted area of KL International Airport, and watching the reception given to Mahathir when he disembarked from his overseas flight. Maybe there were some *toadies* in the welcoming group, but for the most part, it seemed a very friendly and affectionate welcome, and there was much light-hearted banter.

My impression was that Mahathir was not so comfortable with foreigners in large public gatherings but was more relaxed in smaller meetings. However, I think more generally that, despite his long years in public life, Mahathir was also not entirely comfortable mixing with Malaysian people in large crowds.

Mahathir was, undoubtedly, a hard worker. I know we were hard-pressed to come up with answers to a request, put to us by our high commissioner, on Mahathir's non-work interests. There was his family, and we had observed some interest in horseriding, but otherwise there was nothing that came to mind. I had also heard a story, and I am sure it was true, that Mahathir always carried a notebook with him, and he would record anything that he saw that he felt needed fixing or improving and then ensure that follow-up action was taken.

Mahathir could be both a pragmatist and an idealist. For example, in the differences with Australia, two aspects of the relationship were generally quarantined – defence and education. This reflected how important both sectors were to the bilateral relationship and, in particular, to Malaysia. His pragmatism was also seen in holding back where bilateral interests with other important countries might suffer. The United States was a case in point.

To my point of view, his idealism was sometimes misguided. For example, Malaysia was on track to become a developed country by 2020 and some ways of showing they were headed in that direction, were by building the world's (then) tallest buildings, or insisting on developing a domestic car industry. Even though these idealistic projects didn't always make the best sense economically, perhaps they helped to promote a sense of Malaysian national pride.

On the negative side, I believe Mahathir could be vindictive and hold a lengthy grudge. Earlier in his political career, Mahathir had been on the receiving end of his party's wrath, and perhaps this coloured his approach to political rivals later on. Mahathir seemed to pursue those who challenged his leadership, and those he felt had betrayed him, in an even more determined fashion. His former Deputies Musa Hitam and Anwar Ibrahim are two cases that come to mind.

I was working on the Malaysia desk in Canberra in October 2003, when Mahathir made the surprise announcement that he was resigning as prime minister in favour of his designated successor Abdullah Badawi. At the time prior to this, many had believed that Mahathir would not stand down and would probably die in office. In the years following his retirement, I was aware that Mahathir made two private visits to Australia and the feedback I received was that he had enjoyed both visits.

Despite earlier pledges that he would, in retirement, not get involved in politics, Mahathir became an increasingly vocal critic of Prime Minister Najib Razak and the corruption allegations surrounding him.

The final observation I would make about Mahathir, is that I wonder if perhaps he thought there was no-one who was quite as capable as he was to take over the reins of leadership. History may well prove this to be the case. Neither of his immediate successors, Abdullah Badawi and Najib Tun Razak, earned the respect of Malaysians and achieved accomplishments comparable to Mahathir. Overall, Mahathir's legacy to Malaysia was largely a positive one, and certainly he did much to benefit the Malaysian people, even if he left a slightly sour taste in the mouths of some overseas partners.

I wrote many of my above observations back in August 2015. At the time of publishing, in 2024, I must mention that Mahathir produced one more major surprise. Having earlier resigned from UMNO, he joined forces with the political coalition, Pakatan Harapan, and in the May 2018 Malaysian elections, Mahathir led the party as its chairman, with Wan Azizah, the wife of Mahathir's former Deputy Anwar Ibrahim, as his deputy. On 10 May 2018, Mahathir was sworn in again as Malaysia's new prime minister. This outcome was historic for a number of reasons. It was the first time that a party, other than Barisan Nasional, had ruled Malaysia since independence, Wan Azizah became the first female deputy prime minister of Malaysia and, at almost ninety-three years of age, Mahathir became the oldest serving state leader in the world.

While Anwar Ibrahim had ostensibly been pardoned, he still had to wait some years to resume active engagement in politics. Anwar became Prime Minister in late 2022. In the meantime, seen from a distance, Mahathir, for someone his age, maintained a cracking pace as Prime Minister. He stepped down as Prime Minister in 2020. From afar, it would also seem that Mahathir given his age and experience and his disappointment at political developments in Malaysia since his retirement has mellowed considerably. Now aged ninety-nine, Mahathir still speaks out from time to time on political issues.

One anecdote before moving on – there was a widely held belief in Malaysia that as Tuanku Abdul Rahman was the first prime minister of an independent Malaysia, subsequent Malaysian prime ministers would spell out the initials of his name. This indeed happened as illustrated below – Tuanku Abdul Rahman, Tun Abdul Razak, Tun Hussein Onn, Tun Dr Mahathir Mohamad, Abdullah Badawi and Najib Tun Abdul Razak.

More Stories About Snakes and Other Nasties

I have mentioned my experience at the snake temple in Penang, but I've had some other closer than desirable encounters with snakes in Malaysia, and also back in Australia.

Living so close to the jungle in Ukay Heights in Malaysia, it was perhaps not surprising that we had a number of snake encounters at home. One of the first I remember was when Raju, our gardener, called out to me to be careful. Had he not done so, I probably would have been well within striking distance of a green tree snake. It was long and thin and very well camouflaged in the tree where it was hiding. Raju told me it was extremely poisonous, and especially dangerous as it could spit its venom into your eyes.

On another occasion – it must have been a weekend – as we were sitting outside having a leisurely lunch at an outdoor table, under the shade of a tree, when I noticed our dog, Rusty, behaving in a somewhat agitated way at the back of the house. I thought *that's funny* as I had not noticed a long stick there earlier. I went to investigate. It was not a stick, but a pit viper that Rusty had cornered.

A Diplomatic Life

I now appreciate it was the wrong thing to do, but I picked up the mattock leaning against the wall and with one hefty and well-directed swing, decapitated the snake. Had I missed, no doubt the snake would have gone for me.

One morning, I came downstairs to have breakfast when I noticed four wriggling creatures near the front door. At first, I thought that, perhaps, they were a type of giant earthworm. They were thin, dark brown to black in colour and about 20cm long. I quickly realised they were baby snakes, and they must have managed to come in through the gap under the front door.

I cannot remember what I used but I managed to kill all four. Three I asked our maid to dispose of and the fourth I put into a glass jar to take to the office. I was concerned, especially with Alison and Stephanie still young, that it suggested a snake had obviously hatched its young near our front door. I presented the jar to our property officer and asked her if she could check with the company that undertook pest control services for our high commission, what sort of a snake it was. I learnt later that she did not take my request seriously and had been so repulsed by the sight of a small snake in a jar that she had thrown it out almost immediately.

I thought my request was reasonable, as we had been concerned previously that a snake (or snakes) had been stealing fish from the fishpond adjacent to the entrance to our house. I was also to learn later that baby snakes can be as venomous as adult snakes, but because they do not have the capacity to bite as effectively as an adult snake, their bites are usually harmless, or at least less dangerous.

Back in Australia, I came to appreciate that my murderous approach to snakes in Malaysia was wrong and potentially dangerous. If you see a snake, the first thing you should do is to contact the National Parks and Wildlife Service to come and remove the snake.

Although Australia is recognised for its unusual furry marsupials, it is also home to many less lovable creatures. Australia has an abundance of poisonous snakes, including five of the ten most deadly snakes in the world. There are several poisonous spiders, including the funnel-web which can be deadly, and the ubiquitous red-back spiders, which can kill children and make adults quite sick. At certain times of the year, our tropical waters are infested with other deadly species, such as the Portuguese man o' war jellyfish and the well-disguised stonefish. In the tropical forests and waters lurk both fresh and salt-water crocodiles. The latter has shown, in recent years, a particular liking for foreign tourists. Actually, I think the real problem is that tourists do not appreciate how dangerous they are. In rock pools, further south, the deadly blue-ringed octopus can be found.

Of these, probably the species I have had the most threatening direct contact with are the snakes. Although they are not my only encounters with poisonous snakes in Australia, two incidents in particular stand out.

The first happened when I was playing backyard cricket. I was chasing the ball into some longish grass and as I picked up the ball, I froze. This was an instinctive reaction, but as it turned out, was probably the best reaction. There was a snake rearing up off the ground as if preparing to strike me. By freezing motionless, the snake may have sensed I was not threatening and slithered away. Nonetheless, it gave me a good fright.

The other memorable encounter happened one weekend when I was cleaning the rock garden area, near the front water meter. We had been advised to do this, as the local water authority wished to install new water meters. I remember it was July, which in Canberra is mid-winter. There were four or five good-sized rocks which formed the base for some small groundcover plants. I turned over one of the rocks and lying in the hollow was a large common or eastern brown snake, which I believe is the third most-deadly snake in the world. They are very common along the length of eastern Australia. From the way it was coiled, I guessed it was just under 2m long. Obviously, it was hibernating, as the snake was motionless.

I called the Parks and Wildlife Service, and they sent out a couple of their rangers to check. By the time the rangers had arrived the snake had disappeared. One of the rangers was a young woman who had, it appeared to me, an unhealthy attitude towards snakes. There was nothing to worry about, she said. It was just migrating through my property. I had two young daughters and did not fancy the idea of them encountering the snake.

Anyway, the advice the rangers gave me was put my sprinkler hose on for about twenty minutes and the snake would disappear as it would not appreciate getting wet. I followed their advice and resumed my work moving the rocks. The second rock I tried to move revealed the snake had moved there. This time it was not sleepy and, in fact, seemed angry. I do not know who ran faster, me or the snake. Fortunately, we went in different directions. I do not know where the snake went, but thank goodness, I did not see it again.

I could tell more stories about my encounters with some of Australia's deadly creatures but will confine myself to just one. I only once saw a blue-ringed octopus. Generally, I think they get left behind in small rock pools when the tide goes out. I remember thinking it was quite pretty with its attractive blue markings. I found this thought scary, as if a small child saw it, they would possibly be tempted to touch it. The venom from the octopus would certainly kill a child. For me, the lesson was to always take care when walking on the rocky areas near the sea, and to watch small children closely. Whatever you do, do NOT try to touch it.

Hello Uncle Sam

Welcome to Washington. First impressions were not so welcoming. It was the end of winter and everywhere was bleak and grey. Most of the trees looked like dark and naked sentinels. The skies, too, were mostly grey. There was so little colour. At least in a Canberra winter, even when there were cold and foggy mornings, there were often brilliant blue skies after the fog had lifted.

Things changed once we moved from the restricted confines of a serviced apartment, into our own rented house in the suburbs of Maryland, and as spring slowly made its presence felt. Along the Potomac Basin area, the cherry blossoms began to bloom. The original cherry trees were a gift from Japan. In the daytime, we could dispense with our heavy overcoats and enjoy the revitalising rays of the sun.

The post report for Washington had admonished, that while outwardly the United States and Americans might seem very much like Australia and Australians, we needed to remember that the United States was a very different country and culture. Indeed, I found this to be very true. Some of the differences were glaringly obvious, while others were more subtle.

One of the first differences I encountered was the language. I am not talking about the clear difference between American and Australian English pronunciation, but differences in the use of vocabulary.

Early during our time in Washington, I embarked on the task of buying a car. Having navigated my way without too much difficulty through discussion of fenders (mudguards) and trunks (boots), when I signed off on a purchase contract, I was feeling pretty pleased with myself. However, when I was handed my copy of the papers, the salesman stumped me when he said, 'And these are the papers you'll need to get your tags.'

I wondered, *Why would I want tags?* Tags, for me, were name tags you put on your luggage or little cards to indicate recipients of gifts. I asked the salesman what they were, and why I needed them. He answered in a typically helpful and elliptical way, 'You know, tags are tags.' In hindsight, he obviously assumed everyone would know what tags were. I soon discovered *tags* were what we call numberplates, and of course, I did need them.

While on the subject of buying cars, second-hand cars are readily available in the United States, but not as widely purchased as in Australia. One of the reasons for this is that the Americans either like to buy a new car every couple of years, or they lease their car, and the rental company assumes responsibility for maintenance and replacement if required.

There are undoubtedly plenty of dud cars for sale in Australian used car markets, but overall, my impression was that government enforced quality controls and a tendency to hang on to our cars longer meant they were generally better serviced and maintained than many American second-hand cars.

Another reason I held this view, was that during my time in Washington, I saw cars on fire at least five or six times on my way to work. Nearly every week, there would also be one or two traffic announcements on the radio to avoid *such and such* a route, as there was a car on fire. I suspect the cause of most of these fires was poor maintenance, and faulty electrical systems. I also had a more cynical theory, purely my opinion and one I was, of course, unable to substantiate; that American car manufacturers built obsolescence into their cars, so you would be forced to buy a new one every couple of years.

Returning to language, I was pleased when some American friends invited us to attend a 4 July barbecue. It was kind of them to invite us and I welcomed the opportunity to help them celebrate an important day for them. It was also a good chance to meet some other American people.

However, when it came to the food, I was disappointed. I had expected some succulent barbecued steak or grilled prawns, or maybe even a lamb chop, but instead hotdogs and hamburgers cooked over a barbecue was what was served. I later learnt that what we call a *barbecue* is what the Americans call a *cook-out*.

Another experience of language confusion occurred when we visited our host family at their home in Annapolis. The US State Department had a program to designate certain American families to act as hosts to newly arrived diplomatic families in Washington. Our host family had a large house and garden overlooking the waters of Chesapeake Bay. It was quite a peaceful and idyllic location.

At one stage, the husband of our host family was pointing out a few landmarks and, pointing across the Bay, he said, 'Can you see that boo-ee.' I did not know what he was talking about at first, and it took me a while to realise he was pointing to buoys in the water.

Having spent all my working life living in Asia or working on Asia, I appreciated the opportunity to go to Washington and experience life first-hand there. As the global super-power, and the world's leading economy, the United States had a major political and economic influence in the Asia-Pacific region. United States foreign policy, United States exports and United States culture, touched on almost every corner of the region.

However, as I was to discover, this was far from being a two-way process. I was surprised that, even in both Washington and New York, the two most cosmopolitan cities on the East Coast, there was plenty of ignorance about the rest of the world, along with a great deal of parochialism, although not to the extent you might find in the farming communities of the Mid-West.

Working in Asia and Australia, we sought to understand the intentions of US foreign and trade policies, as they affected our regions. However, it was not till I arrived in Washington that I started to better appreciate the influences that helped shape these policies and begin to understand how the US Congressional system worked. For example, I had not appreciated the strength of the various lobby groups. Particularly powerful were the Jewish, Cuban and pro-Taiwan lobbyists. I also came to learn about the strength of the moral Christian right.

Something else which I found hard to understand prior to going to Washington was the level of emotion that made it so hard for the United States to put the past behind and open up its relations with Vietnam – although this did finally happen during my time in Washington. Similar attitudes coloured approaches to Iran. People could not forget, let alone forgive, the taking of American embassy hostages in Tehran.

I believe that if there had been a willingness to open up a dialogue with Iran years ago, the current hostility between the United States and Iran, along with suspicion about its nuclear and terrorism programs, might have been handled in a more sensitive and effective way. Instead, the United States appears, to me, to be locked into a position where its only hope of a real change in Iran, is if the current regime controlled largely by the clerics is toppled or replaced.

Subsequently, President Obama tried to move forward and promote a multilateral nuclear deal with Iran, but early on in his presidency, Donald Trump walked away from that deal.

All of this leads me back to the parochialism which I encountered among so many ordinary Americans. However, it was also reflected in the pages of both *The Washington Post* and *The New York Times*. There are some very good correspondents writing for both newspapers, and there is some good analysis, but all the same, there seems to be too great a tendency to write overseas news stories in a way that is slanted towards the US role or interests and ignores the foreign implications. To me, there also seemed to be a tendency to overlook important news in other parts of the world and to focus on the quaint, the different or the unusual.

In my three years in Washington, I only saw two stories about Australia that attracted more than passing attention. The first related to the New South Wales politician who advocated outlawing domestic cats, as he said they were responsible for the increasing extinction of much Australian wildlife. I don't think this policy ever seriously faced the prospect of becoming law, however, the very idea was enough to prompt demonstrations outside the embassy by American cat lovers.

The second related to the brief flirtation, by the Northern Territory administration, with introducing euthanasia. I guess euthanasia is an issue that attracts quite a bit of debate in the United States, and therefore was an issue of local interest. Again, there was never a strong prospect *at the time* of this becoming entrenched policy.

During my three years in Washington, there were of course short factual reports about political, economic or sporting developments in Australia, but none of these attracted the prominent coverage that the stories on cats and euthanasia did.

Another example of the general US unfamiliarity with the rest of the world was the number of times Americans hearing my accent and knowing I was not American would ask me where I came from. I would tell them Australia. Sometimes this would elicit responses of 'Where's that?' or on at least half a dozen occasions, 'Oh! That's where Arnold Schwarzenegger comes from.' As an Australian and conscious of our alliance relationship with the United States and the importance generally of our bilateral relationship, I was disappointed, although admittedly amused as well, about Australia being confused with Arnold Schwarzenegger, and Austria, where he came from.

One other example that disappointed me was what my youngest daughter, Stephanie, was being taught about Australia at elementary school in Maryland. In the very brief coverage of Australia in her social studies course, she was taught that the main Australian export was wool. This may have been the case in the 1960s, but it certainly was not the case in the mid-1990s when our exports were dominated by coal and iron ore. I found a quiet moment to talk to her teacher and explain that I worked at the Australian Embassy and could provide more recent information about Australia.

Although I sought to be polite and diplomatic, her response was direct and blunt. *How dare I question the curriculum being used to teach the children?* This was set by the Maryland State Education authorities, and I had no right to question the detail. It is no small wonder that American children grow up with some unusual ideas about the rest of the world.

I remember another classic misunderstanding from when I had visited Cairns, many years previously. About this time Qantas had sought to encourage American tourism through TV commercials using koalas as passengers on its planes. It was a cute and inviting advertisement.

I was riding on a boat between Cairns and Green Island and

overheard one American woman tourist speaking to another American woman about her visit to Taronga Park Zoo in Sydney and how pleased she had been to have had her photo taken with one of those cute little 'Qantases'.

In reverse, the United States often doesn't help its cause in promoting understanding about their country. I remember occasionally watching episodes of *Miami Vice* on Australian TV and thinking what a dangerous and dirty city it seemed to be. We visited Miami, when we spent a week or so touring in a rental car driving around Florida. It was a modern and vibrant city and had some attractive areas. It was not the crime-riddled and squalid city portrayed on *Miami Vice*.

Despite the differences, there were many things we enjoyed about life in America.

Our house was located in a small community known as Carderock Springs in Bethesda, Maryland. There were lots of trees and, in one area, there was a small section of virgin forest. Often, we would see deer in this area. Being a quiet and leafy suburb, it was good for bike riding or going for walks. When my parents visited, they too enjoyed going for walks.

At the front of our house, there was a well-landscaped garden which often played host to squirrels, chipmunks and orioles. On one occasion, we found a turtle in our garden – I think it was just passing through. On another occasion, as I was backing the car out of our driveway, I heard a distinctive knocking sound on one of the large trees adjacent to the driveway. There was a woodpecker hard at work. It was the only woodpecker I have ever seen, and I was surprised at how big it was. Woody Woodpecker, of the cartoons, did not do it proper justice.

We had other less welcome visitors to our garden. A couple of times when we came back home in the evening, we found the contents of our garbage tin scattered over the front yard. Our next-door neighbours had managed to take a video of the culprits in their yard. The culprits were not human vandals, but raccoons. I never saw a live raccoon in our garden, but after coming home several times to scattered garbage, I moved the garbage tin to a less accessible place and put a heavy rock on the top so it was not so easy to pry open. This seemed to do the trick.

In Canberra, snow was a rarity, but in Washington it was a more common feature of winter. The blizzard of 1996 was a particularly memorable snow event. On occasions like this, normal daily routine comes to a halt. Schools and offices are closed and public transport ceases to operate. When there was a break in the snowfall, we ventured out to walk around our neighbourhood and admire the white winter wonderland. Alison took advantage of the snow in our front yard to make 'snow angels' – moving her arms and legs in the snow to leave behind an angel shape.

Annapurnas-view from Himalaya Lodge.

For me, I discovered that snow might look pretty and soft, but it was a lot of hard work to clear from our driveway. After all, snow is basically water and when it is a metre or more deep, it becomes very heavy to shovel. The first time, I got so hot I had to remove my outer layers of clothing.

Another memorable snow story was when we had some Japanese friends visit us at Christmas time in 1996. Because of the snow, their flight had been considerably delayed flying from New York to Washington. Fortunately, they arrived before Christmas. On Christmas Day, although there was still plenty of snow around, roads had been cleared and we visited the home of the first presidential family, George and Martha Washington, at Mount Vernon.

As it turned out, it was probably a good day to visit. There were not so many people and there was little hassle viewing the house. Even though it was bitterly cold outside, visitors to the house, on this day, were treated to cups of hot chocolate and freshly made ginger snap cookies. To me, this seemed to represent the spirit of Christmas time in Washington.

As the Australian Liaison Officer in Washington for the Office of National Assessment (ONA), and because my work took me primarily to downtown Washington DC or Langley in Virginia and did not offer travel further afield, compared with other embassy officers, I had the least opportunity for other travel within the United States.

As a result, most of the travel we undertook in the United States was in our own time. The United States has a strong car culture, and it was possible to drive to many places surrounding Washington. We would get in the car and plan on finding a motel where we could stay for the night.

In this way, some of the memorable places we visited included Monticello, the home of Thomas Jefferson – from this visit we came to appreciate the extent of his interests and his inventiveness and ingenuity; Jamestown, one of the early settlements in Virginia – here we learned about the life of the early settlers and the development of the tobacco industry and the legend of Pocahontas; Harrisburg, Pennsylvania – the State Capitol Building was one of the more impressive Capitol

A Diplomatic Life

Buildings we visited – and nearby Hershey was memorable for its street lights shaped like Hershey kisses and, passing through Amish country, including the quaintly named town of Intercourse, allowed us to witness some of their unique culture which eschewed twentieth-century conveniences; and Boston, where we visited Harvard University and were able to photograph Alison standing in front of Harvard Law School, just so she could say she had been to Harvard Law School. Perhaps this was a portent of Alison's subsequent law studies at the ANU in Canberra.

Several times, we drove to New York to enjoy a weekend in the Big Apple. We stayed with one of Christine's cousins who lived in Manhattan and whose apartment was conveniently located for exploring the city. On two occasions, we took advantage of our New York trips to get discounted tickets to shows on Broadway. Accordingly, we were able to see *Miss Saigon* and *Les Miserables*; both very enjoyable. We considered ourselves fortunate to have this opportunity.

A weekend visit to New York was a bit like the occasional weekend trips to Sydney when we were living in Canberra. In both cases, it was exhilarating to enjoy the hustle and bustle of the big city for a short time, but it was also nice to get back to the quieter and less frenetic pace of life in Washington or Canberra.

Three times we also drove to Canada, twice to Toronto and once to Montreal. Excepting food and bathroom stops, these are the longest continuous drives I have made. Christine had relatives living in Canada.

It seemed whenever we went to Canada, we would be snow-bound for part of our visit. During the course of these visits, we were able to visit the Niagara Falls and see it from both the US and Canadian sides. My impression was that the view from the Canadian side was more spectacular. We also drove from Montreal to Ottawa one day. Much of the route was covered in snow, and for the most part, was flat and largely featureless scenery. Ottawa was, however, worth the trip and we had an interesting visit to the Canadian Parliament Building and stopped to look at people skating on the frozen river running through Ottawa.

In Toronto, near where Christine's 'aunt and uncle' lived – not really relatives, but very close friends of her parents – it was like visiting little Hong Kong. The population seemed predominantly Chinese, the shopping centres had many Chinese shops and many good Chinese restaurants. We ate very well while we were there, though we hardly felt we were in Canada.

The other memorable thing we did in Toronto was ascend to the viewing platform in the Toronto Tower. The Toronto Tower stands way above everything else and on a clear day affords panoramic views of the city and surrounding countryside. What really struck me was the number of people who crawled, hesitantly on their hands and knees, out onto the section of glass floor, an area of about 2-4m square, some too scared to look down. I assumed the building management would not let you go out onto the glass floor unless it was considered safe. I walked out onto the floor and took a few photos of the view below. Some 342m down.

Canberra – Interlude

After returning from Washington to live and work in Canberra, I first worked for about three years in South Asia and then, for a bit over four years in Southeast Asia (Philippines, Singapore, Malaysia and Brunei).

South Asian Nuclear Tests

The day I started working in the South Asia area, 12 May 1998, was the day after India conducted a nuclear test. What a great way to start! For the first couple of weeks, it was in the office by 4:30am every morning to work on media briefing for Foreign Minister Downer.

An initial priority was to try, against the odds, to encourage Pakistan not to follow suit and also carry out a nuclear test. It so happened that a Pakistani parliamentary delegation was visiting Canberra, and we sought to use their visit to point out the moral high ground Pakistan could claim, if they did not follow suit after the Indian test. I think we realised we were battling uphill, but it was worth a try. We were not surprised when Pakistan soon after tested their own nuclear weapon.

They were busy and interesting times, as we had to review our relations with both India and Pakistan, but also seek to limit negative fallout (pardon the word) on non-strategic aspects of our bilateral relationships.

One such task was to push through the ratification of an Investment Promotion and Protection Agreement (IPPA) with Pakistan. I had to attend a meeting of the Joint Parliamentary Committee on Foreign Affairs, Defence and Trade to advocate the case to push forward with early ratification. We considered it even more important to have an IPPA in place, given the extent of Australian mining interests in Pakistan in particular, and the uncertain political environment on the Indian subcontinent.

I was asked some questions about the IPPA, but a major focus of the questions I received was whether the scheduled Australian cricket tour to Pakistan in October 1998 would go ahead. I confirmed we were in regular touch with the Australian Cricket Board about the security situation in Pakistan, but at the end of the day, the decision was theirs as to whether the tour would go ahead.

That afternoon when I got back to the office, I received a copy of a wire service report claiming I had told the committee that the cricket tour would not be going ahead. I had said nothing of the sort. I had said the final decision was for the Australian Cricket Board to make, but DFAT would continue to provide advice on the security situation in Pakistan. The next day I received a further copy of the wire service report on which Foreign Minister Alexander Downer had annotated, 'My sympathies, Mr Lade. This sort of misreporting happens to me all the time.' I think this was the only time in my career in the department that I had received such a hand-written note from the minister. I now wish I had kept a copy.

The cricket tour did go ahead. As it turned out, I was on an official visit to Islamabad while the Australian cricket team was in Pakistan. Unfortunately, my schedule did not overlap with theirs and I didn't get a chance to see any of the play.

A Diplomatic Life

While I was in Islamabad, the second test match between Australia and Pakistan was being played in Peshawar. In this Test, the Australian captain, Mark Taylor, scored 334 runs, equalling the highest test score by Sir Donald Bradman, the greatest Australian batsman of all time, and at that time the highest test score by an Australian cricketer. Having reached that score, Taylor declared the Australian innings closed.

A day or so later, I had a meeting at the Pakistan Ministry of Finance and was quite surprised and touched by the comments of the boy operating the lift taking us up to our meeting. Knowing that our group were Australian, the lift boy said to us, 'That Mark Taylor, he is fantastic. Such an honourable man as he declared (the innings closed) and did not try to outscore Sir Donald Bradman.' These were unexpected comments, but not entirely out of keeping with the serious way the people of South Asia follow their cricket.

In the wake of the South Asian nuclear tests, the dilemma for the Australian government and other governments as well, was how to react and show our displeasure, but also how to develop strategies to discourage further tests and to work towards normalisation of relations with both India and Pakistan. It was a full and challenging agenda.

I remember attending a conference at the University of Canberra which was focused on looking at Australia-India relations. My friend and colleague from the Office of National Assessments, Mike Hillman, aptly characterised the history of Australia-India relations since Indian Independence in 1947, as being like the children's nursery rhyme, The Grand Old Duke of York.

The nursery rhyme went:
'Oh, the Grand Old Duke of York,
He had ten thousand men,
He marched them up to the top of the hill,
And he marched them down again.

And when they were up, they were up,
And when they were down, they were down,
And when they were only halfway up,
They were neither up nor down.'

Over the years since Indian independence, different Australian leaders had bursts of enthusiasm to strengthen and expand links with India, but, in-between such bouts of enthusiasm, relations were tempered by disillusionment. The three Cs that Australia and India shared in common – Commonwealth, cricket and common institutions – were not enough to serve as building blocks for a more substantial relationship, although they helped to some extent. Far too often, both Indian perceptions that Australia did not really matter in terms of its broader strategic interests, and Indian policy developments that ran counter to Australian interests, stymied efforts to develop a stronger and closer relationship.

If we were to build a more substantive relationship with India after the nuclear tests, we knew we had to demonstrate to India that Australia was of strategic value to India. Since my time working in South Asia, there does seem to have been some progress on this score, and certainly Australia's value to India in economic terms as India seeks to promote economic development and industrial growth, has strengthened considerably.

With Pakistan, the challenges were somewhat different. While Pakistan also largely shared the three Cs with Australia, it did not have the same strong democracy as India and this presented challenges to the British Commonwealth. The Pakistan budget was largely devoted to debt repayments and defence expenditure, not the basis for healthy economic growth. Accordingly, Pakistan did not offer the same economic potential as India, nor did loss of trade with Pakistan risk major injury to Australian business, as loss of trade with India would have

A Diplomatic Life

done. Obviously, the situation was more complex than this quick outline.

In short, the initial imperatives to strengthen relations with Pakistan were not as compelling as those with India. This was only really to change post 9/11 (11 September 2001, by which time I was no longer working in South Asia). The need to address fundamentalist Islamic terrorism provided the incentive to try and develop relations with Pakistan, as a bulwark against such terrorism. That is another story and not one I was closely involved in.

Returning to responses following the South Asian nuclear tests, one approach was the establishment of a task force of like-minded countries, which wanted to see no further proliferation of nuclear weapons, to encourage India and Pakistan to renounce the first use of nuclear weapons and hopefully become parties to the Nuclear Non-Proliferation Treaty (NPT) and find other ways to support confidence building measures between India and Pakistan. The membership of this task force comprised the five established nuclear powers (USA, UK, France, Russia and China), countries such as Japan, Australia and the Republic of Korea that had a strong interest in nuclear disarmament, and Ukraine, which had renounced nuclear weapons following the break-up of the Soviet Union.

I attended three meetings of the task force – in London, Tokyo and Kiev. There was some interesting and constructive discussion at these meetings, but our objectives were always going to be difficult to achieve. Realistically India and Pakistan were unlikely to be persuaded to sign on to the NPT and, even though the task force produced some interesting ideas on confidence building measures, it was a tall order to find a way in which these could be successfully promoted to India and Pakistan.

For me, apart from attendance at the task force meetings themselves, the most interesting thing was the chance to visit Kiev. I had never previously been to a country that was part of the former Soviet Union, although I had previously been to communist states – China and Vietnam. The visit therefore provided an opportunity to see a part of the world I was not familiar with, and I found it quite eye-opening.

Getting to Kiev was not so easy. En route, I stopped to visit our high commissions in Colombo and Dhaka. From Dhaka, I took an Emirates flight to Dubai and then a Turkish Airlines flight to Istanbul, and another Turkish Airlines flight from Istanbul to Kiev. The only feasible airline connections into Kiev meant I had to arrive a day and a half before the start of the meeting. A colleague from Canberra, Adam McCarthy, also could only arrive in time for the meeting by arriving just over a day early. So, for just over a day, Adam and I were able to enjoy being tourists. It was the beginning of summer in Kiev, and surprisingly hot.

The old part of Kiev city had many attractive buildings and parks. The new part of the city, mostly across the river, was, in one word, ugly. One of the places in old Kiev that Adam and I visited was St Michael's Monastery. It had been largely destroyed during the Soviet era (I believe in about 1935) but was being rebuilt. When we visited, much of the reconstruction had been completed, although there continued to be some construction activity. If the reconstruction is a faithful rendition of the old monastery, then the old monastery must have been even more impressive, as it was considerably larger. As it was, the blue walls and gold domes were a spectacular sight.

Near St Michael's we found a plaque in front of a very heavy and austere-looking Stalinist-style building which advised that part of St Michael's had previously existed in that location but had been knocked down to make way for the building standing in front of us. The plaque indicated, that originally, this building had served as the headquarters

A Diplomatic Life

of the Ukrainian Communist party.

By way of digression, this reminds me of a story I heard on Canberra radio many years back. The former Secretary-General of the Soviet Communist party was Nikita Khruschev. He had started his Communist party career in Kiev. Prior to politics, his trade had been that of a plumber. The Canberra radio announcer joked that, by comparison, you could never imagine a plumber in Australia working his way through the political party ranks to become prime minister of Australia as he would not be able to afford the drop in income.

Returning to my visit to Kiev, the next morning, when we were picked up from our hotel to go to our meeting, we were surprised that we were taken to this same ugly building. It turned out it was now being used as the Ukraine foreign ministry.

Our hotel in Kiev was called the Dnipro Hotel. There was a coloured pamphlet extolling the amenities the hotel had to offer. One such amenity listed was air-conditioning. It was claimed *all rooms* had air-conditioning. I looked carefully about my room to find the air-conditioning outlet and controls, but they were nowhere to be found. It was the start of summer and surprisingly warm. I figured the only air-conditioning I was going to get was to open the large room windows, which I did, and hopefully get some cooling breeze.

Another amenity listed was a hairdryer *in every room*. Again, my room was sadly lacking, not that I really wanted to use a hairdryer. However, I figured that if you wanted a hairdryer, you would just stick your head out the opened window and dry your hair in the breeze.

One feature, which I guess was a carry-over from the Soviet era, was that at the foot of the stairs to every floor, there was seated a hotel security employee who would make a note in their notebook every time you walked past. Obviously, they were intent on monitoring all movements in and out.

It was recommended not to drink the tap water, but no bottled water was provided in the room. I went down to the front desk and asked where I could buy some bottled water and was told to go to the adjacent bar. I walked into the bar to buy some water, but before I reached the counter, an attractive local woman came up to me, offering her services for the night. She no doubt was disappointed when I told her that all I wanted was to buy some water. For me, I got my water.

Next morning at the hotel dining room for breakfast, there were a number of Japanese men, presumably businessmen, and they all had obviously accepted the hospitality of the local women, and each had a blonde Ukrainian woman in tow.

In post-Glasnost Ukraine, there were some signs of Ukraine opening up to the wider world. There were modern imported cars on the roads and lavish advertising for expensive brand-name products, such as French cosmetics and perfumes. The window display of one department store I walked past held out the promise of imported luxury goods being on sale. However, when I walked inside, the shelves were scantily and uninterestingly stocked with local produce.

We went one night to a surprisingly good Thai restaurant, apparently the enterprise of a local businessman who had invested substantially in the venture. The Indian and Greek restaurants we had already tried were disappointing. Any resemblance to real Indian or Greek food was purely coincidental. However, perhaps reflecting the exposure to globalisation, the Thai food proved to be reasonably authentic, but was expensive, even by Australian standards.

Prior to going to the Thai restaurant for dinner, the Australian delegation fitted in one last sight-seeing excursion. We went to the magnificent St Sophia Cathedral. This was declared a UNESCO World Heritage Site in 1990. Architecturally it was most impressive, but the interior was apparently not a touch on what it used to look like. We learnt that many fine art works had been removed during the Soviet Era and taken to St Petersburg. We did manage to climb the viewing tower from where there were great views of Kiev.

At the time of our visit to Kiev, we were told that the radioactivity levels in the Dnieper River, which runs through Kiev, still remained unacceptably high following the Chernobyl nuclear reactor disaster in 1986.

Despite that, and despite not knowing where the fish had come from, I opted for fish at the lunch hosted by the Ukrainian Foreign Ministry as the alternate option of chicken Kiev looked too oily for my liking. We were, in fact, served a lavish and hearty meal, but too much for someone like me who normally prefers only a light lunch. There was borsch (beetroot soup – which was indeed tasty), masses of bread, potatoes, potato dumplings and other foods high in carbohydrates.

Obviously, the sort of diet that helps the Ukrainian people build up their resistance to the severe Ukrainian winters. For the record, the fish was actually quite good, regardless of whether or not I glowed in the dark afterwards.

While working on the South Asia desk, I had the opportunity to visit both Sri Lanka and Bangladesh briefly.

I have written separately about my missing suitcase on arrival in Colombo and how this may have caused the breakdown of the marriage of the man who inadvertently took my suitcase.

One other memory of my visit to Colombo was a more poignant one. My last meeting on the first day was with a prominent Tamil politician, who was seeking to work with the existing predominantly Sinhalese Sri Lankan government. The politician had squeezed our meeting in with him just prior to his departure for the airport to take a plane to the United States. About two weeks later, just after his return from the US, he was assassinated by the Tamil Tigers. I realised I must have been amongst the last few people to have seen him alive in Colombo. His assassination was one of the many tragic losses of life resulting from the long, drawn-out ethnic conflict in Sri Lanka.

My final memory of Colombo was a more pleasant one. Kathy Klugman, the Australian Deputy High Commissioner, suggested we go for a beer at the Galle Face Hotel in Colombo. The Galle Face is a grand old hotel, founded in the 1860s, and many famous people have stayed there over the years. Some of the prominent Australians listed on the hotel board included Sir Donald Bradman, the former Lord Mayor of Brisbane, Sally-Anne Atkinson, and one of my own bosses at the time, Foreign Minister Alexander Downer.

Befitting a hotel steeped in such tradition, it was hard to beat the atmosphere of sipping a beer and watching the sun set over the Indian Ocean from the hotel verandah. It was indeed a fitting way to end my short visit to Colombo.

My visit to Dhaka, capital of Bangladesh, was similarly rushed, but not anywhere near as dramatic as the preceding visit to Colombo.

One of the most memorable events from that visit was going to the heart of Dhaka city for a meeting with the ANZ bank and witnessing the frenzy of people and rickshaws. I don't think I had witnessed so many rickshaws before – it literally seemed as if there were about ten thousand of them crowded into a busy square. How their drivers could all make a living was hard to imagine, given the other overt signs of poverty everywhere. Probably many of them either just scraped by or could not earn enough money to support their families.

My other memory of that trip to Dhaka, was visiting the Australian High Commission Social Club prior to heading out to the airport to watch the start of the Cricket One Day World Cup final between

Australia and Pakistan. I only got to see the first innings and then had to head to the airport. At the airport, I met the local manager of operations of the Australian fashion company, Country Road, in Bangladesh. I had not realised until I spoke with him that Country Road's dinnerware, at that time, was made in Bangladesh.

On boarding my Emirates flight headed to Dubai, I was anxious to try and find out what had happened in the cricket. There was a Bangladeshi businessman sitting next to me and he was also keen to know the result. I asked the steward, who was from Hong Kong, if there was any chance for the captain to find out when he was in touch with ground control, but I was not entirely sure this was possible. However, the steward came back some minutes later and said that the captain had advised that Australia had won. I thanked the steward and said that sounded like some celebration, perhaps some champagne, was in order. The steward replied that he did not think celebrations would be in order, as the captain was from Pakistan!

Travel to Brunei and the Philippines

This had been my first visit to Brunei. I had not been quite sure what to expect, but during the course of my two working days, I managed to fit in a lot of meetings as well as see most of the major attractions before my flight to Manila on the Sunday afternoon. I found a visit to Seria, the heart of Brunei's oil and gas industry, quite revealing.

It was quite a surreal landscape, remarkably arid for a tropical country, and dotted with little oil derricks everywhere. However, more than the discussions with government officials and business back in the capital, Bandar Seri Begawan, it helped me appreciate how vital the oil and gas industries were to Brunei's economy. I came away realising that what was good for Shell was generally good for Brunei.

On Sunday, Elena Balogh from the high commission escorted me around most of Brunei's major sights of interest. The small museum was packed full of history and proved interesting. The visits to the two main mosques left me awe-inspired. Both were impressive in different ways – one for the lavishness of its golden decoration, the other for elegance and comparative simplicity, but also its sense of dignity. My visit to the museum containing some of the royal treasures was a bit rushed, but enough, again, to impress me with the opulence of some of the royal belongings or items for ceremonial use.

Another lasting impression of my short visit to Brunei was the seeming paradox in a predominantly Islamic country of Valentine's Day being so ostentatiously celebrated at the Sheraton Hotel where I was staying.

When I arrived, the hotel lobby was festooned with red balloons and hearts, and there were signs everywhere highlighting the scheduled Valentine's Day celebrations. Of course, this should not really have been so surprising, as there are a significant number of ethnic Chinese amongst Brunei's population and there was a very large Filipino contingent amongst the guest workers. In fact, it was in Brunei where I first encountered the Philippine fast-food institution, Jolibee.

Nonetheless, I was told that the Islamic authorities kept a close eye on the Bruneian Muslim population, to ensure they did not over-step the mark on Valentine's Day and leave themselves open to charges of being in unacceptable close proximity with the opposite sex.

One other notable memory from Brunei was of some of the impressive infrastructure in and around Bandar Seri Begawan. Much of this was attributed to the efforts of the then-disgraced Prince Jeffrey, brother of the Sultan. Part of this legacy included modern buildings for government ministries, some excellent roads, the Empire Hotel, and an amusement park that opened, I was told, late afternoon and into the early hours of the morning because it was generally too hot during the daytime to appeal to the locals.

The Empire Hotel was a self-styled six-star hotel. I went there one night for dinner. The entrance foyer is massive with polished marble everywhere and enormous pillars that seemed big enough to drive a truck through, if they weren't solid marble. The hotel has its own golf course, man-made beaches and numerous other amenities that set it apart from the usual luxury hotel. It is the largest and most lavish hotel I have seen, anywhere. However, for all that, our seafood buffet dinner was surprisingly inexpensive and had a good selection of quality seafood.

Checking in for my flight to Manila, I noticed there were only two Royal Brunei flights scheduled that Sunday afternoon. One was going to Manila, the other to Kota Kinabalu in Sabah. Thus, on arrival in Manila, there was no suitcase waiting for me on the baggage carousel. As Royal Brunei later confirmed, while I was still at the airport, my suitcase had gone to Kota Kinabalu and the next Royal Brunei flight to Manila would not arrive till the following day. After several hours confirming details and filling out paperwork, Royal Brunei presented me with just over US$100 to buy some emergency supplies, to tide me over until my suitcase turned up.

Miles Armitage, the deputy at the Australian embassy in Manila, had met me at the airport and raced me into the city to check into the Peninsula H Hotel in Makati and then to go shopping. It was almost closing time at the shopping mall that Miles took me to. The first clothing shop we went to would not let me in as they were closing. We then went to Marks and Spencers, the British chain and certainly not one of the cheapest places to shop in Manila. When I told them my story, they agreed to let me in to choose a few items.

I bought a shirt, a pair of socks and a pair of underpants and had only a few cents change from my Royal Brunei money. Miles lent me a tie, so at least I was respectable for my work meetings the next day. However, waist down, I had to wear the blue jeans I'd been wearing on the flight to Manila. At least, my dress, and the reasons for it, provided a good conversation starter for my meetings in Manila.

It had been a bit over twenty years since I'd last visited Manila. Makati remained the modern showcase, as more and more new buildings had gone up since my last visit. Modern, sprawling air-conditioned shopping malls were a new feature. Construction of new roads and overpasses helped ensure that traffic congestion remained a feature of Manila's traffic.

As this was my first work-related visit to Manila, I perhaps had not been quite as conscious of the difficulties of planning travel times before. One morning, we had a meeting scheduled with some senior military personnel at Camp Aguinaldo. It took us about two hours to get there and we were, of course, late for our meeting, but our meeting host agreed to wait for us even though it was cutting into his lunch time.

After our meeting, we had a hurried lunch nearby and then headed off to our next meeting with the protocol officer at Malacanang Palace. As our driver could not predict how long the trip would take, he recommended we get going as soon as possible. We had a dream run and encountered very light traffic, arriving at Malacanang over an hour early. What to do? We decided to risk the traffic and visit the National Museum of the Philippines. Just under an hour was probably not enough time to do justice to what was then, a good museum, and today is even better. However, we did not want to be late back to Malacanang and we weren't.

At the end of a long day, we went back to the Peninsula Hotel and thankfully, my suitcase was waiting for me. I only had a few morning meetings the following day before heading off to the airport to catch my flight back to Australia via Hong Kong.

Travel to Singapore and Malaysia

I had several work-related opportunities to visit Singapore and Malaysia. One visit to Singapore was for the Singapore-Australia Joint Ministerial Committee Meeting. I recall this involving a couple of late nights trying to fine-tune the joint statement to be issued at the end of the Meeting. However, after the departure of the Australian Ministers, I joined other Australian officials in going to the east coast, not far from the airport at Changi, for a chili crab dinner. This is one of the most memorable food delicacies in Singapore. It was messy, but truly delicious.

Another visit to Singapore was for general orientation on the political and economic situation in Singapore. One element of this visit involved going to the Institute of Southeast Asian Studies. There I met with two prominent academics, one a Singaporean who was ethnically a Sikh, and the other was a Malaysian who was ethnically a Tamil. As it turned out, I didn't have to intervene much in the discussion as there was quite a lively discussion between the two academics.

At the time of my visit, there was considerable debate in Singapore about whether Muslim girls could wear the hijab (Islamic head-dress) at school. Generally, the official thinking was that to allow them to do so would encourage more fundamentalist Islamic views to take root, something considered undesirable with the growing Islamic fundamentalist involvement in terrorism. The Singaporean academic believed banning of the hijab for girls at school was appropriate. Perhaps, partly to be provocative, the Malaysian academic argued, wondering how was this any less acceptable than allowing Sikhs to wear turbans, including by Sikh schoolboys. The

Singaporean academic, being a Sikh, was of course wearing a turban and rejected this analogy. This led to a very lively discussion. I observed quietly, but the discussion left me thinking afterwards how easily misunderstandings can develop.

One of my visits to Malaysia was related to preliminary discussions on a bilateral free trade agreement. As with our already concluded free trade agreement with Singapore, liberalisation of services trade was one of the most contentious issues. Our Australian team argued that one sector, in which we would like to see trade opening up, was architectural services. We were aware that for many big architectural projects, the Malaysian firm of architects often sought consulting services from foreign architectural firms. However, these foreign architects could not be registered to practise in their own right in Malaysia.

Discussion revolved around what the Australian side saw as an anomaly. If an Australian architect had provided significant advice to a Malaysian architectural firm for the design of a bridge, and the bridge were to collapse either during or after construction, the Malaysian firm had to wear the responsibility for any design fault and the foreign firm could not be held accountable, even if it was wholly or partly responsible for the design fault. For the Australian team, this seemed illogical. Surely it would be better to allow Australian firms to be registered in Malaysia and enter into joint ventures directly with Malaysian firms. For their part, the Malaysians wished to preserve exclusivity for Malaysian architectural firms. I remember this discussion going round and round in circles.

When I was able to get a break from the official discussions, I liked to meet up with my good Malaysian Foreign Ministry friend, S K Choo. Soon after our arrival in Malaysia, Choo had introduced us to *cendol* (a shaved ice dessert) in Malacca. Often when we met during my return visits to Malaysia, it was for a cold beer and a few satay sticks.

After more than seven years back in Canberra, it was time to move on and do something else.

Mission to the Last Hindu Kingdom

Having worked for just over three years in the South Asian region, I was interested when head of mission jobs were advertised in 2005 for Bangladesh and Nepal. I threw my hat in the ring for both positions.

Some months later, I received a phone call advising I had been selected to be appointed as Australian ambassador to Nepal. In keeping with Australian practice, but not the practice of a number of other countries which hold public confirmation hearings for ambassadorial appointments, I was sworn to confidentiality until Agrément for my appointment had been received from the Nepalese government.

Although I was unable to disclose where I was going, I had to begin enrolling in the numerous mandatory courses required before proceeding overseas. These included courses on finance, media handling and consular work, to name but a few, as well as a course specifically tailored to prepare for head of mission assignments. There were also numerous personal chores that had to be attended to, but fortunately Alison had agreed to stay on in our house and that saved me from the major tasks of having to prepare goods for going into storage or putting the house up for rent.

Most importantly, I needed to learn more about Nepal and Australian interests. I already had some knowledge of Australian interests and some of the major political developments in Nepal, although things had moved on somewhat since 2001 when I had previously been responsible for Nepal. I had in fact still been responsible for Nepal when the gruesome massacre of the Nepalese royal family occurred in 2001. However, Kathmandu was the only one of the South Asian posts I had not visited when director of the South Asia section. I therefore had very little sense of what Kathmandu and Nepal were really like.

In December 2005, when Agrément had been received, I was able to commence a concerted program of activities involving meetings with relevant government departments in Canberra, such as AusAID, Australian Federal Police, immigration, education, Office of National Assessments and a few others. I also spent a few days in Sydney and Melbourne meeting with organisations that had interests in Nepal, such as Fred Hollows Foundation, the Australian Himalayan Foundation, World Vision, Austcare and a number of individuals who had been involved in medical or other assistance in Nepal. I also spent some time with Les Douglas, one of my predecessors, who was then working for the Snowy Mountains Engineering Corporation, which was pursuing one of the potentially largest engineering projects to be undertaken in Nepal. There was much to cover in a comparatively short time.

From my time working on Nepal, I had some general sense of the country's geography. Namely, that Nepal was divided into three main regions – the plains, or *Terai*, in the south, the hilly country in the middle where the Kathmandu Valley and the old cities of Patan, Kathmandu and Bhaktapur were located, and the north, home to the mighty Himalayas.

I had not, however, really appreciated that Kathmandu was at a similar altitude to the peak of Mount Wellington in Hobart. Yet by contrast, the weather conditions in Kathmandu were very pleasant most of the year, compared to the windy, unpredictable and often snowy conditions on Mount Wellington. Accordingly, I was not surprised at the number of people who I met prior to departure who suggested I needed to be prepared for cold and snowy weather ... and perhaps I should take my skis – even though I was not a skier.

As I found out, living in Kathmandu, in winter the temperature sometimes dropped close to freezing, but snow was extremely rare. In fact, during my time in Kathmandu, it snowed once, and it was remarked that it was the first snowfall in the Kathmandu Valley for sixty years.

My daughters Stephanie and Alison with Himalayas in the background.

There was a clever cartoon in one of the local papers that recorded this rare snowfall. Maoist leader, Prachanda, had boasted that within ten years under Maoist rule, Nepal could be like Switzerland. The cartoon quipped alongside the image of Kathmandu under snow that Prachanda must be a genius as, already, Nepal had become like Switzerland! Such was the rarity of snow in Kathmandu and, in fact, in winter, daytime temperatures were often quite mild despite regular cold nights.

One other common misconception was the number of people who encouraged me to pursue the objective of introducing the Nepalese to playing cricket. As South Asian countries Nepal and Afghanistan were seen as the two main stand-outs where cricket was not a national obsession, though I had been aware of some interest in cricket in Nepal because the Australian Cricket Board had provided some coaching assistance. On arrival in Nepal, I found that cricket was the fastest-growing participation sport and people, just like in India or Pakistan, would play makeshift games on any available piece of land.

One of the previous administrative officers in Kathmandu recommended I take my bicycle, as there would be plenty of opportunities to use it. I had not expected such advice as I still understood that much of the Kathmandu Valley was quite hilly. However, as I was soon to learn, there were also many comparatively level areas.

My bicycle was much travelled. I had bought it in Malaysia but used it much more extensively going for bike rides with Alison and Stephanie around Bethesda, Maryland, and then back in Canberra. However, as it turned out, I only had a few opportunities to ride my bike in Kathmandu. I agreed that my cook could borrow the bike when he went grocery shopping. One day, he came to me most distraught. He had stopped at a stall to buy some vegetables and, although the bicycle was parked only a metre or so away, in the instant he averted his eyes to pay for the vegetables, the bicycle was stolen. He reported the theft to the police, but of course the bicycle was never seen nor heard of again.

I was aware that there was a swimming pool and tennis court at the embassy and my predecessor, Keith Gardner, encouraged me to take my tennis racquet. He even identified a couple of partners for me to play tennis with. Reflecting this, Alison and Stephanie presented me with a new tennis racquet for Christmas. It was to get a lot of use.

One of the potential tennis partners Keith had mentioned was Abraham Abraham, the Head of the United Nations High Commission for Refugees in Nepal. Abraham and I became regular tennis partners, as well as very good personal friends and close work colleagues in regard to Bhutanese and other refugee issues.

Keith provided me with helpful advice on things I should do prior to going to Kathmandu and on other things I might take to Nepal, as well as on things I did not need to take. Keith's advice greatly simplified my inventory of goods for shipment to Nepal. Apart from paintings, photos, books, CDs and DVDs, clothing and some personal knick-knacks to give the embassy residence my own flavour, I took comparatively little to Kathmandu. It was all packed into three wooden crates and, probably, the paintings and my bicycle took up the most space.

I was now ready to head to Kathmandu. I departed Canberra on Friday the thirteenth for Bangkok where I was to spend one night before flying to Kathmandu the next day. As our Thai international flight approached Tribhuvan International Airport in Kathmandu, I was fascinated to observe the rugged hills (hills by Nepalese standards, but mountains by Australian standards), the communities nestled in the valleys or on the sides of the hills, and the large number of brickwork chimneys, given the preponderance of bricks in local construction. To my right, out the plane window, I was also blessed with my first glimpses of the awesome and mighty snow-capped Himalayas.

Arrival in Kathmandu

On disembarking, Linda Trigg, the deputy head of mission at the Australian embassy in Kathmandu at the time, greeted me at the satellite arm of the airport, near where our plane had parked. She introduced me to someone from the protocol area of the foreign ministry and they both escorted me to the airport VIP room. Immigration processing and baggage collection were quite quick, and I was soon meeting the ambassadorial driver, Rabi, and getting into the ambassadorial Range Rover for the trip to the Australian embassy compound at Bansbari in Kathmandu.

I had no preconceived expectations of what Kathmandu was like as we drove to the embassy. The most lasting impressions I have of that first trip were of the large number of four- to six-storey brick buildings, many of which seemed to have an unfinished floor on top, lots of dust and lots of colour, as people, especially the women in their bright saris, went about their Saturday chores. I was also struck by the congestion and chaos of the traffic, although it was only later that I came to appreciate some of the unique features of Kathmandu traffic.

Therefore, when we entered the gates of the Australian embassy compound, it was like coming upon an oasis with its expansive grounds, big trees, colourful flowers and, most of all, its quiet.

Waiting at the residence front door were Ganga, Mishree and Leela, the three domestic staff who worked at the residence. As I got out of the car, they welcomed me in the traditional Nepalese way with a *Namaste* (the usual Nepalese and Indian word of greeting, said with palms pressed together in front of your chest as you bow slightly from the waist), garlands of marigold flowers around my neck and *khada* (white cotton or silk cloth which is draped over your shoulders). I was also introduced to Orsa, the German shepherd dog I was inheriting from my predecessor.

After putting my bags down and having a quick tour of the house, I was shown to the verandah off the living room, to sit down for a cup of tea. This verandah became one of my favourite features of the house as it opened onto the front garden and provided a great space for entertaining guests or preparing barbecues.

However, that first time, Orsa decided to make herself better known to me. Most dogs will chase a stick or a ball, but not Orsa. She brought me a stone to throw. When I threw the stone, she would retrieve it and bring it back to me, to be thrown again ... and again and again.

Next day, being a Sunday, Rabi came to collect me to take me shopping for a couple of essentials. One thing I found I did not have was an alarm clock. I asked Rabi if he knew where I might be able to buy one and he took me to the Bluebird Department Store near the Radisson Hotel. There were indeed some alarm clocks for sale, but the selection was quite limited, and they were all really intended for children.

As Rabi had advised that Bluebird was probably the best place to find a clock, and of course not knowing what else, if anything, might be available, I chose the sturdiest looking clock available out of choices really intended for children. The one I chose had a pink cover and a picture of Snoopy on the clock-face. This is not normally what I would have wanted, but it did prove a reliable clock. I later learned there was a much better selection of alarm clocks available in Kathmandu than my first exposure to Bluebird had led me to believe.

In many senses, this experience was typical of Kathmandu. If you knew where to go, you could buy almost anything you were familiar with in Australia. During my time in Kathmandu the sophistication of some of the supermarkets and department stores, and the range of goods they stocked, both improved dramatically. I was told that many Indian tourists to Kathmandu came to buy electrical goods or other household items to take back, as the range and availability was better than in India. However, by the time I left Kathmandu, this was a less common practice, as availability in India had apparently improved greatly.

That afternoon, Rabi took me for a bit of a drive around the city and we ended up at Swayambhunath or the Monkey Temple. This ancient Buddhist stupa and temple is probably the iconographic image of Kathmandu. Sitting atop a hill, with its four-faced tower above the stupa, Swayambhunath can be seen for miles around. On each face of the tower are painted the eyes of Buddha, a third all-seeing eye, and, although it might look a bit like a nose, the Newar symbol for unity. Within the temple grounds, wild monkeys run everywhere, hence its alternative name of the Monkey Temple.

Swayambhunath is one of the most common images of Kathmandu, and certainly, it was one I was familiar with. By coming to this temple, in particular, I felt I had truly arrived in Kathmandu.

Work begins

Monday morning, I made the 30m walk to the office and met the embassy staff. This was basically a short introduction as a welcome drinks function was organised for later that week to allow me a chance to get to know them better. Several of them I came to rely on extensively – Sanjana, my principal assistant, Manju and Kumudh on consular matters and Tara on Australian aid to Nepal.

Sanjana had already been in touch with the foreign ministry, and one of the first tasks was for me to meet with the chief of protocol to discuss arrangements for the presentation of credentials.

Credentials are the formal letter of appointment from your head of state to the receiving country's head of state, advising that you will be the representative of your country and recalling the credentials previously handed over by your predecessor. In the Australian case, the credentials are printed on beautiful thick paper, printed in colour with the Australian coat-of-arms and signed by the governor-general. The receiving country organises a ceremony for the hand-over of your credentials to the head of state, and it is only when that ceremony has been held, that you officially become the ambassador to that country and can conduct your full range of duties.

The meeting with the chief of protocol took place soon after my arrival in Kathmandu, but the bad news was that the chief of protocol could not tell me when I would be able to present credentials. The King was currently holidaying in Nepal, outside Kathmandu, and it was not clear when he would return. I just had to wait.

The chief of protocol also advised that normally they liked to have at least three ambassadors at each credential's ceremony. He said I was the only Kathmandu-based ambassador waiting to present credentials and there were no others immediately on the horizon. *However, not to worry, as there would probably be several accredited from New Delhi who would wish to present their credentials.*

At this time, the chief of protocol was very strict about what I could and could not do prior to presentation of credentials. I could meet with my ambassadorial colleagues, and I could meet business people either at the embassy or in their offices, but I could not meet officially with any government personnel apart from himself and other designated staff in the foreign ministry. I could also not attend any public events where Nepalese government officials might be present.

This precluded me from attending the National Day function organised by the Sri Lankan ambassador. That I could readily understand, however, it also precluded me from attending a piano recital organised by the Russian embassy and which involved a visiting Russian pianist. The reason was that it was possible Nepalese government officials might be present.

Perhaps reflecting the political changes that took place in Nepal after April 2006, these restrictions on me were generally more relaxed for ambassadors who arrived after me. For me, I had to work within these strict guidelines.

Accordingly, my first few weeks in Kathmandu were spent

familiarising myself with the work of the Embassy, making introductory calls on my ambassadorial or UN agency counterparts, meeting with some members of the business community with links to Australia and meeting at the embassy with Nepalese representatives of alumni or friendship groups. I also attended a couple of private welcoming lunches or dinners in my honour.

Although I was able to meet most of my ambassadorial colleagues early on at a lunch hosted by Mohinder Singh, the Malaysian ambassador, in his residence garden. I felt a bit out of touch with much of the lunch-time conversation as they were talking about people or events that were largely unfamiliar to me. Nonetheless, I was grateful for this chance to start putting faces to names. Mohinder himself was to become one of my closest colleagues in the diplomatic corps.

When I arrived in Nepal, I only knew a few people. This included my assistant Sanjana who had attended a staff training course in Canberra. Amongst others, were the Pakistan Ambassador Sohail Amin and his wife Shahnaz, whom I had known quite well from Canberra, where Sohail had served as deputy high commissioner. I remembered Sohail as a keen bushwalker, until he heard about all the snakes in the Canberra bush in spring. Sohail was one of the first ambassadors I called on and I was impressed to hear that his bushwalking exploits had advanced in Nepal to some serious trekking activity.

There are a couple of other calls worth mentioning specifically. Both the Russian ambassador, Andrei Trofimov, and the UN resident coordinator and head of the United Nations Development Program, Matthew Kahane, invited me to their homes to pay my introductory call and both provided a nice afternoon or morning tea. This impressed me as allowing a greater level of informality on the one hand, and a greater sense of personal rapport on the other.

I decided that when it was my turn to start receiving newly arrived ambassadors in Nepal making their introductory calls, I would receive them at the residence and offer some home-made afternoon tea. I followed this practice with all new ambassadors, except once, when there was some major repair work going on at the residence.

The other call of note was on the Myanmar ambassador Aung Khin Soe. He had been the last ambassador before me to have presented credentials. He had set something of a record in the time taken to present credentials following his arrival in Kathmandu. He'd had to wait almost four months. I know they say that records are made to be broken, but this was one record I hoped I would not break. As a footnote, Aung Khin Soe was subsequently appointed as Myanmar ambassador to the Philippines, where I caught up with him in 2009 and 2010.

In most of my introductory calls on other ambassadors, a major point of discussion was the current state of Nepalese politics. I was impressed, although not at all surprised, that the four South Asian ambassadors – Shiv Mukherjee for India, Sohail Amin for Pakistan, Humayun Kabir for Bangladesh (later Bangladesh high commissioner in Canberra for a year before going as Ambassador to the United States) and Grace Asirwatham of Sri Lanka – followed developments very closely and knowledgably. I found their comments especially persuasive and interesting. The British Ambassador, Keith Bloomfield, the US Ambassador, Jim Moriarty, the Norwegian Ambassador, Tore Toreng, and the Danish Ambassador, Finn Thilsted, seemed also to follow developments closely and were well informed. Apart from this group, other ambassadors I called on also helped reinforce the key impressions I gained from these meetings.

Essentially, the message I was given was that I'd arrived in Nepal at a time of political stalemate, where neither the King nor the political party leaders of the Seven Party Alliance, as it then was, were prepared to compromise with each other and that this impasse was likely to continue indefinitely. Many offered the view that things were unlikely to have advanced notably by the time my assignment was due to end, three years hence. This represented a very gloomy outlook for both the future political and economic development of Nepal. I hoped it would not prove to be the case.

As the subsequent events of April 2006 demonstrated, things could, and did, change rapidly and dramatically. However, these events were completely unforeseen at the time I was starting out in Nepal.

In these early days prior to presentation of credentials, there were a number of people I was grateful for, helping me to meet Nepalese people and to better understand Nepalese society.

At the end of my first week in Nepal, Bruce Moore, who was an Australian long-time resident in Nepal and who was leasing the third house on the Australian embassy compound, hosted a dinner in my honour. The dinner was notable for two reasons – the food and the company.

Bruce had invited Sangeeta Thapa, daughter of a prominent banker and manager of one of Kathmandu's leading private art galleries, the Siddhartha Gallery. Her husband, Sunil, was also present. He was the son of a former Nepalese prime minister and was employed by the United High Commissioner for Refugees. As such, it was not often that he was back in Kathmandu for an extended period. Other guests included Abhinav Rana and his wife, Sweetie. At the time, Abhinav was acting general manager of the Radisson Hotel. The final guest was Geeta Basnyet, who was a senior medical officer, later medical general in the Nepal Army. Her husband, Buddha, was not present, but he was a prominent local doctor who specialised in altitude sickness, and it was not to be long before I met him too.

All of these people were generally ones I came to know well, both professionally and personally, and were mostly people I maintained contacts with after leaving Nepal.

As for the food – it was my introduction to Newari cuisine. This is quite different to the more Indian-inspired cuisine which is widely available in Nepal. It was developed over many centuries by the Newar people who inhabited the Kathmandu Valley. I recall our dinner that night included buffalo tongue, battered and fried buffalo lungs (which actually tasted better than it sounds), buffalo brains (this was not for me), wild boar and a range of other exotic vegetarian and non-vegetarian dishes served with beaten rice. Some of the dishes were quite appetising, but others were very much an acquired taste. Nonetheless, I was grateful for this introduction to the local cuisine.

Someone else I was grateful to was Keith Bloomfield, the British ambassador, and at the time Dean of the Diplomatic Corps, who hosted a lunch in my honour to which he invited a number of prominent businessmen and local politicians. This was my first real exposure to some local business people and politicians, and I found the discussion very revealing, in particular, on the outlook for the Nepalese economy.

One of the businessmen argued that politics was not the main reason holding up economic development in Nepal, but that wealth was in the hands of a comparatively small group of people, who failed to pay back the debts they owed the government. Although I don't think it was quite as simple as this, it was an idea I carried with me during my time in Nepal and it did come up again from time to time in discussions I had with the World Bank and other economic analysts.

Another memorable dinner during this period was hosted by Kiran Shrestha, his wife and two daughters and Arpan Sharma. Kiran and Arpan ran Nepalaya, an organisation aimed at raising social awareness. One of their main means for doing this was through the band they managed, Nepathya, with front man Amrit Gurung. Nepathya concerts would target audiences of disadvantaged or disabled children and seek to empower them and make them realise they were the same as everyone else. However, through movie-making and other activities, they also sought to raise social awareness at the political level as well.

Kiran's wife was an excellent cook, and we had a very tasty meal and some interesting and lively discussion. Kiran explained some of his close calls at the hands of the Maoists, but he was also keen not to attribute all human rights violations to them, as he acknowledged there were also reports of abuses by the Nepal Army.

The last memorable dinner I recall during this period was hosted by Dr Sanduk Ruit and his team at the Tilganga Eye Centre. Other staff from the embassy were invited as well. This marked the beginning of what was to become a lasting friendship and close association with Tilganga throughout my time in Nepal and beyond. Both I and other members of the embassy were made to feel like family. As I have written elsewhere, Dr Ruit is a remarkable man and I truly valued, and still do, the association with him and Tilganga.

Presentation of Credentials

A date was finally set for my presentation of credentials ceremony, about four weeks after my arrival in Kathmandu. Gratefully, I was not going to break the Myanmar Ambassador's record. I was to present my credentials to King Gyanendra on 11 February 2006 (I had not appreciated at the time that this was in fact, my partner, Odette's birthday) along with ambassadors from Morocco and Zambia, accredited from New Delhi.

King Gyanendra had assumed the throne of the Hindu Kingdom of Nepal following the death of his brother. (The former King Birendra, and other members of the royal family were killed in a massacre engineered by the late Crown Prince Birendra on 1 June 2001.)

In the wake of the continuing Maoist insurgency, on 1 February

2005, King Gyanendra suspended the constitution and assumed full authority. This led to an ongoing stalemate between the king and the deposed parliament seeking its restoration. This was the situation at the time I presented credentials. Little did I know that I would be among the last few Ambassadors to present their credentials to the king.

Because I was based in Kathmandu, I was invited by the Foreign Ministry's Protocol Department to attend a rehearsal for the presentation of credentials ceremony. Sadly, the chief of protocol had died suddenly, and it meant the officers remaining in the protocol department had little direct experience of organising the arrangements for the ceremony.

I could sympathise with these protocol department officers, and I knew they had my best interests at heart. However, for me, the rehearsal seemed like an episode from the British comedy program, *Yes Minister* and there were times I found it hard to keep a straight face. As one protocol department officer acted out his understanding of procedures, another would say he was wrong and take his place in acting out procedures. There were differences of opinion over how many steps I would have to take before I bowed before the king. After watching this performance for over half an hour, they had more or less reached agreement on the process to be followed.

There were also differences of opinion as to whether the Minister for Foreign Affairs, Ramesh Nath Pandey, would be present and, if so, where he would stand. There was uncertainty as to whether I would be travelling to the Narayanhiti Palace in an open roof carriage. It was suggested that if the weather was good, I might travel in the open roof carriage, otherwise it would be an enclosed sedan. I was also told I needed to bring a white handkerchief, as this would be presented to the king to sprinkle it with some sacred oil.

After the rehearsal, I was still left with some doubts as to the actual

A Diplomatic Life

procedure to be followed, but I was not concerned as I knew I would be escorted the whole way. One thing I did do was to go out and buy a white handkerchief, as I did not have one. This was one vestige of the Hindu Kingdom that I considered would be unique to Nepal and it was something I looked forward to.

On the day of the ceremony, I went to the Annapurna Hotel accompanied by my deputy, Linda Trigg, and met for the first time with my Moroccan and Zambian counterparts. We, again, ran through the procedures for the ceremony. By now, there seemed to be firm agreement on the process. We were also told that there would be no open roof carriage as that was reserved for use in the warmer months. I was also disappointed to learn that there would be no anointing of my white handkerchief with sacred oil.

As I was the only resident ambassador, I was the first to go to the palace. A black Mercedes was waiting for me at the entrance of the Annapurna Hotel and drove me the short distance, maybe 300m, through the gates of the Narayanhiti Palace and to an entrance at the side of the palace. Perhaps because of my excitement at the time, I cannot remember if we walked up one or two flights of stairs to the large reception room where the king was waiting at the end of a short red carpet. I also was so focused on the ceremony I paid little heed to my other surroundings. I was escorted the whole way by a palace official and, in a sense, the number of steps I took became irrelevant. He prompted me every step of the way. I had to walk to the end of the red carpet and bow to the king.

The king greeted me and invited me to present my credentials. While I thought they were very smart-looking on their thick polished paper and embossed in colour with the Australian coat-of-arms, I thought the smart green folder that the Moroccan ambassador had for his credentials would have been a nice feature for me too. We were advised that the king would talk to us for two to three minutes and then I should retreat a few steps backwards to where the foreign minister was standing – yes, he was there and standing to my left rear – bow and then depart in the company of the foreign minister. At the door to the reception room, the foreign minister returned to his place for the next presentation ceremony, and I was again escorted by a palace official to the waiting car and back to the Annapurna Hotel.

I had prepared a few points for my discussion with the king, but time did not permit me to raise more than three, very short points. The king was obviously accustomed to these ceremonies. He started the short conversation with a few personal comments about his previous links with Australia and sought to put me at ease. The time passed quickly, and it seemed almost no time before I was back in the waiting room at the Annapurna chatting with my colleagues from Morocco and Zambia, nibbling on a couple of canapés and sipping a fruit juice.

I hoped it was a good omen for me, but as I left the Annapurna Hotel to return to the Australian embassy, I caught a glimpse of the snow-capped peaks of the Himalayas. As I was to find, it was not such a common sight to see the Himalayas from Kathmandu as they were often shrouded in cloud or obscured by dust or smog. Therefore, when the mountains were visible from the city it was a truly magical sight.

I was now official and could commence my full range of official duties. However, they were going to have to wait a few days, as that weekend I was due to fly to New Delhi for a meeting of Australian Regional Heads of Mission.

Commencement of Official Duties

Apart from the letter of credentials, Australian ambassadors received one other important document that guided their duties overseas. This was the ministerial directive, which was a short letter signed by both the Minister for Foreign Affairs and the Minister for Trade. It briefly outlined the key objectives and priorities and set the basic parameters for what the main focus of activities should be.

In my case, the focus was on supporting the effective delivery of Australian economic assistance, supporting Australian commercial interests, especially the efforts by the Snowy Mountains Engineering Corporation to develop a major hydropower project in Nepal, and to ensure that consular services were delivered efficiently and smoothly. All such directives also included a statement on the Head of Mission having ultimate authority and responsibility for the proper and efficient running of the post's administration.

In reporting back to Canberra on the post's performance each year, it was important to show the post was meeting the guidelines laid down in the ministerial directive. However, within the guidelines set by the Ministerial Directive, there was still scope for Heads of Mission to imprint their own particular style on how to do the job, in a way that best met Australian national interests. More significantly, as I found in Nepal, there were other issues not specifically addressed in the Ministerial Directive that assumed high priority during my time in Nepal.

Two such issues were Bhutanese refugees and Nepalese students in Australia. These were issues that came to occupy quite a lot of my time and attention but were not early priorities following my presentation of credentials. Rather, a major early focus was the momentous political change taking shape, and the implications this had for our consular travel advisories, in particular.

Within two weeks of arriving in Kathmandu, I experienced my first bandhs (strikes) and curfews. Bandhs are a widely used political tool in South Asian countries, but personally I think they are now rather out-dated, as they cause most disruption and inconvenience to the ordinary people; the very people whose sympathy and support they are supposedly trying to win over. A common feature of bandhs was to burn rubber tyres, mainly to deter vehicular traffic. Burning rubber gives off an awful acrid smell which probably also served as a deterrent to pedestrians.

One of the main impacts of a bandh is the restriction it places on daily traffic. In some cases, all traffic is prohibited. In other cases, essential services such as ambulances or water delivery are permitted, along with media transport, as the media is needed to report on the bandh. Often, diplomatic vehicles are allowed freedom of movement, although in my time when such movement was permitted, it was not always guaranteed in all parts of the city. A government-imposed curfew meant that access to and availability of basic food stuffs was severely limited.

Bandhs and curfews created challenges for us to maintain the usual embassy services and flexibility was required to ensure that Nepalese staff could get safely to and from the embassy. They could not use their normal private transport arrangements. Accordingly, at such times, when it was safe for diplomatic vehicles to be on the roads, we would collect staff immediately after the end of the morning curfew and get them home before the commencement of the evening curfew. Occasionally, our vehicles would encounter roadblocks that would not allow them to pass, and they would have to retrace their route and find an alternative way.

The Australian embassy was located about 400ms from the Narayan Gopal Chowk intersection, where the ring road divided Maharajgunj, which headed towards the city and Bansbari which headed up to Budhanilkantha. Narayan Gopal Chowk was a favourite gathering place for protestors and other activists and, if travel restrictions during bandhs were being strictly enforced, it meant we had to use alternate routes to travel to and from the embassy.

Less than two months after the presentation of my credentials, the impasse between the king and the Seven Party Alliance was becoming increasingly tense. The Seven Party Alliance sought in April 2006 to turn up the pressure against the king by encouraging mass protest activities and supporting curfews throughout the whole country. Taking advantage of this situation, the Maoists and their sympathisers began to lend their support to the mass protest movements. Rumour had it that many people were being bussed into the city, often with the lure of a meal, a new T-shirt or a few rupees.

On the first day of concerted protest activity, it was almost like a festival atmosphere. We did not realise, at the time, that this was the start of Jana Andolan II, the revolution that was to change the shape of Nepalese politics, in much the same way Jana Andolan I had led to the implementation of the 1990 democratic constitution.

We witnessed the events as they developed, to and from Narayan Gopal Chowk. Crowds of protesters, mostly young men, but including quite a few young boys aged between about seven and twelve, would charge down from the Heart Hospital/Budhanilkantha direction towards Narayan Gopal Chowk where they would face a wall of policemen, all with their metal shields raised. As the barrage of stone-throwing by the protesting mob weakened, the police would charge at them with shields and batons raised and force them back up the hill towards the Heart Hospital.

I and other embassy staff took turns watching the action from the safety of the security desk at the front gate of the embassy. At first, it was like a game. Both the protesting mob and police flashed broad smiles as they made their respective charges and, despite the stone throwing, the atmosphere did not really seem overtly hostile.

However, by the end of the day, tempers were starting to fray. Most of the police had been on duty all day and many had not had proper food or water. Even among the protestors, there were some signs of tiredness and irritation. I witnessed one or two incidents towards the end of that first day of police dealing harshly with some of the protestors, whose stone-throwing was possibly getting too close to the mark. What I saw was a couple of protestors being detained and manhandled, including one or two strokes of the baton.

In the evening, I would try and watch some of the Nepalese language TV news coverage, although I could not understand what was being said, the moving images helped tell the story. I would also watch the Nepalese TV English language news coverage. I tuned into the BBC news coverage, which throughout remained of a high standard.

Even on this first day, the TV news coverage indicated what we had seen near Narayan Gopal Chowk was not atypical, but it also revealed there had been some much harsher clashes in other parts of the city. Over the coming days, the trend was to continue, gradually escalating both in terms of numbers of participants and the numbers of violent incidents and casualties. By the end of the protest activity, at least twenty-five people were estimated to have been killed and many hundreds more were seriously injured.

Apart from a respite of a couple of days to coincide with Nepalese New Year, the protest activity continued unabated for almost three weeks. However, as the protests continued, they became more inclusive with all sections of the community participating, as people saw the chance of a popular revolution helping to bring about a restoration of democracy and a prospect of lasting political change in Nepal. On 24 April, the king relented and called for the restitution of the disbanded parliament.

In the ensuing weeks, events unfolded rapidly. The Maoists came in from the jungle and joined the emerging political process. The sight of truckloads of Maoist supporters waving the red Maoist flag with a white hammer and sickle became increasingly common. Mass rallies, openly organised by the Maoists, took place in Kathmandu. Undoubtedly there was a hard core of Maoist supporters, but there were probably a fair number of people curious to see what the Maoists had to offer. Increasingly, there were stories of Maoist coercion and intimidation of ordinary citizens in Kathmandu, including some of our own embassy staff.

However, the crucial factor was that talk, rather than guns had become the principal weapon of political change. And the Maoists were firmly part of this process. Apart from the Norwegians who had actively sought private contact with the Maoists beforehand, other embassies now openly began to get to know the Maoist leaders. The exception, at first, was the United States, for whom the Maoists were still listed as a terrorist organisation.

I remember some of the first meetings I attended at which Maoist leaders were present. I came away with mixed impressions. I was impressed at the modification of some of the hard-headed rhetoric reported from their public mass meetings and party documents, and a willingness in some areas to compromise. I was also struck by a lack of understanding of reality in some areas. For example, I recall one meeting at which Dr Baburam Bhattarai, the Maoist deputy leader, proposed moving the capital away from Kathmandu. This was something that would have been strongly resisted by the most populous city in the country, and challenged the long recognised view of Kathmandu as the established centre of government. It would have opened a potentially divisive Pandora's box regarding the fragile ethnic composition of Nepal. I also foresaw the seeds of more entrenched positions that would lead to difficulties, as the peace process moved forward. One such issue was the uncompromising stand the Maoist leadership took in relation to their troops.

The other key point of interest was to observe the dynamics within the senior echelons of the Maoist leadership. Their leader, Prachanda, did exude a confidence as the Maoist leader, although as subsequent events were to show, his continuation as leader was dependent on a skilful balancing of conflicting views and factions within the Maoist party. Baburam Bhattarai, perhaps reflecting his own background, displayed a better understanding of economics. While seeking to place the future Nepalese economy in a Marxist setting, he did show some appreciation of economic realities. Baburam's wife, Hisila Yami, was an interesting figure. She could be outwardly charming but leave you wondering what her real intentions were.

On 18 May 2006, the reinstated parliament adopted the first of a series of lasting changes to the political landscape of Nepal. They

A Diplomatic Life

resolved to strip the king of his main powers and declare Nepal a secular state. No longer would Nepal be a Hindu kingdom. However, it was not until June 2008 that the king departed Narayanhiti Palace. He had been given an ultimatum about leaving the palace and it was strongly implied, but not clearly specified, that measures would be taken against him if he failed to comply.

I recall sitting with Odette, who had joined me in Kathmandu in January 2008, and watching these events unfold on television. While it may have been the King's stubbornness that had helped create the atmosphere for the political change unfolding in Nepal, the way he handled his departure from the palace was dignified and, as far as we were concerned, impressive. I think many Nepalese also felt the same way.

In the months from May 2006 onwards, a peace agreement was signed, an interim constitution was adopted, and agreement was reached to hold elections for a constituent assembly with the aim of drafting a new constitution to replace the 1990 constitution. Not surprisingly, each step of the way forward was not easy, and there were many threats from one or more parties to withdraw from the process, until last-minute compromises were reached. I came to feel this was the norm for every step forward.

For me personally, it was an interesting and exciting time to be in Nepal. At first, there were times of great optimism, but invariably these were soon frustrated. It was also a time where talk, even if it was seemingly going nowhere, prevailed. And so the country generally observed a level of peace, unparalleled during the ten years of the Maoist insurgency. It was also a good time to try and pursue some of Australia's major commercial and other interests in Nepal.

Despite this changed political atmosphere in Nepal, I still had a lengthy battle in convincing Canberra that the travel advice for Nepal could be relaxed. I knew that after the experience with the Bali bombings, downgrading travel advisories were handled with greater care and caution. However, the six months following May 2006 were probably overall the calmest and most peaceful times I experienced during my three-year assignment in Nepal. This made it more and more difficult in explaining the continuing reluctance to amend the travel advice to Australian travel agents who, like me, saw the ever-improving calm throughout Nepal. After several months, we did succeed in achieving a down-grading of the travel advice.

One direct consequence of this was that it opened the way for me to travel more extensively in Nepal and, in particular, visit a greater number of our more distant direct aid program projects.

Working in the Shadow of the Himalayas

Settling In

As I have previously indicated, my first few months of living and working in Kathmandu were quite dramatic and exhilarating times as the momentous political changes unfolded. They were also times when I was settling into my job and becoming acclimatised to life in Kathmandu. I was also acclimatising physically, as in my first three months I came to think it was quite normal to have diarrhoea at least once a week. My stomach did in fact settle down after that.

Kathmandu and its surrounding areas offer some splendid scenery and many fascinating and historic sights, including the old Malla Kingdom cities of Patan and Bhaktapur, as well as central Kathmandu itself. In spring, the colours of the jacaranda trees in the city and the red rhododendrons in the forested areas added a welcome splash of colour. Much of the time, however, the sky was hazy, dusty or smoggy and visibility was limited. Even when there was blue sky, the Himalayas would often be playing coy and hiding behind a coat of clouds. However, when you did get the rare clear days, and could see the snow-capped Himalayas clearly in the distance, it was a magical sight and lifted your spirits.

One of my first priorities in the job was to pay introductory calls to senior political leaders and ministers with portfolios that impacted on Australian interests. I was soon to learn that getting to and from such appointments was not always easy. My assistant, Sanjana, to her credit, was a stickler for punctuality and liked to ensure sufficient allowance was made for potential traffic delays. Punctuality was something I, too, valued. It was almost impossible to claim traffic congestion as an excuse for being late in Canberra. However, Kathmandu was a different story.

The roads in Kathmandu were often narrow, pot-holed and congested. The congestion had a uniquely Nepalese flavour. Cows nonchalantly strolling the streets, goats being herded, likely to slaughter, men carrying furniture on their backs, over-loaded bicycles or push-carts, school children walking on the road to and from school (because there were no or inadequate footpaths), tuk-tuks and mini-buses stopping anywhere they pleased – these all contributed to slowing down traffic movement. Added to this, the occasional mass protest, often in support of demanding compensation for a road traffic accident victim, meant it could be difficult to predict how long it would take to get to and from appointments.

Between Sanjana and my driver, Rabi, they did a good job of calculating how much time would be needed. Only a couple of times during my stay in Kathmandu did I have to phone and apologise that I would not be able to make appointments within a reasonable time. A few times the traffic even proved lighter than expected. If I was going to meetings at UN Headquarters in Pulchowk, across the Bagmati River in Lalitpur or other locations close by and was very early, I would either drop into the Himalaya Hotel for a cup of tea, or Pilgrims Bookshop opposite to kill some time.

There were some common themes that emerged from my meetings with ministers and political leaders. I was asked to ensure the continuation of the Australian Community Forestry Project. When I had met them in Canberra, AusAID had alerted me to their plans to discontinue the project. The SMEC West Seti hydropower project was often raised. This had been listed as a priority in my ministerial directive. Generally, there was support for the proposed project, but not much sense of real hope as to how it might be realised.

Other issues raised included requests to reinstate a visa issuing office at the embassy in Kathmandu, and the commencement of Qantas flights to Kathmandu, as a way to increase tourist numbers. The Australian Department of Immigration had withdrawn its office in Kathmandu as there was insufficient workload to justify the cost of keeping it. Visa applications were sent to New Delhi and, if bona fide, were turned around in five to seven working days. Student visas were approved in Australia and the fact they were sent to New Delhi had little bearing on the outcome. Australian tourist numbers dropped off during the period of the Maoist insurgency, but did start increasing during my time in Kathmandu. At the end of the day, it was a commercial decision for Qantas, but the numbers would not have made a Qantas service commercially viable.

Australian Community Forestry Project

The Australian Community Forestry Project, or as it was called at this time, the Nepal Australia Community Resources Management and Livelihood Project (NACRMLP), was to prove to be one of the most difficult issues I had to address in my early months in Kathmandu.

Counting the involvement of the Australian National University before the Australian government became involved in supporting community forestry in Nepal, the project had been running for close on forty years. For a project to run such a length of time was almost unheard of and it was the longest-running aid project AusAID had been engaged in. I believe AusAID appreciated the high Nepalese regard for the project, and I know it was not a decision taken lightly. However, finally, at some stage a project does have to end, and the local people have to assume responsibility.

As I was to discover, it was not as simple as it sounds. First, as I have noted, I was to be reminded repeatedly during my introductory calls of how much it was hoped the forestry project could be continued. I was struck by the high level of emotion and strength of feeling in some of these presentations. I did my best to explain that after forty years, it was time for Australia to move on and for the Nepalese to manage things themselves.

One human side I became aware of from my initial meetings with the NACRMLP team, ably led in Nepal by Mike Hawkes, was that there was a dedicated and capable team managing the project in Nepal. If the project ended, most of them would be thrown out onto the job market looking for new employment. Mike encouraged me to pay early visits to Khavre and Sindhupalchowk Districts, which had been the focus of the project for over forty years. Arrangements were made for this to happen.

Visiting Khavre and Sindhupalchowk, it was hard to envisage that the sites of the forestry project activities had previously been barren and eroding hills. Almost everywhere you looked, there were now pine forests. Meeting with the local communities, I got a very real sense of their emotion, but I also got a more realistic picture of what the project had achieved.

The project had pioneered the concept of community forestry in Nepal and the establishment of community forest user groups, where the local community took responsibility for the management of the areas of forest within their area. It had proved to be a successful model, not just in terms of forestry management, but also in terms of social and community awareness and development. It was a model subsequently applied throughout Nepal, also adopted in a number of other countries, including Bangladesh.

I was made aware of an edition of the Lonely Planet Guide for Nepal which held up the Australian Forestry Project in Nepal as an example of how an aid project should be run, in terms of the benefits to the people. In my time in Nepal, I could not help but be struck by the almost universal recognition of Australia in Nepal for its contribution to the forestry sector. Australia and forestry in Nepal were basically synonymous. From my contacts with the Forestry Ministry, I came to appreciate the strength of the forestry relationship resulting from the fact that some two hundred Nepalese officials had studied at the Australian National University's School of Forestry.

One site we visited in Khavre, we met an old man who, remembering the past barren hillsides, was proud of his beautiful trees. Yet Mike, as a forester, sought to explain that you needed to cull the thinner and weaker trees so your remaining trees would grow even stronger. However, this old man became emotional at suggestions that some of the weaker trees should be cut down and removed. He began to cry, saying he did not wish to lose any of his beloved trees.

In one sense, this example highlighted some of the strengths and weaknesses of the project. One of the key, firmly entrenched outcomes of the project, was that it had addressed the problem of deforestation and eroding hills. This objective was clearly understood and appreciated by the local communities.

Aside from this, we would have met with a dozen or more different community forestry user groups. It was clear they were at different levels of development. A couple had developed sophisticated financial plans and put in place subsidiary industries to earn additional income. Generally, they had a fair understanding of sustainable management of the forestry resources and were exploring managed commercial utilisation. These groups inspired confidence for the future.

There was one community forestry user group that particularly impressed me. This community had introduced a training program for Dalit women in their community. (Dalits are the lowest caste in the Hindu caste system and often are referred to as untouchables.) I met with about twenty women who had been undergoing a year of training. They were a self-confident and articulate group. They told me that at the commencement of their training, they had been shy and reserved and there was considerable opposition from their families, especially their husbands, about their leaving home to attend the training. They said that now their husbands welcomed the training, as they had introduced improved health and hygiene practices into their homes, as well as improved animal husbandry and horticultural practices. Their husbands had seen the benefits, and they, too, were practising improved health and hygiene methods.

There were some eight hundred community forestry user groups in Khavre and Sindhupalchowk alone and, from memory, by June 2006, only seventeen had reached the advanced stage of financial planning and management, although perhaps another thirty or so were well on the way. This meant over seven hundred user groups still had a way to go.

For these seven hundred, termination of the project would mean their ability to carry on was dubious at best. The project had more than adequately met the objective of raising awareness on how important the forestry plantations were to protect and enhance the environment. However, the ability to manage the resource in a sustainable way, including for the use of timber, was still not sufficiently developed.

Personally, I was conscious of the high standing Australia was held in, for having played such a long-standing and pioneering role in the forestry sector in Nepal. It seemed the final phase of the project was heading in the right direction in terms of leaving a legacy that the community forestry user groups could build on, but I was concerned its coverage was not yet wide enough, and I doubted that the Forestry Ministry had the resources to carry things forward, even if it had the will.

I was also conscious of a number of other aid donors, notably the UK, Switzerland and Denmark, supporting forestry activities in other parts of Nepal, who would be happy to gain kudos at Australia's expense.

I fully understood why AusAID wished to terminate Australia's involvement in the forestry project. After forty years, it was time to move on and encourage local communities to take on the responsibility. AusAID were also seeking to change the way aid was being delivered in Nepal because limited human resources made it difficult to continue with project-based assistance. In fact, AusAID wished to put more emphasis on education and health, both equally important sectors in a developing country like Nepal.

I hoped we could find some way to provide a soft landing for terminating the forestry project, so it would not look as if Australia was turning its back and walking away from the community forestry user groups. Much to my relief, we did identify such a way and it was accepted by AusAID.

The soft landing involved providing support to the already established UN Development Program (UNDP) on Micro-Enterprise Development (MEDEP). This meant bringing in the Forestry Ministry as an additional ministerial partner in the program and focusing on community forestry user groups in Khavre and Sindhupalchowk as new elements to the existing MEDEP program.

We planned a dinner reception to mark the termination of the project, but rather than portraying the event as the end of forty years, we sought to portray it as a celebration of what had been achieved and a turning point in looking to the future.

We had arranged for one of the leading English newsreaders on Kathmandu television, Issa Moktan, to act as our master of ceremonies for the night. She proved an excellent choice. Not only did she provide a sense of dignity based on her experience as a newsreader, she showed herself to be a smart and dedicated operator as well. She had asked the embassy to provide her with some basic materials on the forestry project. When I met her, I was impressed that she had prepared a well-thought-out script for the evening which, for the most part, accurately reflected the project and our objectives.

However, it was the first time I had worked with an event organiser. She wanted to change Issa's presentation. Without consultation, she changed drink and canapé service arrangements, also changing the time for dinner service. This disrupted the flow of the evening program. I was not impressed.

On a more positive note, Issa lived up to expectations and did an excellent job as master of ceremonies. In addition, an exhibition of photos on the forestry project by noted local photographer and director of the Indigo Gallery in Kathmandu, James Giambrone, was nicely set up outside the ballroom and attracted many favourable comments. But perhaps best of all, and something I had not anticipated beforehand, was that the event brought together many people who had worked on the project at various times over its forty years, and therefore served as a happy reunion for them.

It proved to be an emotional evening for many of the guests, as they were reunited with former colleagues, reminiscing about the project and life in Khavre and Sindhupalchowk. I think the message about the project's achievements came through clearly and I hoped people were left thinking they were witnessing the start of a new chapter.

On a sadder note, forestry minister Rai, the main guest, and his wife, were killed a couple of months later in the Taplejung helicopter crash, in which the cream of Nepal's wildlife conservationists, as well as a number of international experts, were killed.

For me, the end of the forestry project was quite an emotional experience. My predecessors had basked in the glory of the profile that the project had given Australia in Nepal. While I understood why the project had to come to an end, given the strength of feeling I had encountered in Nepal, I felt a bit like the villain who had brought the party to a close.

Although, perhaps, I should not have felt this way, I also felt some sense of responsibility for the project team who were forced to look for new jobs. We tried to help a number of the staff find new jobs by drawing their credentials to the attention of UN agencies or other embassies. For similar reasons, I was determined to closely monitor progress of the activities under MEDEP.

I visited MEDEP project sites amongst community forestry user groups a couple of times in Khavre, although I was not able to visit any sites in Sindhupalchowk. I remember one eventful trip to Khavre. The first community we visited were developing a number of subsidiary industries, including making *sal* leaf plates and bowls (the *sal* tree is a tree indigenous to Nepal and common especially in lower lying areas) and separately producing honey and rhododendron juice. The rhododendron is Nepal's national flower, so it was interesting to see it being used in this way.

I think the initial intention was to popularise the juice, like fruit juices, but I found it had a medicinal flavour and perhaps needed some added sugar if it was to be popularised. After visiting several more communities where rhododendron juice was also being produced, I must have consumed about five glasses of the juice. One of the communities had produced a small card extolling the health benefits of rhododendron juice. It was good for just about everything, including respiratory diseases, stomach pains, period pains and earache – *and it would cure you from wanting to eat dirt*. I had not been aware of any cravings to eat dirt, but after five glasses of rhododendron juice, I was sure I was cured for life.

On our way back from this series of visits, there had been a landslide as a result of some very heavy rain while we'd been up on the hillside. One section of the road was completely covered in stones, and we could not pass. I often felt a bit embarrassed by the police escorts provided when I travelled outside of Kathmandu, however, on this occasion, they proved a blessing in a most unexpected way. About a dozen police set to work, even though it was still raining, to clear stones from the road so we could pass. They worked quickly and diligently, and within twenty minutes the road was sufficiently cleared for us to continue on our way.

Because this police effort was beyond the call of normal duty, I wrote a letter to the head of the Nepal police expressing my gratitude for their endeavours, praising them for acting beyond their normal duty requirements. I certainly hoped this message was passed to the policeman directly involved.

Generally, the MEDEP activity did seem to be making a useful contribution, and it was agreed to extend Australian support beyond the initial period of involvement.

West Seti Hydropower Project

The West Seti hydropower project also provided many challenges for me. I had a supporting role consistent with the ministerial directive of providing assistance to an Australian business to try and secure its business objectives in Nepal.

The Snowy Mountains Engineering Corporation (SMEC) had done a preliminary assessment in 1994 on the feasibility of building a dam on the West Seti River in far western Nepal and developing a hydropower project to produce electricity for sale to India. In 1997 SMEC was granted a management licence by the Nepalese government to bring the project to fruition. The project was worth in the order of US$1.5 billion and, if materialised, would have been the biggest engineering project undertaken in Nepal. It would demonstrate that Nepal could earn substantial revenue from the properly managed utilisation of its hydropower potential. After Brazil, Nepal was considered to have the second greatest hydropower potential in the world, yet this potential was hardly utilised.

By the time I arrived in Nepal in early 2006, SMEC had already undertaken much work in trying to bring the project into being, likely having invested millions of Australian dollars. Agreement had been reached on the sale of the electricity to an Indian power company. An environmental impact assessment had been undertaken. Much effort had been expended on seeking political support for the project across the whole spectrum of Nepalese politics and on seeking the support of the local communities, who would be displaced as a result of the dam construction, including detailed plans for their relocation. A Chinese company had been identified to undertake the construction work. By the time of my arrival, the main focus was on finding the required funding to support the project.

As an Australian, I was proud to be able to support SMEC in its endeavours in Nepal. Development of hydropower represented the most promising way to promote economic development in Nepal, both through the sale of power to India and then through the use of some of the hydropower to encourage environmentally friendly industrial development in Nepal itself. The SMEC concept would involve Nepal working closely and cooperatively with its two major neighbours, India and China. I was proud that SMEC, as an Australian company, was acting as the broker in helping to promote closer collaboration between the three countries.

SMEC arranged an agreement with the Asian Development Bank. This was probably a worthwhile step to try and confirm both Nepalese government support for the project and also to attract necessary additional foreign investment in the project. The downside, however, was that to satisfy the ADB's requirements, it meant having to redo much of the work that had already been done.

Principally, a new environmental impact assessment had to be undertaken. Satisfying this, and other ADB requirements, meant delays in proceeding with commencement of the project. The project also had to receive the formal endorsement of the ADB Board, and it seemed that ADB Board consideration kept being delayed, as newly identified requirements had to be satisfied.

Meanwhile political developments in Nepal required SMEC to reaffirm political support for the project. Given power shortages in Nepal, there was a lot of pressure to change the conditions of the agreement and provide more power directly to Nepal, rather than money. They also had to deal with increasingly active environmental groups, some of the most active of which were controlled by foreign interests. These groups were encouraging the local community to seek rewriting of the terms of treatment for those communities. And yet, despite all this, SMEC had to continue its efforts to encourage further foreign

A Diplomatic Life

investment interest in the project and seek the required risk insurance.

As an outsider looking on, it was frustrating to see new obstacle after new obstacle emerge. To me, the potential benefits of the project were clear. If the project could be materialised, it would demonstrate that a project on this scale was possible in Nepal and could possibly open the way for further foreign investment in the power sector. This, in turn, would lead to increased income generation for the Nepalese government through power sales and generation of more power to meet Nepal's own energy needs. Also, given the often-competitive nature of Nepal's dealings with China and India, it was a good opportunity to show that the three countries could work together cooperatively.

In seeking to support SMEC in bringing the project to fruition, there were basically three areas where I could assist. The first was in arranging buffet dinners at the residence, to which we invited as many of the key stakeholders as possible; relevant ministers, political party leaders, the ADB, Chinese and Indian ambassadors and senior embassy officials, as well as other banking and commercial representatives and officers from other organisations with some collateral interest in the project. I organised three to four such functions and these usually coincided with visits by the SMEC manager responsible, Bill Bultitude, the local SMEC representative, Himalaya Pande, who was often travelling overseas with Bill, and visiting ADB teams from Manila, or representatives from Chinese financial or construction interests.

The second role was assisting with visas at short notice for Himalaya Pande. Often meetings were arranged in China at short notice, or once to Bermuda, to discuss risk insurance. As a Nepalese, he required visas for both China and Bermuda (through the UK embassy). I approached my Chinese and British colleagues, both of whom were well aware of the West Seti project, to assist in facilitating early visa issue.

The third way I sought to assist was to raise the issue in the course of my meetings with Nepalese government ministers, senior politicians and senior officials of the ADB. I had many occasions to meet the finance and water resources ministers, either formally or socially. Generally, there was an understanding of the potential benefits of the project, and I recall the finance minister telling me the project had been endorsed by the cabinet of the day. I tried arguing that it would be good as a sign of confidence in the project if the government could publicly indicate its support, but apart from a commentary piece in one of the newspapers, written by someone close to the water resources ministry, this never happened. With the ADB, my main objective was to reassure them of SMEC's credentials in other engineering projects and seek clarification of when the issue would be considered by the ADB Board.

Several times during my time in Nepal, there were promising signs that, perhaps, some preparatory work might be able soon to commence, but at the end of the day another obstacle always seemed to emerge. While personally I was disappointed, I'm sure things must have been even more disappointing for Bill Bultitude, in particular. I was always impressed with Bill's patience, calmness and persistence, even in the face of the many uphill battles he had to fight. These included with the Nepalese government, the ADB and ultimately with his own SMEC Board.

From my perspective, I was puzzled, and to some extent disappointed, at the number of senior Nepalese politicians or business people who were negative about the project, perhaps in part because they did not understand its scope and ramifications. However, in part, I believe it was also because they were not in line to receive the kudos from the project if it succeeded. Perhaps the most blatant example was a senior Nepalese businessman who told me, after a few too many whiskeys, that he would do all in his power to see that the project never saw the light of day because he wasn't getting a cut.

It was disappointing for me to see that both SMEC and the ADB subsequently dropped out of the project – although I understand why. I heard that efforts were underway for it to go ahead as a Chinese funded project, aimed at producing electricity for Nepal.

It's a little disheartening after all the hard work and energy that Bill Bultitude, Himalaya Pande and many others put into trying to make the original project concept happen, and all the compromises, changes and extra work and obstacles they had to try and overcome. I hope that maybe someday in the future, the hard work they put into developing a model for hydropower development in Nepal might be taken up by a future Nepalese government. The potential of the hydropower sector, if properly and carefully managed has the potential to contribute substantially to Nepal's economic development in a way that no other sector can come close to matching.

Cricket Diplomacy

There was a SMEC connection in my first real taste of cricket diplomacy in Nepal. Himalaya Pande called on me to advise that SMEC had received a cricket bat autographed by the then Australian captain, Ricky Ponting. It turned out that a close family member of Ricky Ponting's wife was a long-time employee of SMEC and had assisted in arranging for the bat to be presented in Nepal. The presentation of the bat was intended to encourage further interest in playing cricket among young Nepalese. Ricky Ponting also stipulated one condition for the recipient of the bat – namely the bat had to be used and not just put on display as a trophy piece.

By coincidence, the Nepalese under-nineteen team had just won the plate competition at an international under-nineteen tournament in Sri Lanka. Himalaya's suggestion was that the ideal recipient of the bat would be the captain of the Nepalese under-nineteen team, Kanishka Chaugai. I was happy for the embassy to be the venue for the presentation, as I saw it as an opportunity to get some good publicity for Australia, for SMEC and for cricket.

Little did I realise that this would prove to be the best attended media conference organised by the embassy during my time in Nepal.

A Diplomatic Life

We had reasonable attendance at a media event subsequently organised at the embassy during the visit by Professor Ian Frazer, the developer of the cervical cancer vaccine and 2006 Australian of the Year, but this was probably only about a third of the number who showed up for the cricket bat presentation.

We had about thirty-five separate media representatives turn up, including all the main TV companies and all the main print media. What is more, they all turned up on time. I was to discover this was a rarity, as sometimes media representatives would turn up much later than the scheduled time and still expect to get the story. Admittedly, this was often due to traffic delays, but not always.

One practice I established at this media conference was that the journalists should be offered morning tea, including such Australian staples as lamingtons and ANZAC cookies. I felt it was important the journalists feel they were being treated hospitably, even if on some occasions they did not give high priority to the story we wished to promote. That, however, was not a problem with the presentation of the cricket bat. We had widespread TV and print media coverage. Some of my South Asian colleagues told me they were impressed, almost jealous, at how good the coverage was that we'd achieved.

Cricket provided an additional bond between me and some of my South Asian counterparts Shiv Mukherjee of India, Sohail Amin of Pakistan, Sumith Nakandala of Sri Lanka and Imtiaz Ahmed of Bangladesh. During my time in Kathmandu, neither British ambassador was particularly interested in cricket, but surprisingly the French ambassador, Michel Jolivet, showed some interest, although he was much more fanatical about rugby. Michel's interest in both sports had developed from his extended service in Fiji and New Zealand.

My next experience with cricket diplomacy related to support the embassy had provided to the Nepalese blind cricket team. Through the embassy's direct aid program, we had supported the blind cricket team to get uniforms and some cricketing equipment to enable them to participate in an international blind cricket tournament in Pakistan. The event was held to welcome the team back to Nepal and announce other programs of support for them. Unfortunately, I never got to see them play, but I heard them explain how they relied on their sense of hearing to play cricket. This media event was organised by the then president of the Cricket Association of Nepal, Binaya Pandey. Again, there was very good media coverage.

Odette and me at the entrance to the old city of Patan, Nepal-Patan.

When I returned to Australia for mid-term consultations, I called on the Australian Cricket Board to discuss if there was further scope for direct support of development of cricket in Nepal. The ACB had, already, prior to my arrival in Nepal, provided some coaching assistance to the Nepalese team. One outcome of my discussions, and separate discussions the Cricket Association of Nepal had with the ACB, was assistance with running a coaching clinic for umpires.

A Diplomatic Life

The embassy lent its support to two applications from organisations in Nepal for Australian government sports development grants to support the development of cricket among disadvantaged groups and through school-based programs. Both applications were successful, but I left Nepal before having a chance to observe how successful the implementation of these programs proved to be.

During my time in Nepal, the names of Ricky Ponting, Adam Gilchrist and Brett Lee were well-known in Nepal. The embassy supported an education and food fair in Kathmandu, where we had some blown-up photos of these three players. The photos attracted almost as much interest as the food and education booths. We had numerous requests from people wanting to have one of the photos.

Brett Lee was particularly popular following the release of the video of his singing a duet with one of India's most popular Bollywood singers, Asha Bhosle. There was serious talk that Brett would visit Nepal to promote a new energy drink and hopefully participate in some coaching classes. Unfortunately, his visit did not materialise, but had it occurred, I'm sure the Nepalese would have treated him like a major Bollywood movie star.

My final notable sortie into cricket diplomacy was when Binaya Pandey asked me to help officiate at the opening of the Nepalese girl's cricket competition. The opening ceremony included Binaya bowling me an over of his spin bowling. It was a long, long time since I'd wielded a cricket bat before such a large crowd. Befitting my prowess as a batsman, I only got bat onto two balls. One shot was a defensive prod; the other was a bit more elegant and trickled gently into the covers. However, neither Binaya nor I demonstrated much skill compared with the impressive form of some of the players who followed us onto the pitch.

Before heading to Nepal, I'd been told by a number of people that I should encourage the Nepalese to take up the game of cricket. I found when I got to Kathmandu that the game of cricket was already well-established and was, in fact, the fastest-growing participation and spectator sport in Nepal. Cricket diplomacy offered good returns for small investments and proved a useful tool in drawing public attention to Australia and its support for development of cricket in Nepal.

Education

I've previously mentioned the ministerial directive outlines and the main priorities a head of mission should pursue at each post, but sometimes major issues emerge that are not covered by the directive. In my case two such issues came to light. One related to Bhutanese refugees, and efforts to find a durable solution for the many who had been waiting over fifteen years in refugee camps in Nepal. This was a significant issue, and later in this book, you'll find my thoughts in a case study on the search for a durable solution.

The other issue was education, and the interest of Nepalese students wanting to study in Australia.

When I met with the immigration department before travelling to Kathmandu, I was told there were around one thousand Nepalese students studying in Australia. When I arrived in Kathmandu, there were as many as three hundred education agents offering support for Nepalese students wishing to study overseas, not just Australia, but also including the UK, USA, Canada, New Zealand, Japan, Germany and the Scandinavian countries. Efforts were underway to develop a code of conduct to better regulate the activities of these agents.

Two things happened that saw this change, suddenly and dramatically. The first was the changed political environment in Nepal, whereby it became easier to go overseas to study, although many students saw study abroad as an avenue to obtaining residence overseas, away from the political uncertainty in Nepal. The second factor related to the comparatively cheaper cost of education in Australia, compared particularly with the UK and USA, as well as changes in the student visa provisions in Australia, which allowed certain courses to offer permanent residence subject to other requirements being met.

Almost overnight there was a massive growth in the number of education agents in business in Nepal, and Australia quickly became the number-one preferred destination of choice. By the time I left Nepal in early 2009, there were almost eighteen thousand Nepalese students in Australia and over one thousand education agents seeking to cash in on the overseas education bonanza, not just for Australia, but other countries as well.

This rapid increase in growth also came with problems. The additional education agents were competing for business and there was a proliferation of inaccurate or misleading advertising, and an increase in unscrupulous behaviour. I was concerned that if students were misled or duped by education agents and found out, as a number of them were, that the agents could not guarantee visa issue, deliver on places at schools, provide meet-and-greet services and arrange suitable accommodation, the students and their parents would come away with a negative impression of Australia.

Admittedly, it was not all the fault of the education agents in Nepal. There were also avaricious operators in Australia, and some schools could not deliver on their promises. There were a number of instances of schools in Australia being closed down or collapsing, with the majority of affected students either Indian or Nepalese. A number of concerned families contacted the embassy seeking assistance, but there was little we could do other than refer them back to the education department in Australia, which had arrangements in place that were intended to protect or compensate students in the event of such closures.

I was forced to go into overdrive to try and find strategies to address these concerns. There were three umbrella organisations representing education agents. The majority of their members were the longer established agents, although even they were not immune from misleading or unlawful behaviour. One strategy I pursued was to work with them to try and strengthen their code of conduct arrangements and ensure adequate enforcement of breaches. I also spent a lot of time educating them with accurate and updated information on Australian immigration and education matters. In this, I was greatly assisted by the immigration and education representatives in New Delhi, who also sought to increase the frequency of their visits to Nepal.

Another strategy was to take opportunities offered by education fairs, pre-departure seminars, and the like, to talk to prospective students and seek to ensure they had accurate and up-to-date information. Generally, there were few problems with students enrolling in undergraduate or postgraduate university courses. In speaking to them, a major focus was on helping them to try and get the most out of their education experience.

The biggest problem was with the vocational courses, such as cookery and other hospitality courses, hairdressing and beautician courses, and to some extent IT and accountancy. It was in this area that there had been considerable misleading advertising. It was implied, for example, any cookery course would guarantee you permanent residence. Some other agents claimed they could *guarantee* you would get a visa. I recall one case of an agent advertising a discount on the visa processing fee.

As the number of prospective students went up, so did the trend for presentation of more fraudulent documentation. We heard of agents who told students that if they had a failing grade on any of their Nepalese education documents, this would make them ineligible for an Australian visa. Accordingly, the agent obliged by providing forged

A Diplomatic Life

education records. Other scams became prevalent, such as inventing false spouse documents, so another person could obtain an Australian visa as the supposed spouse of a bona fide student.

Our immigration authorities became concerned about the ease with which prospective students seemed to be able to obtain bank loans. A detailed examination of the accredited banks was made, and this led, at one stage, to all but two banks being de-listed as accredited banks.

I spent a lot of time using the education fairs, programs about overseas education on television and other media opportunities to try and provide more accurate and up-to-date information, as well as alert prospective students to some of the pitfalls and traps on the education marketplace. In this, I was very fortunate to have the support of one of the main TV education program producers. He provided me quite a number of opportunities to be interviewed and to try and spread key messages.

Some of the key messages I sought to get across to prospective students were talk to returned students about their experience in Australia and ask which education agents they used; use the older established agents with a proven good track record; if what an agent was offering sounded too good to be true, it probably was; avoid any agent who claimed they could guarantee issue of a visa as no agent had this power – it was purely the prerogative of the immigration officials; be wary of claims that permanent residence was guaranteed, as often it was not; be wary of agents offering financial or other incentives; and so on. I also advised that much basic information could be obtained by searching the official Australian education and immigration websites and that this was available free. Prospective students could also contact the Australian Education Office in New Delhi. I also pointed out that students did not have to go through an agent. They could apply directly themselves, although I also noted that good agents offered a more convenient way of doing things.

There were two other key messages. The first was to try and educate Nepalese people that free information and advice offered by Australian government officials was trustworthy. In part, there was a tendency in both Nepal and India to be uncertain about the reliability of information provided by the government. However, there was another issue which needed to be overcome. This was the tendency in both Nepal and India to believe that if you were paying for a service, you were getting a better deal. I sought to point out that the longer-established agents and the ones with the better track records, generally did not charge a service fee as they covered their costs through the commissions earned by placing students in certain courses.

The other message I sought to convey was how important it was that students returned to Nepal where there was a growing need for well-educated people to contribute to Nepal's economic development. I cited two examples. One was the comment by one of our leadership award scholarship applicants that she had a great incentive to return to Nepal. She said that if she sought to stay on and work in Australia, she would just be a small cog in a big wheel, but if she came back to Nepal, she would be the key driver and would gain a much greater depth of experience. This would, in the longer term, help her future career development.

The other example I referred to was that of Dr Sanduk Ruit. Dr Ruit had studied at the University of New South Wales under the renowned Australian ophthalmologist, Professor Fred Hollows. Dr Ruit came back to Nepal and not only applied what he had learned but adapted his knowledge to the conditions of Nepal, as well as developing innovative approaches to address the specific needs in a developing country like Nepal. Dr Ruit had received world-wide recognition of his achievements in Nepal and had become a major educator of ophthalmologists in many of Nepal's Asian neighbours. He was a good example of how he had not only used his Australian education experience, but expanded upon it to the benefit of Nepal and people in many other developing countries.

Given the problems with the proliferation of agents, a group of about sixteen agents that represented predominantly Australian interests and predominantly the higher university end of the market, formed their own umbrella organisation, NAAER (the Nepal Australia Association of Education Representatives) – this was one of the three umbrella organisations I referred to previously. NAAER did not include two of the largest agents involved with Australia and some of its own members needed to adopt more rigid standards. However, NAAER was prepared to work with us in improving the quality of their code of conduct and assist in a number of other ways – the key one of which was to offer a free information and referral service to address enquiries from prospective students. This service was offered on a neutral basis and was not linked to any particular NAAER member.

We sought Canberra's approval for NAAER to be allowed to use one of the vacant rooms adjacent to the front gate of the embassy compound to provide this service. Although the numbers availing themselves of this service were not great, it did offer another avenue for providing accurate and up-to-date information to prospective students.

The other key strategy I sought to pursue was to work with the Nepalese government in developing a stricter regime for the registration of agents. It was very easy to establish a new education agency. Basically, all that was needed was to register the business name with the Ministry of Industry and ensure it did not duplicate an existing business name and to obtain a tax number. There were no clear organisational or operating guidelines. As a couple of examples showed, it was also not easy to obtain a prosecution for an agency that had been found to be involved in illegal activities.

I had numerous meetings with the 'several' ministers of education who held the portfolio during my last eighteen months in Kathmandu. I also had several meetings with the ministers of industry. I had even more meetings with key senior officials. Generally, there was an appreciation that the current situation was unacceptable, especially given the increasing level of misleading information and illegal activity. There was some discussion about which Nepalese ministry should take the lead on the issue.

Odette with Jacaranda tree in Australian Embassy residence grounds in Nepal.

Ultimately, a couple of months before I was due to leave, the Ministry of Education advised that they would set up a joint committee involving officials from relevant ministries and include some representation from the executives of the umbrella organisations of agents and some embassy representation. A couple of other embassies did express interest in being involved. However, the first meeting of the committee was yet to take place at the time of my departure from Nepal. This would be something for my successor.

However, events in Australia, where there was growing concern about agents and educational institutions rorting the system precipitated a crack-down and changes to the courses that might lead to permanent residence. Almost immediately there was a rapid decrease in the number of Nepalese students seeking to go to Australia. For a time, the UK became the preferred destination of choice. While this development did lead to a reasonable number of the unscrupulous agents going out of business, it still fell short of addressing the basic concerns I had about agents indulging in misleading advertising and being able to establish new agencies too easily, without a proper regulatory framework.

I kept in close touch with one of the major agents handling Australia, and he told me that he hoped, and was reasonably confident, that these developments would lead to an enhanced focus on students seeking a quality education at an Australian university. In the short-term there was, he said, a drastic reduction in numbers going to Australia because of the decline in students entering vocational training courses. This experience had probably also tarnished Australia's reputation as a destination for overseas students, although a number of other factors also came into play in India, with reports of violence against a number of Indian students. In the longer term, my agent friend believed the opportunity now provided for increased emphasis on quality studies in Australia, would see a gradual increase in student numbers again. I hope he was right.

At the end of the day, the shake-up was, I believe, a good thing because the uncontrolled proliferation of agents in Nepal was fuelling increased document fraud and other abuses, and things were just growing too fast and unsatisfactorily. If the trend had continued as it was in 2009, Australia's longer-term reputation as an education destination would probably have suffered irreparable damage.

My efforts to address the problem were a bit like trying to put out a bushfire with a watering can. Nonetheless, I very much appreciated the support I received from the departments of Immigration and Education, either directly from Canberra or mainly through their representatives in New Delhi. They shared my concerns, and they provided a lot of useful factual data for me to use in my efforts in Nepal. This was not an issue foreseen when I left Canberra, but it was one that came to take up a great deal of my time, especially in my last two years in Kathmandu.

Subsequently, after watching a *Four Corners* program on ABC Australia network, I became concerned that some of the negative trends regarding overseas students were re-emerging.

Nepal – A Case Study on Finding a Durable Solution for Bhutanese Refugees

As I have written separately, I was keen to visit Bhutan while based in Nepal. Odette and I had a wonderful experience during our visit and came away with much admiration for Bhutan and its people. Bhutan's reputation is richly deserved, with its pristine and spectacular scenery, its determination to maintain its culture and its emphasis on gross national happiness. These set Bhutan apart as a unique and admirable country, and one seeking to resist the entry of undesirable foreign influences. As the story of the Bhutanese refugees demonstrates, however, no country can be perfect in everything.

Before leaving for Nepal to take up my position as Australian ambassador, I received briefings from both the Department of Foreign Affairs and Trade and the Immigration Department on the subject of Bhutanese refugees. The main thrust of these briefings was that there were about 100,000 'so-called' Bhutanese refugees living in Nepal and that they had been there for over fifteen years. Talks had taken place between Nepal and Bhutan regarding possible repatriation of these people to Bhutan, but at that stage no consideration was being given to possible resettlement in third countries. Nonetheless, this was a situation I was told I should monitor.

Some months after my arrival in Kathmandu, the issue did start to attract increased international attention. Largely I believe at the initiative of the Norwegians, a contact group of interested countries was established in Geneva. The interested countries comprised Australia, Canada, Denmark, Netherlands, New Zealand, Norway and the United States. Working in conjunction with the UN High Commission for Refugees, the contact group sought to identify and facilitate ways to find a lasting solution for this group of refugees. In part, this was because the problem had dragged on for so long without an imminent solution in sight and in part because there were clear signs of growing donor fatigue in having to continue providing funding support for these refugees.

A counterpart group of Kathmandu-based representatives of the contact group was set up in Kathmandu at the initiative of the Norwegian embassy. Chairmanship of the group was rotated every six months in Geneva, and it was agreed that the Kathmandu group would seek to replicate that. There was however one snag. The Netherlands, New Zealand and Canada did not have embassies in Kathmandu, although both the Canadian and Netherlands retained aid offices that looked after some other national interests.

Regrettably, the Netherlands aid officer became very ill, and in fact, subsequently died, and so, for much of the period, the Netherlands was not directly represented at the meetings of the Kathmandu-based representatives of the contact group. However, the Canadian aid officer was a regular participant.

Despite this, when Canada chaired the Group in Geneva, I was asked by the Canadians to continue chairing the Kathmandu-based group, having already chaired it on behalf of both Australia and New Zealand. I was also asked to continue chairing it a few months more following a change-over of US ambassadors, until the new US ambassador was properly settled in. In all, therefore, I chaired the Kathmandu-based group for the best part of thirty months. This proved to be a period of intense activity in seeking a lasting solution for the Bhutanese refugees.

I had to visit New Delhi at least once a year to meet with Australian government agencies that covered Nepal from India, to meet with the Indian Ministry of External Affairs, and to meet with education agents who had an interest in Nepal. One other important duty was to call on the New Zealand, Canadian and Dutch Heads of Mission, all of whom were accredited to Nepal. This provided an opportunity to brief them on developments regarding the Bhutanese refugees as well as to take on board any concerns or queries they may have.

I found the first meeting with the Dutch ambassador particularly memorable. However, this was not because of our discussion on Bhutanese refugees, but because we met at his residence; a building of some historic interest as the former home of the emerging Pakistani leader Jinnah. (I have written about this earlier.)

However, I digress. Therefore, at this stage it might be useful to provide some background on the Bhutanese refugee issue.

Large-scale settlement by ethnic Nepalese in southern Bhutan commenced in the early twentieth century, although there was some limited Nepalese migration to Bhutan before then. These Nepalese settlers in Bhutan were called Lhotshampas. The Nepalese settlers pioneered agricultural development in the southern regions of Bhutan, and some of them became influential in other aspects of the Bhutanese economy.

There were some concerns within Bhutan about the growing

number and influence of these Nepalese settlers and so in 1958, the Bhutanese government enacted a citizenship act. According to this, an amnesty was provided to those settlers who could prove their presence in Bhutan dated back more than ten years. New Nepalese settlers were to be banned.

However, because there was insufficient labour to build the planned Thimphu-Phuntsholing Highway, immigrant workers had to be recruited from neighbouring areas of India. As it turned out, many of these workers were ethnic Nepalese and this added to the Lhotshampa population in Bhutan.

The Bhutanese government, conscious of the increasing illegal migrant population, promulgated a number of directives to try and address the issue. This included a determination that if a person could not prove residency prior to 1958, they were deemed to be illegal. Another less than successful initiative was to offer cash payments to persons who intermarried with locals. As it later proved, this favoured Nepalese women who married Bhutanese men, but not the other way around.

Under a revised Bhutanese Citizenship Act of 1985, all residents were required to wear Bhutanese national dress and speak the Bhutanese Dzongkha language. Nepalese language would no longer be permitted as a subject in schools for the ethnic Nepalese communities. Coinciding with a national census in 1988, some ethnic Nepalese were deprived of their property, some were unable to obtain proper documentation and others, perhaps reflecting inadequate training of the census takers, were incorrectly categorised, including apparently some ethnic Bhutanese.

This led to growing protest activities by ethnic Nepalese people, including some who were genuine citizens of Bhutan. One prominent Lhotshampa, Tek Nath Rizal, who held a senior official position in Bhutan, became involved in these protest activities and fled to Nepal.

He was kidnapped and brought back to Bhutan, prosecuted on charges of treason and sentenced to prison. On release, he ended up back in Nepal where he became a strong advocate of repatriation of Bhutanese refugees to Bhutan. Many other protesters were also jailed.

Conditions for the Lhotshampa people were seen as becoming more and more difficult, with constraints placed on their ability to speak Nepalese, own property and practice their own religion. The overwhelming majority of the Lhotshampa people were Hindu. The Bhutanese are virtually all Buddhist.

The protest activities continued, and the tensions grew stronger, resulting in the exodus of about 100,000 Lhotshampa people by 1992. The Bhutanese claimed these people left voluntarily. The Lhotshampa claimed they were forced to leave. The exodus continued to dribble on through much of the 1990s. If anything, conditions seemed to become more and more difficult for many of the Lhotshampa people and there were claims that children were restricted in going to school only up to grade eight.

Initially, the Lhotshampa people transited India, and some melted into existing ethnic Nepalese communities there. There is no shared border between Nepal and Bhutan. The refugees claimed that the Indians accordingly assisted in transporting them to the Nepalese border, putting them on buses or trucks.

It was on this basis that subsequent efforts to encourage Bhutan and Nepal to reach agreement on a lasting solution were seen as perhaps being facilitated by seeking to engage Indian assistance. At best, the Indians offered some encouraging rhetoric but argued they could not do more, as Bhutan was an independent country. Most international observers considered this disingenuous as Indian influence on the Bhutanese government was seen as very strong.

Those refugees who made it to Nepal were settled in refugee

camps under UNHCR management in Jhapa and Morang districts in south-eastern Nepal. By 2007, many of these refugees had been in the camps for over fifteen years, some even longer.

By that time there had been sixteen rounds of high-level bilateral negotiations between Bhutan and Nepal on the refugee issue. For the most part, progress remained dead-locked.

For their part Bhutan argued that the majority of the refugees were not Bhutanese. It also indicated concerns about the politicisation of some of the refugees and that their goal was to cause political unrest in Bhutan. There was some justification to such concerns as there were Maoist sympathisers and some troublemakers amongst some of the refugees.

Scenes inside Beldangi settlement for Bhutanese refugees.

Nepal, without specifically using the term ethnic cleansing, argued that people had been forcibly evicted from Bhutan and Bhutan had to demonstrate its willingness to allow at least some repatriation before other possible solutions could be considered. Nepal was concerned that Bhutan not be allowed to get off 'scot-free' for having created the problem in the first place. as it feared this may encourage Bhutan to make life even more difficult for remaining Lhotshampa people in Bhutan, encouraging the exodus of even more refugees.

For Bhutan, as indicated above, there were concerns about the growing influence of the Lhotshampas; understandable in a nation that prided itself on its unique culture and determination to maintain that culture. For Nepal, there were concerns about being left to absorb a group of people who, in many cases, were no longer familiar with Nepal and able to contribute constructively to the country. As the saying goes, *it takes two to tango*, but Bhutan and Nepal were seeking to dance with different steps, and this complicated efforts to try and reach a suitable accommodation despite numerous rounds of talks.

Over the course of the sixteen rounds of negotiations, Bhutan and Nepal reached agreement on categorisation of the refugees into four groups and Bhutan had indicated willingness to consider repatriation of a small group who had clear claims to Bhutanese citizenship.

By 2000, some two hundred people suitable for repatriation had been identified in Khudanaburi Camp, but riots ensued when Bhutanese officials sought to visit Khudanaburi to process these people. Both sides blamed each other for causing the riots. As a result, by 2007, no further attempts at advancing repatriation had taken place.

The general assessment was that no repatriation to Bhutan would occur within the foreseeable future and the time had come to start looking at other options for a lasting settlement. In-country settlement in Nepal was not a feasible lasting solution as this was strongly resisted by the Nepalese government, both on political grounds because it was letting Bhutan off the hook, and because of some genuine concerns about such a large group being harmoniously absorbed into the local communities. This left third country resettlement as the only other possible option.

In late 2006, the then Nepalese Foreign Minister, Mr K P Oli, had indicated that he wished to make one last try in getting Bhutan to repatriate at least some refugees, but after that would be prepared to consider third country resettlement. Unfortunately, he became seriously ill and had to stand down from his job, so he could focus on getting medical treatment for himself.

This, however, proved to be one of the key turning points in terms of international engagement in efforts to find a lasting solution to the Bhutanese refugee issue.

I was only able to visit the camps once, as part of a UNHCR coordinated program to look at the condition of the camps and to witness refugee registration processes being conducted by the Home Ministry, with the support of UNHCR.

Our visit took in a couple of the Beldangi sites. I remember the day of our trip well. It was a beautiful, clear sunny day and we had fantastic views of the Himalayas, including Mount Everest, as we flew to Biratnagar. We then drove from Biratnagar to Damak, where the local UNHCR office was based, and from there drove to Beldangi I.

My impression of Beldangi was that the huts in which people lived were very close to each other and provided little scope for privacy. In other respects, the sanitation and health situation seemed generally good and people at the time of our visit seemed to be getting adequate food.

Our visit started with a general meeting with camp leaders from most of the camps. This meeting revealed some strident differences between the camp leaders and elders who continued to seek repatriation to Bhutan, and others who felt that fifteen to seventeen years living in a camp were more than enough, especially for children who had known no other existence, and that it was time to explore other options for a lasting solution.

One of the most ardent supporters of repatriation as the only solution was Tek Nath Rizal. There were a number of groups who supported his objectives and, whether or not directly with Tek Nath Rizal's support, sought to intimidate people in the camps who expressed a preference for third country resettlement. There were also, as mentioned before, pro-Maoist sympathisers, as well as other criminal and thug elements.

All of this meant that the security situation in the camps had become a major cause for concern. Physical intimidation and assault were common. Rape was also quite common. Along with occasional murders. Clearly these security concerns needed to be addressed if there was to be any movement on third country resettlement.

Another issue was that statistics on the camp population had become outdated and inaccurate. There was a need therefore to find out just how many genuine refugees there were in the camps as over the years there had been considerable fluidity with people leaving the camps and heading to Kathmandu or other places for work or study, children being born in the camps and other undocumented arrivals.

The registration process being conducted by the Home Ministry at the time of our visit was intended to obtain an updated and more accurate database on the refugee population and seek to identify extended family linkages. The work that we witnessed during our visit was being carried out in an efficient and orderly manner, but there were still challenges including accurately mapping extended family lists, taking photos of young children and the occasional security threat.

This was important work, not just for providing a good database for when third country resettlement processing might be able to commence, but also in clarifying the exact number of people who were in the camps, dependent on food, health and other UNHCR and NGO assistance. It was also hoped this would assist in persuading countries that were showing signs of donor fatigue to continue providing funding support.

Consideration of the Bhutanese refugee issue began to receive increasing attention both in Geneva with the contact group there and amongst the Kathmandu-based representatives of the contact group.

In my role as Chairman of the contact group in Kathmandu, I found that the most convenient time to ensure full representation at our Kathmandu meetings was to host working breakfasts. I am not normally a fan of working breakfasts, but they proved effective in getting much business done in a short timeframe. Ganga, my cook, ensured a tasty breakfast of fresh fruit, quiche or scrambled eggs, bacon, grilled tomato and some fresh vegetables or occasionally a piece of grilled Tasmanian salmon, and these were promptly served so that we could concentrate on the business at hand.

On one occasion the UN High Commissioner for Refugees, Mr Antonio Guterres, a former prime minister of Portugal, joined us for one of these working breakfasts. One important outcome of this meeting was that the high gommissioner underlined the importance of maintaining donor funding support for the refugee camps in Nepal even after resettlement commenced. We needed to show the Nepalese government we were not deserting them and were committed to ensuring a lasting solution that did not leave Nepal with unwanted responsibilities and costs. It was also important in gaining Nepalese support if, as expected, at the end of the day there was a residual caseload of persons wanting to stay in Nepal and obtaining Nepalese agreement for that.

In general, the working breakfasts provided an opportunity to exchange information on recent developments or progress, consider input for position papers being developed in Geneva and agree on actions that should be taken in Nepal. For example, we provided significant input to public statements being developed in Geneva seeking to encourage movement by both Bhutan and Nepal.

Statements for Bhutan sought to encourage Bhutanese willingness to take some of the refugees back and those for Nepal commended Nepal for its hospitality in providing a safe haven for so many refugees for so long, and encouraged Nepal to maintain its hospitality towards the refugees, while gently encouraging Nepal to look at alternative durable solutions.

As chairman, I was tasked to set up occasional joint meetings for our Kathmandu-based group with Nepalese ministers or senior officials, or to draft letters on behalf of the group to be sent to ministers or officials. I ended up writing many such letters. Separately, when I was meeting bilaterally with ministers or officials on other matters, I was delegated in my role as chairman to raise issues in regard to the Bhutanese refugees.

Another key turning point on the refugee issue was the statement by US Assistant Secretary of State for Refugee Affairs, Ellen Sauerbrey, in October 2006, that the United States would be willing to resettle sixty thousand Bhutanese refugees. The US Ambassador in Nepal, Jim Moriarty, then began working hard to try and sell this proposal to the Nepalese. His efforts were ultimately rewarded with a statement by Nepalese Prime Minister G P Koirala that Nepal would be prepared to allow resettlement.

Koirala's statement was certainly a big step forward, but for the Kathmandu-based representatives of the contact group and UNHCR it remained unclear on what basis third country resettlement would be allowed and when. I had been seeking a meeting with the prime minister for many months in relation to a number of important bilateral issues, but the Bhutanese refugee issue ended up opening the door for me to secure an appointment in my role as chairman of the contact group.

I was able to confirm with prime minister Koirala that the process of resettlement was not dependent on progress on repatriation, although the prime minister remained concerned about the need for Bhutan to honour its international obligations and take some of the refugees back. The problem was, at the time, there was no unequivocal public record of the prime minister's position and so relevant senior ministers, and senior officials, continued to insist there was a need for either some prior repatriation or at least some repatriation in concert with the commencement of resettlement.

Jim Moriarty, the UNHCR country director (my good friend and tennis partner), Abraham Abraham and I all went into overdrive to try and lock in support for the prime minister's position at other levels of the Nepalese government.

I remember a meeting that left me somewhat frustrated. With a continued push for some prior repatriation and not wanting to stand in the way of resettlement, the Nepalese government representative suggested, in all seriousness, that we could perhaps transport the refugees through Bhutan, en route to their resettlement in other countries. This and other comments left me wondering as to how well the problem was understood.

A meeting had been arranged on the basis that resettlement was now Nepalese government policy, and that the main purpose would be to discuss the modalities for implementing a resettlement process. We were therefore surprised, when the foreign minister, Mrs Pradhan, reverted to old arguments about the need to hold another round of consultations with Bhutan. US ambassador Moriarty was furious, claiming he'd been misled by the Foreign Minister and if she was not prepared to discuss modalities, he would end his involvement in the meeting.

I interjected in my role as chairman of the Kathmandu-based representatives of the contact group. I sought to play the good cop to Jim Moriarty's bad cop and argued that the Prime Minister had confirmed resettlement was to be allowed, that the time had been reached reluctantly to put the attempts to achieve a political solution to one side and focus on the clear humanitarian needs of the refugees. Our good cop/bad cop performance seemed to work, and the meeting ended with Mrs Pradhan indicating that we could proceed with putting in place the modalities for resettlement.

Another key turning point occurred when respected journalist and social activist, Kanak Mani Dixit, organised a gathering of refugee leaders, senior Nepalese officials (including Mrs Pradhan and Dr Dinesh Bhattarai, the Director-General for the International Organisations and Law Division of the Foreign Ministry and Mr Koirala, a mid-ranking official from the home ministry), myself as Chair of the Kathmandu-based contact group, Abraham and other officials from UNHCR, other embassy representatives, several academics and a couple of trustworthy journalists. He had also asked some of the pro-repatriation refugee leaders to join the meeting, but they declined. Perhaps as it turned out this was for the best.

Scenes inside Beldangi settlement for Bhutanese refugees.

The meeting provided a good outlet for the refugee leaders to express their views for the first time as a group to senior representatives of the Nepalese government. A number of the refugee community leaders proved very eloquent and persuasive speakers. They argued that seventeen years living in a refugee camp was not the way to live; they wanted to have a real life. They supported our contention that the time had been reached to put aside efforts for the time being on trying to achieve a political solution and focus on the humanitarian needs of the refugees. It was clear that Dr Bhattarai now fully understood their position and it also seemed to have had an influence on Mr Koirala of the home ministry.

Following this meeting, things started moving and we had foreign ministry support for putting in place the modalities for resettlement.

Things also started moving at the home ministry. A meeting with a group of senior home ministry officials. The meeting started a bit awkwardly as they had not completely confirmed their support. However, by the end of the meeting, they started talking a different language. They said third country resettlement was now official Nepalese government policy, and I could be rest assured that as the Hhome ministry was to be the principal implementing agency, they would do everything in their power to ensure the policy was a success and effectively implemented.

With the main hurdle of reaching agreement on commencement of third country resettlement overcome, the next step was implementation. The US had to go to tender to select an organisation to do much of the processing work for them. This process took the best part of six months. The successful tenderer was the International Organisation for Migration (IOM). This benefited countries like Australia and Canada also as we had used IOM in other refugee processing situations.

With agreement on third country resettlement, there was an increase in attempts at disruption by the pro-repatriation lobby groups. At first, it was not possible to readily spread the word and encourage people to sign up for resettlement. The majority of refugees who had indicated any interest in possible resettlement, would be harassed, intimidated and occasionally, physically assaulted. We sought to spread the word orally through sympathetic refugee community leaders.

However, it was also clear at the outset that physical security at the camps was inadequate. Abraham and his UNHCR team and the home ministry worked well together, and despite the intervention of the Dassain religious holiday, it was impressive the speed with which they were able to reinforce fences, improve lighting and increase the number of security personnel.

During this preparatory phase, I was occasionally required to call on the home ministry and the foreign ministry, but the next main phase for me was helping to prepare the ground for Australian processing of refugees for resettlement. I developed a very close working relationship with Paul Windsor, the head of the Australian immigration team in New Delhi, and Joanne Eyre, who headed the refugee processing operations and was in fact Paul's spouse. We had several long phone calls, exchanged many emails and had quite a few opportunities to talk things over at working dinners in Kathmandu.

Australia was slightly later getting started than the Americans and Canadians because of debates within government circles in Canberra about what quota of Bhutanese refugees Australia might take. However, Joanne worked with such efficiency that we quickly caught up and had people ready for movement to Australia not long after the first small groups of departures for the US and New Zealand.

I was also kept busy during this period by meeting with Bhutanese refugees based in Kathmandu or had travelled down from Jhapa and Morang to see me. As much as possible, I tried to encourage them to come and see me in groups. I did not want to turn people away as the refugees had many questions and few answers given the difficulty of disseminating information in the camps. It took up more of my time than I would have wished, but I felt it was important to help the refugees get accurate and up-to-date information. Later Joanne Eyre agreed to field some of their enquiries directly.

I also felt it important to show the refugees that potential resettlement countries were interested in offering them a real opportunity for a better life. This was because the anti-resettlement groups were spreading all sorts of falsehoods. One of the more implausible ones was that once they were airborne on their way for resettlement they would be dropped into the ocean. More plausible were concerns that they would be required to stay locked up in refugee camps once they reached a third country.

The refugees had many questions. *Would they be required to repay the cost of their travel? Would they be able to work?* Or, several times, because some people were keen to be able to stand on their own feet as quickly as possible, *Would they be able to work both day and night shifts?* There were many questions about education, both for their children, but also in terms of improving their own skills.

There were two particular refugees whom I had contact with that warrant further mention. One was a young man called Indra Rizal. Indra was preparing a thesis on Bhutanese refugees for his master's course at Tribhuvan University. He came to me seeking my assessments in view of my role as chairman of the Kathmandu-based contact group representatives.

What set Indra apart was that not only was he a diligent and intelligent student, but he was totally blind. I met Indra many times over the course of almost two years. I was impressed with the dexterity with which he used his Braille board to take down notes, along with his enthusiasm in wanting to use his studies to find ways to improve the lot of other refugees.

When Indra approached me for some funding assistance to enable him to type up and print his thesis, I willingly assisted. His gratitude was demonstrated by his achieving the highest marks ever by anyone, sighted or blind, for a thesis in Tribhuvan University's political science faculty. The media picked up on this story. Originally, I had wanted my financial support for him to be a private matter between him and me, and so was disappointed, at first, when I saw this referred to in the media.

However, by coincidence two Australian ladies were visiting Kathmandu at the time looking at ways they could, perhaps, become benefactors to the Tilganga Eye Centre. Because of my close links with Tilganga and Dr Ruit, I met these two ladies, Mei Wen and Merci Kusel. They asked me about Indra Rizal and offered to assist him obtain a place to further his studies in Perth, should he be accepted for resettlement in Australia, which he subsequently was.

The other refugee I want to mention is Ratan Gazmere. I met Ratan many times. He was a Bhutanese refugee community leader, and quite outspoken. When I first met him, he was a supporter of repatriation, but when resettlement emerged as an option he quickly got on the bandwagon and made it clear he wished to go to Australia. He had been a teacher in Bhutan and while working as a teacher had had the opportunity to visit Queensland for work-related purposes.

Ratan could be very persistent, and I know this persistence at times annoyed the UNHCR Office. I found him to be a very personable fellow with a good sense of humour. He was someone you could explain a point to and know that he understood the point, even if he did not always agree with it. I was confident he would accurately represent what I had told him to other refugee colleagues. He too was ultimately selected for resettlement in Australia. I know our immigration team hoped, that with his good English and prior experience in Australia, he might play a useful role in helping other refugees to adjust to life in Australia.

Many of the other refugees who came to see me were impressive individuals, as the majority of them had shown considerable drive and energy to get educated and learn skills. I am sure these refugees would be a credit to wherever they were resettled.

My involvement in the quest to find a durable solution for the Bhutanese refugees came full cycle when I was asked by IOM to meet and brief the first two groups of refugees headed for Australia. Odette came with me to the first session, and she had some useful insights based on her experience as a foreigner having to adjust to life in Australia.

Much of the briefing of the first group focused on the logistics of their travel and what would happen when they transited Singapore en route to Australia. I don't think any of this group had previously travelled by air. The refugees in this first group were going to Adelaide and Launceston.

Issues such as housing, education and employment were ones at the top of their minds. However, other issues that clearly vexed them were whether they would be able to practise their Hindu beliefs in Australia and, in this context, whether they would be able to take their portable shrines to Australia with them. Another concern was whether they could take their ceremonial *kukri* (a curved knife used to great affect by the Nepalese Gurkhas in past battles). IOM officers and I advised them that there were weight limits on how much baggage they could take on the plane, and that while we could not guarantee whether the shrines and *kukri* would be permitted entry by Australian Customs, it was important that they honestly declare such items to Customs if they decided to take them.

A Diplomatic Life

Something else a number of the Bhutanese women were concerned with was whether they could take their pressure cookers with them. Both the Bhutanese and Nepalese heavily relied on their pressure cookers for preparing everyday meals. Some of the women wanted to carry their pressure cooker on the plane with them. This reminded me of my experience just over twenty years earlier, when I witnessed refugees being prepared for departure at Ho Chi Minh City's airport prior to boarding the Air France flight that would take them to a new world under the Orderly Departure Program. Many women on that flight were carrying their metal kettles.

By the time of the second group, IOM had recruited someone to provide more formal orientation on travel to Australia and the questions, therefore, were less about logistics and more about life in Australia. Some of this group were going also to Adelaide, and others to Albury/Wodonga and to Darwin.

Having continued to live overseas till November 2020, I was not able to track how the Bhutanese refugees were adapting to life in Australia. I sincerely hope they are doing well.

I have since had the opportunity while living in Melbourne to meet some Bhutanese community leaders and learn how well settled and organised they are.

Off the Beaten Track in Nepal

Nepal is a beautiful country with much spectacular scenery. Its people are friendly and hospitable. My opportunities to travel, as widely or immerse myself as deeply in the culture as I would have liked, were limited in part by the proscriptions imposed by the Travel Advisory, and in part because there always had to be one Australia-based officer contactable, not so easy when there were only two of us.

The embassy's direct aid program afforded some opportunities to visit places less travelled. It also allowed a more hands-on and grass-roots approach to development assistance than was generally possible under formal aid activities. This is not to diminish the importance of these formal activities, as they were much larger and usually could have a bigger impact nationally.

The direct aid program during my time in Nepal generally allowed for grants of up to AU$10,000 for projects that would either be self-sustaining or lead to lasting developmental benefits. We tried to spread the areas covered by the projects to as many different regions of Nepal as possible. However, for the most part we also sought to

A Diplomatic Life

focus on projects we could visit and observe the practical contributions the supported projects were making to local communities. I sought to visit as many projects as was practicably possible. These visits provided many uplifting experiences and good memories.

One memorable such visit was to Sindhupalchowk District. Our starting point was near the town of Melamchi. Odette and her son, Miko, as well as Sanjana, my assistant, and Rabi our driver, made the trip with me.

We stayed in a very basic hotel, but supposedly, the best in the area. The beds in the room looked as though they had been hammered together by a weekend handyman who didn't know what he was doing. They were very rough and hard to sleep on. The room itself was swarming with mosquitoes, despite the use of mosquito coils. The bathroom and toilet were outside the main hotel building; perhaps manageable if it hadn't been pouring with rain. Instead, we had to manoeuvre huge puddles of water and try and keep dry under an umbrella. Both proved impossible and I was drenched by the time I returned to our room after using the toilet and cleaning my teeth.

Next morning, we were to make our way up the hill behind the hotel, to visit the community we were assisting under the embassy's direct aid program. We had to ascend an altitude of about 300-400m up to the village. Because of heavy rains the usual access path had been washed out and we had to climb up towards the village along the rocky bed of what would have been a fast-flowing stream at the height of the rainy season.

The first part of the ascent was very steep, at times it seemed it was like a 50° incline and involved a lot of hard work. When travelling out of Kathmandu, it was quite usual for ambassadors to be accompanied and watched over by local police units. This trip was no exception. I had a troupe of about a dozen willing and friendly police accompanying me. None of us were wearing the best shoes for climbing up and over rocky creek-beds.

The police were very solicitous of me and clearly wished to ensure I safely made the trek up, and later down. However, I think the police-issue shoes were more of a hindrance than my rubber-soled leather shoes. Several times as the police sought to guide me safely up, they slipped and once or twice, both a policeman and I fell. Fortunately, other than perhaps a few bruises, no damage was done.

Me with police escorts while trekking at Sindhupalchowk, Nepal.

When we reached the end of the rocky creek-bed, we stopped to catch our breath and have a cool drink. I was worried also that my assistant, Sanjana, was looking quite troubled and seemed to be having some problems breathing. After resting for a while, I am pleased to say that Sanjana was able to continue on the ascent to the village.

The village people, who were mostly Tamang people, welcomed us to the village, where they had laid out a lavish spread of food. A full-time chore for some of the village people, was

trying to fan away the flies. I don't think I had seen so many flies since when I was a student at school in Canberra, before the city was so built up and where a popular recreation period past-time was slapping someone on the back and counting the number of dead flies in your hand.

After lunch we had another walk of almost 2km to the school, which was the recipient of our DAP funding. Most of this walk was along the ridge of the hill and did not involve any real difficulty. It did offer, however, some great views across the valley below.

As we walked through the gates of the school, there was an honour guard of children lined up to greet us. As is customary at such events, there was a lengthy list of speeches and there were some cultural performances involving singing and dancing by some of the students. It was then time to go down to the classrooms to inaugurate the new school computers. As luck would have it, there was a power black-out, so we couldn't do the launch proper justice. However, this was really an anti-climax compared with the drama and physical struggle involved in climbing up to the school.

I was, however, starting to get a bit concerned about getting back downhill. I could see storm clouds building and time was getting on. I certainly didn't fancy having to climb down the rocky creek-bed in fading light or rain. I think because of the concerns about an impending storm, my police escorts were keen to try and get us back down as quickly as possible. One of them did actually take a tumble, but no harm was done, and another very nearly brought me down as well. Needless to say, we made it otherwise safely down, and it was then time to pose for some photos with the police on the rickety wire suspension bridge taking us across the river to where our car was parked.

This visit to Sindhupalchowk was probably the toughest walk I had to undertake in all my time in Nepal. I don't remember any section of our trek in the Annapurna region coming close in terms of difficulty. I remember the first time I went to Hatiban, just outside Kathmandu.

I found this a very arduous walk, but this was as much because I was suffering from a bad cold at the time, as from the difficulty of the actual walk.

I twice visited projects in Baglung in central western Nepal, both of which were equally memorable.

On the first visit, we stayed overnight in Baglung at the Peace Hotel. My assistant, Sanjana, thought this was a most inappropriate name as the hotel was anything but peaceful. All night there was never-ending noise. It was also incredibly cold, even with extra blankets, and I had trouble staying warm. It was not a good place if you wanted a good night's sleep.

Having learned our lesson, next time we visited Baglung, we stayed overnight in Pokhara and made an early morning start from there to reach Baglung at a reasonable hour, undertake our program and then return to Pokhara the same day.

The road to the DAP recipient villages in the hills behind Baglung represented a real challenge. The second trip was probably more difficult as we encountered some heavy rain, but the road during the first trip was not much better. For both trips, I was glad we were in the embassy Land Rover, and not in an Indian Mahendra four-wheel drive, as they did not seem to have as good road-holding capabilities. We saw several Mahendra vehicles slipping and sliding badly and sometimes going very close to the edge of the road.

Even for the Land Rover, it was challenging. The roads up the mountain to the project site were wet and muddy, and therefore slippery. Several times we skidded. The roads were also narrow which made life interesting when we encountered traffic coming in the opposite direction. Sometimes we would have to reverse to a wider spot to allow another car to pass. In places, landslides had gouged holes out of the side of the road, leaving an even narrower space to get through. Of

A Diplomatic Life

course, to make things more exciting much of the road skirted the mountainside, so there were steep drops on one side.

Both trips required all of our driver Rabi's skills to negotiate safely. It was an uncomfortable ride of about two and a half hours to cover roughly 20km.

The first trip I made to Baglung involved completion of gabion work; a netted cage made of strong metal and filled with heavy stones or rocks, which when lined up or stacked on each other, helped to create a barrier to protect against landslides. It also included a pipeline enabling fresh water to be piped from a reservoir higher up the hill to one of the villages. These visits allowed the local people to show their gratitude, and the ceremonies on both occasions in Baglung were memorable.

On the first occasion, I think the whole village turned up. There were musicians playing traditional woodwind instruments and horns, lots of garlands of marigolds placed around our necks and red *tikkas* smeared on our foreheads. Children from the village performed dances and songs. There were innumerable speeches. At the end of the formal presentation, we were asked to stay for dinner. Out of politeness, we agreed to stay for a very short time, and ate a little food, quickly, as we were concerned with the time, and didn't fancy driving back down the mountain in darkness.

Odette was with me on the second trip to Baglung, and she rates it as one of the scariest drives she experienced in Nepal. The welcome by the villagers, of course, made us forget about the scary drive until it was time to make the return trip. However, on this occasion, it started pouring with rain as the proceedings got underway and people rushed off looking for shelter. I was under a tarpaulin, but unfortunately, it had a dip in the middle that allowed the rain to collect and every so often would overflow with large torrents of water streaming down. I think I was wetter than some of the people who braved staying out in the rain. As a result, when it was my turn to speak, I did not wish people to have to endure staying out too much longer and kept my speech short.

Fortunately, I had a dry shirt in the car and dried myself as best I could, changing shirts as we drove along, though I had to stay in my wet trousers. Odette and Sanjana had managed to stay better protected from the rain and were not too wet at all.

It was on the return trip when I saw some movement just to the side of the road and a spotted tail sticking out behind bushes. I was convinced it was the tail of a leopard. That was the closest I came, the whole time I was in Nepal, to seeing a leopard in the wild.

In Udaipur, me with local politician Dr Narayan Khadka showing us both heavily endowed with red tika paste and laden with marigold wreaths.

I remember meeting Chandra Gurung, one of Nepal's leading environmentalists, who tragically died in the Taplejung helicopter crash in 2006, and him telling me that there were some encouraging signs of a possible increase in leopard numbers in Nepal, although the snow

A Diplomatic Life

leopard continued to be highly endangered. Leopards are known to frequent areas around the Kathmandu Valley.

On a visit to Kakani, I met someone at the international training centre who told me that a leopard (or leopards) had taken a number of their dogs. They knew this was the case from footprints and animal droppings. Even closer to home, maybe 3km from our residence, the residential compound of former Prime Minster, Surya Bahadur Thapa, was visited by a leopard during my time in Kathmandu. Efforts to restrain the leopard with tranquiliser darts failed and, when the leopard lashed out at the people trying to help it, it was unfortunately shot and killed.

One disappointment from my two trips to Baglung was that I never got to see Mount Dhaulagiri, the seventh highest mountain in the world, standing over 8,000m high. I had been told it was an impressive sight and that when the skies were clear, you could get some wonderful views of Dhaulagiri. My two trips were characterised by rain, mist and low cloud. Perhaps Dhaulagiri was just being shy, as many of the mountains of Nepal often seemed to be.

One of the first DAP projects I visited was in a village in a rural area of Lalitpur, one of the adjoining districts close to Kathmandu. In better times, the village had earned considerable income from fishing in the adjacent river. However, the fish had disappeared because of pollution further upstream. As a result, many of the village menfolk had either migrated overseas or to Kathmandu in search of work. The village was therefore largely run by the women, and they were doing a very good job.

The project in this village had involved support from a local NGO, the Green Society, to install simple toilets. The village essentially provided the labour to build the toilets, and the NGO provided the knowledge and the materials, drawing on DAP funds. From memory, twenty-four toilets were installed comprising the actual toilet and attached septic tank. In addition to the toilets, however, the NGO provided basic health and hygiene instruction. Some of the key results of this were that the women understood the importance of washing their hands after using the toilet and before preparing food. They also had got into the habit of dumping rubbish in one location so that it could then be collected and transported away. Previously, we were told the rubbish was thrown anywhere convenient.

The women of the village took great pride in their toilets and seemed to keep them spotlessly clean. One elderly lady kept her toilet under lock and key to prevent just anyone going in to use it. She proved quite a character. She said before getting her toilet and adopting the better hygiene and rubbish disposal practices, she would frequently visit a lady in a nearby village. 'Not anymore!' she said. She now found that village *disgusting!*

We supported a subsequent DAP application to provide toilets to the remaining households in the village. Additionally, however, these new toilets sought to convert human, animal and plant waste into biogas that could provide at least two hours' gas supply to the home each day.

This was a great innovation, as it provided a clean and cheap energy source and more importantly, did away with the need for a cooking fire in the centre of the downstairs room of the standard house. Such fires in the past had been the cause of many terrible accidents, involving children who had burned themselves while their mothers were busy cooking. Because of the lack of access to high-quality medical care, many of these children developed horrific burn scar problems that left limbs deformed.

From time to time, medical teams from Australia as well as other countries assisted in providing burn scar tissue surgery to help correct some of these deformities.

Accordingly, it was inspiring to see what DAP grants of about AU$10,000 per time could achieve by providing sanitary toilets and effectively using waste to produce biogas and improve health and hygiene. It really did provide an excuse to get excited about toilets.

Another way in which DAP money was used, was to assist rural villages to build basic roads. For many villages, the lack of roads limited their ability to get their farm produce to market. Without roads, the villagers were forced to walk long and difficult routes, with heavy baskets of produce on their backs.

The first such project I visited was in Gorkha District. The NGO sponsoring this project had arranged free survey and engineering services. The main cost was the hire of a grader, to come in and cut a basic road from the village to the nearest main road. There were some other costs, for example, materials needed to build basic bridges across streams.

Welcoming at the entrance to Hadiya Village, Udaipur.

For a cost of about AU$9,000, the village was able to get about 7km of a basic road. The grader produced a dirt road free of trees and large rocks. It was certainly a bit rough, but it served its function. It was passable by four-wheel drive vehicles or tractors pulling carts laden with produce. We used the road to get into the village.

With the road completed, the villagers could transport their produce to the intersection with the main road and off-load the produce onto trucks to take it to market. Conversely, the villagers could bring goods into the village by the same means. The difference created by the road was dramatic. Not only did this mean less physical labour, but it also meant being able to deliver more produce to markets and thus earn more income.

In a number of DAP projects, we supported people or organisations seeking to help persons with disabilities. Perhaps the most inspiring of these people was Govinda Dhakal.

Govinda contracted polio when he was young and became permanently disabled in his legs. However, he did not let his disability get the better of him and he sought to pursue a normal life. He obtained a good education and became a high school economics teacher. He got married and had three well-behaved and charming children. Most of all, conscious of the limited funding available to support disabled people in Nepal, and the fact that most such people tended to be hidden away out of sight, he was determined to assist other physically disabled people to achieve respect and some worthwhile role in society.

Several times we supported him through the Australian embassy's Direct Aid Program, to provide training in sewing to similarly disabled people. The aim was to teach them how to sew, so they could return to their home village with this knowledge and a sewing machine, and make clothes that could then be sold to earn some income. The training courses that took place during my time in Nepal proved largely successful. In most cases, the people indeed went back to their villages with a useful skill, but also with a much-enhanced level of self-confidence.

A Diplomatic Life

I visited Govinda and his family a number of times in Dhading, and he made a point of coming to see me most times he was in Kathmandu, to show me photos and update me on the progress of his training programs. Odette was with me during one of these visits and we were made to feel very welcome, enjoying a home-cooked meal with Govinda, his wife and children.

Another memorable visit was to celebrate Dashain (the most important spiritual holiday in the Hindu calendar, and in that sense akin to Christmas for Christians) with Govinda and his family. James, one of the embassy drivers came with me. Again, we shared an enjoyable meal, but Govinda, with great pride, took us down to meet his landlady and her family. James and I were both honoured in the traditional way at Dassain with *tikkas** on our foreheads and bits of special grass in our hair. *(The *tikka* is a Hindu custom in which red paste is applied to the forehead for auspicious occasions.)

After lunch, we joined Govinda and his family on a family outing, Govinda in his wheelchair and the rest of us walking along the banks of the nearby river. We finished off the visit by stopping at a cafe and treating everyone to ice-cream. I participated in a number of Dassain celebrations during my time in Nepal, but this visit with Govinda and his family was undoubtedly the most relaxed and enjoyable.

What I found most inspiring about Govinda was the fact that despite his own disability, he was one of the happiest, if not the happiest person I have ever met. He embarked on all his endeavours with great enthusiasm, whether it be training for other disabled people, his school teaching or his family. He was always smiling and always had such a positive outlook on life.

Govinda did not wish to be dependent on anyone for his own livelihood. He probably had the strongest shoulders of anyone I have met. He would steer his wheelchair, with great dexterity, wherever he wanted to go. His house was on the second floor of a building in Dhading. Govinda would climb up and down the stairs numerous times each day, just using the strength of his arms and shoulders. He could go up and down about as fast as I could go with my healthy legs.

I found Govinda such an inspirational person because he never let his disability get in the way of pursuing his dreams, and he was always so happy and contented with his life. I thought that Govinda could teach many of us healthy people, who often seem burdened with worries and trying to keep up with society's consumerist demands, a lesson about living life to the fullest and being happy. I wish more people could be exposed to Govinda and be infected by his enthusiasm for life.

More Adventurous Pursuits

Apart from DAP-related visits, a completely different sort of adventure in Nepal was going white-water rafting in support of efforts to raise awareness about the need to clean up the Bagmati River; the sacred river that runs through Kathmandu. Megh Ale, one of the promoters of the clean-up campaign, was also one of the leading proponents in Kathmandu of sustainable eco-tourism. He convinced me to join this adventure.

In its upper reaches near Kathmandu, above the Golkarna Golf Course, the Bagmati was still in pristine condition. However, unfortunately as it flowed further downstream through Kathmandu, it became increasingly polluted and filled with rubbish. Yet the Bagmati is a sacred river. It flows past the Pashupatinath temple complex, one of the holiest shrines of Hinduism, and certainly the only Hindu site outside of India accorded such status. Pashupatinath is where there are *ghats* (ritual stairs leading down to the Bagmati River) adjacent to which funeral pyres are built and Hindus are cremated. Being such a holy site, many Hindu devotees bathe in the river or, as we saw from time to time, brushed their teeth in its waters. However, 50m or so downstream from Pashupathinath, litter sullied the Bagmati's waters.

Dr Sanduk Ruit with Odette's Mother during the formal opening of Hetauda Hospital.

Our white-water rafting adventure, of course, took place in the pristine upper reaches of the river. I had originally hoped I could join the raft being navigated by a group of the Australian Youth Ambassadors for Development. Megh had other ideas. I was to join the VIP raft. Our crew included politicians from the Nepali Congress Party, including representatives from the faction that supported Prime Minister Koirala and from the faction that supported former Prime Minister Deuba, a representative of the Communist party – United Marxist Leninist, and a representative of the Maoist party.

Megh gave us some rudimentary instruction in the skills required to row and navigate our raft, but this proved of little value as the politicians engaged in heated political debate most of the way, and all the rowing and navigating was done by Megh and me. Occasionally they sought my opinion, but for the most part I just listened and rowed.

We were, of course, one of the slowest rafts coming down the river. However, despite the active political debate onboard, it was quite peaceful watching the river and the vegetation along its shores, listening to the abundant birdlife. And then there was the occasional rush as we forded down another rapid. I was quite enjoying the experience.

Perhaps it was at such a peaceful time, Megh told me about a proposal that had been put to him. He, of course, wished to see sustainable eco-tourism given more support in Nepal, as there was undoubtedly massive potential. However, money and official support were lacking. Megh told me he was seriously looking at a proposal that had been put to him by some interests in the UAE. *If they could create a man-made river suitable for white-water rafting, would he be willing to develop the eco-tourism opportunities this then provided?*

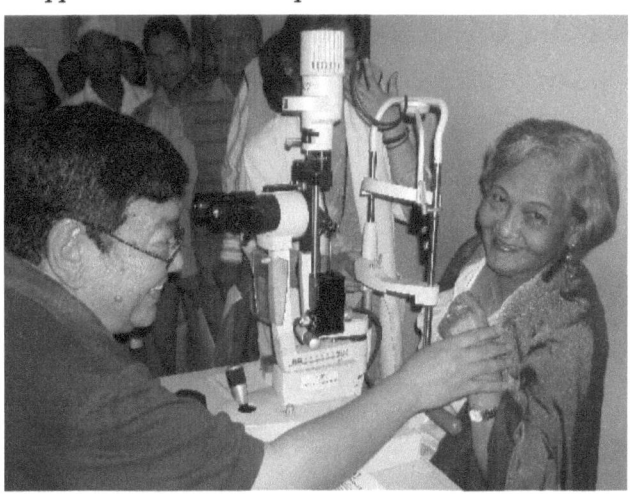

Dr Sanduk Ruit with Odette's Mother in Nepal.

Then we came around a bend in the river and our goal was visible, as were the TV cameras. I am sure politicians are the same the world over and if there is a chance to play to the TV cameras they will take advantage of it. Suddenly, the politicians in our crew picked up their oars and began rowing frantically. We really spurted to that finish line and I am sure the moment was well-captured by the TV cameras, although I never actually got to see it for myself.

I wondered afterwards if our white-water rafting experience might be an allegory for future Nepalese politics. I was certainly familiar with the constant posturing and endless political debates and differences. No-one really seemed to focus on the end goal which was achieving a better and more prosperous Nepal. However, I hoped that, perhaps, when there was a common and realistic appreciation of that goal, that, just as on our raft, the politicians might come together and work as a team for the common good of the country. I was probably being too idealistic, but Nepal and the Nepalese people deserve such a future.

My experience with the white-water rafting adventure did not finish there. I had agreed to come back the next week and officiate at the prize-giving ceremony. I turned up at about 11am and preparations were still being made for the ceremony.

Formal opening of new eye hospital in Hetauda with student performers.

A Diplomatic Life

When the ceremony got underway, there were about fourteen persons, representing different political interests, who wanted to get up and have their say. All being politicians in actuality, or at heart, meant that none of them could keep their remarks short and to the point; every speech ran for at least ten to fifteen minutes, and if was difficult for me to keep up with, as it was all in Nepali. Another concern for me was that I had another appointment at 3pm and had to allow sufficient time to get there.

Fortunately, the organisers agreed to bring forward the presentation of prizes so I could get to my next appointment and, thankfully, this spared me having to listen to the remaining speeches.

Another hair-raising car journey was when we travelled by road from Kathmandu to Hetauda and took a less direct road because of concerns about congestion on the main road which passes through Naubise and Daman. Odette and her mother were with me on this trip. Large sections of the road were under construction or repair and so much of the road was bumpy. Parts of the road were also steeply winding and, in a few places, quite narrow.

I think for Odette's mother in particular it was quite an unnerving experience. As a result, to distract herself from the scary drive, she talked non-stop. When we reached Hetauda about five hours after leaving Kathmandu, our driver Rabi commented that he did not think anyone could talk uninterrupted for that long.

That same trip we also travelled to Rautahat District to inspect some of our DAP projects providing support for adding additional school rooms in what was a very poor and under-serviced area of Nepal. As a former schoolteacher, Odette's mother relished the opportunity to mingle with the students and visit their classrooms.

We also travelled to Udayapur where we met with a good friend, Narayan Khadka, who was a member of parliament representing that district. Narayan wanted us to visit his electorate and hopefully see how much in need one of the district high schools was, so we could lend some support under our DAP program. We did in fact subsequently agree that its needs were worth supporting. Apart from the obvious developmental needs another compelling factor was the large number of minority ethnic Rai people in the district and the number of Rai children that would therefore benefit from support for the school.

Front view of the eye hospital in Hetauda during the opening ceremonies.

Everywhere I travelled in Nepal, I was greeted with great warmth and hospitality. The visits to Rautahat and Udayapur were no exception. However, what was most memorable about the trips to these districts was the abundance of *tikka* paste that was applied to our foreheads. At one stage in Udayapur my whole forehead and much of my hair was covered in red. I have a photo of Narayan and me laughing together with our almost totally red faces. It was one of those special and enjoyable Nepal experiences. The one downside was that it took almost three months for the red colour to completely disappear from my hair.

For our return travel to Kathmandu, we did take the sealed road

A Diplomatic Life

through Daman and Naubise.

This was certainly much smoother. However, we were delayed for almost two hours en route on a mountain-side section of road, where two trucks going in opposite directions had both tried to go around a bend at the same time. The bend proved not quite wide enough, and the two trucks scraped together. Both drivers refused to back up and let the other pass.

I understood from Rabi that the main issue was determining who was in the wrong and how much money that person had to pay the other driver. The negotiations went on and on while traffic continued to bank up on both sides behind the trucks. Eventually a settlement, or truce, was reached and one of the trucks did back away to a wider section of road. Neither truck was badly damaged, but the altercation certainly had wider repercussions with the number of other drivers who were seriously delayed.

We stopped late afternoon in Daman. Daman is probably the place closest to Kathmandu where you can get the most extensive view of the Himalayas – on a clear day. The skies were thankfully clear when we got there, and we had some fantastic views. On a really clear day you supposedly can see from Dhaulagiri in the west to Everest in the east. We were not quite so fortunate. We had great views of the Annapurnas and Langtang, but we could not quite see Everest. Nonetheless, we counted ourselves lucky that we got a good view, and as we drove away from Daman, we continued to get glimpses of the sun setting over the Himalayas. This, itself, was a spectacular sight.

When Odette joined me in Kathmandu in January 2008, we had two principal priorities. One was to visit Chitwan National Park and hopefully see a tiger. The other was to undertake at least one mountain trek.

Regrettably we only managed to do one proper mountain trek in the Annapurna region as time did not permit doing another trek in the

Everest region. The timing of our trek coincided with the major religious Dassain festival in Nepal. While it was a good time to get away from Kathmandu, as the city was very quiet over this holiday period, it did limit the number of trekking options available to us.

I obtained a number of quotes and in the end opted for the package offered by Steve Webster at Escape2Nepal in conjunction with Ker and Downey. His price was only $25 more than the cheapest other quote I obtained. The difference was that Steve's package availed of the Ker and Downey cottages which provided proper beds, hot water and decent bathrooms as well as a warm open fire to sit around in the cool of the evening. The cheaper quote offered hole in the ground toilets and sleeping on the ground in tents. Maybe the purists might say we missed out on the full trekking experience, but I am glad we stayed in good accommodation. Odette had developed a cold, so it was good for her to be able to sleep in a proper bed. I also appreciated having hot water showers every day and proper flush toilets. We also enjoyed the assistance of several willing and able Sherpas who carried water and other supplies for us while we carried light backpacks.

One other good thing about the trek we undertook was that although we were forced much of the time to follow the main tourist tracks, wherever we could, we diverged from these tracks and got away from the main tourist beat, walking through farmlands and on less frequently followed hill paths. What was good about this was that we seldom saw other foreign trekkers on these routes and our main people-to-people contacts were with the local communities.

When we did venture onto the main tourist tracks, we were able to observe the different mental approaches to trekking of the different nationalities. We passed quite a few German trekkers. Their objective for the most part seemed to be to walk as fast as they could, and they sought to overtake you as soon as they could. For me, this approach may test your physical capabilities, but you may miss out on enjoying some of the main attractions of trekking in the Himalayas.

We enjoyed looking at the mountains towering above us. We enjoyed looking at all the different plant life; a wide variety of different trees, shrubs and colourful flowers. We enjoyed trying to spot the different birds and butterflies, although the most exotic wildlife we encountered was a monitor lizard about 40cm long. Most of all, we enjoyed the meetings with the local people, dropping into local schools and speaking with the children, or watching the adults go about their daily farming chores. We made small donations to several schools to purchase notebooks, pencils and the like.

We met an Israeli couple. The man had severely sprained his ankle and was struggling but determined to complete the trek. I wondered if, perhaps, he had sprained his ankle because, like the Germans, he initially had tried to go too fast.

Near Sanctuary Lodge, where we stayed one night and which offered spectacular views of the sacred Macchupuchre or Fishtail Mountain and relaxing views of the nearby Modi River, we ran into a group of about a dozen trekkers from Singapore. They seemed to be marching rather than trekking, almost with military precision. They were fully kitted out in expensive looking trekking gear. I wondered afterwards what they would take away from their trek.

However, we did meet quite a few people from the UK, France, Belgium, Australia and Japan who, like us, seemed to want to enjoy the atmospherics of the Himalayas and its natural wonders. Until you have done such a trek, it's hard to imagine the beauty and wonderment of the Annapurnas. When there was clear blue sky, you could marvel at the Annapurna Range towering over you and look across deep and expansive valleys, as well as absorb something of the culture and traditions of the villages you passed through. Much of the daytime, the mountains were shy and hid behind a veil of clouds. I guess this made us appreciate them even more when we were able to get clear uninterrupted views. Early morning was usually the best time. The Himalayas certainly do weave a magical spell over you; you always want more.

There were three particularly magical mountain views. The first we got to appreciate was that of the sacred mountain, Macchupuchre, which from certain angles you could understand why it had been named Fishtail Mountain, as you could see the splitting near its summit into a fish-tail like shape. It is the mountain you see from the city of Pokhara, which is the starting point for most Annapurna treks. Macchupuchre seemed to follow us, off and on, for much of our trek.

It was wonderful to see Macchupuchre at different times of day with the rising sun or the setting sun reflecting off its snow-covered peak. It does have an allure about it, given its very distinctive shape, and it is small wonder it became the source of legends. It's also no surprise that it is regarded as a sacred mountain by the local people. Accordingly, it's off limits to climbers and has not been summited since organised mountaineering began in Nepal.

Another special view was having breakfast, each of our two mornings at Himalaya Lodge, at Ghandruk. We sat out on the lawns in front of the lodge quarters to eat breakfast with sensational views of Annapurna South, Annapurna 1, Gangapurna, Hiunchuli and Macchupuchre towering over us. Apart from the appetite which trekking gives you, breakfast these two mornings assumed an added flavor, with the crisp mountain air and stunning scenery. One morning, we shared the breakfast experience with a group of French people and I know they found it as magical as we did.

From the Himalaya Lodge we made a trek one morning higher up the mountain. When we got to a small temple at the top of a hill, we

A Diplomatic Life

were treated to fantastic views of Hiunchuli. It may not be as high as many of its neighbouring mountains, but from our temple vantage point on this particular morning, it stood out like a sentinel, standing clearly outlined against the bright blue sky, made more dramatic when viewed between the orange marigold flowers and branches of the trees that surrounded the temple.

That same afternoon we trekked down from Himalaya Lodge to the town of Ghandruk. Ghandruk is a town that played a central role in the recruitment of many Gurkha soldiers and still maintains strong links with the Gurkhas. From a distance overlooking the whole town, it is a picturesque sight with white-washed mud brick buildings climbing up one side of the hill overlooking the centre of town. There was a small museum in the centre of the town. It presented aspects of the life of the mainly Gurung people who lived in the area and provided some insights into the role of the Gurkhas.

One other notable memory was as we trekked to Ghandruk. The afternoon had been punctuated by brief rain showers. It made the route a little slippery in places. However, when the clouds lifted and the rain ceased, we were treated to a spectacular double rainbow arching over the valley to our right.

Overall, our trekking experience was most enjoyable. It was arduous at times, but for the most part I think the regular yoga classes Odette and I had been attending in Kathmandu ensured we were not left panting when trying to go up some of the steeper inclines. Much of the walk was quite gentle. In fact, the hardest part of the experience was one long and steep descent. Even though we were on a well-worn and maintained track, the hardest part of trekking is to stop yourself going too fast downhill. Our trekking walking sticks came in most useful in slowing down our pace and helping to protect our knees from potential damage if descending too fast.

Graeme Lade

Full view of Palace. Home of Bhutanese Royal Grandmother Dechenchholing Palace, Thimphu, Bhutan.

From Left_ Granddaughter Kesang, Consul General Maria Lourdes Salcedo, Bhutanese Royal Grandmother, Mr Graeme Lade and Daughter Pem-Pem.

A Diplomatic Life

Receiving a gift from Bhutanese Royal Grandmother.

Chitwan National Park
– Observing Wildlife

We were able to visit Chitwan National Park in early April. It was already hot, but not as hot as it would normally get from late April onwards. We flew with Buddha Air from Kathmandu to Bharatpur and were met by our guide from Temple Tiger Jungle Lodge. The sky was a clear and bright blue and we had fantastic views of the Himalayas as we flew to Bharatpur. I hoped this was a good omen and that the tigers would be on hand to welcome us.

Meeting us at the airport were Odette's friends, Rexona and Shristhi, whom she had met at a training program for election poll-watchers in Kathmandu run by the US funded National Democratic Institute. Rexona and Shristhi presented us with bouquets of flowers and accompanied us on the 50km or so drive from Bharatpur Airport to our Narayani River crossing to get to the Temple Tiger Jungle Lodge. We had a simple lunch together and then said goodbyes as Rexona and Shristhi headed back to Bharatpur with the driver.

Temple Tiger Jungle Lodge is located inside the Chitwan National Park and 'theoretically' offered some of the best opportunities to see wildlife. The lodge derived its name from the exploits of famous British writer and hunter, Jim Corbett, who sought to track down and kill man-eating tigers, but preserve other tigers in the wild. We did not get to see it, but apparently there was a small temple that had provided the location for one of these man-eating tiger hunting expeditions. I had read some of Jim Corbett's books when I was about eleven.

During our time at the lodge, we ended up undertaking four elephant safari rides into the jungle. Each trip was generally in a different direction. We saw patches of elephant grass where the elusive Royal Bengal Tiger was supposed to lie in wait for its prey. During our four trips, we saw wild boar, monkeys, deer and the endangered one-horned rhinoceros. In addition, there was an abundance of interesting bird life. Our guide proved to be an incredible mimic of the different bird noises.

During our first elephant safari ride, we had a slightly unnerving experience when our elephant became a bit restless and anxious. My initial reaction was that it must have sensed a tiger nearby. We were told this was not the case, rather, our elephant was concerned for her baby elephant as she sensed a rogue bull elephant not far away. Shortly after, mother and baby were reunited and our elephant calmed down.

After our first elephant safari ride, we were ecstatic that we had already seen about half a dozen rhino, including a mother and child. Returning to the lodge, we had a cool drink on the wooden deck overlooking the pond, which was a favourite locale for rhino to come and have a wallow. We saw another two rhinos. In the distance, we also saw the wild bull elephant crossing the built up track that straddled the pond, heading back into the jungle. We had yet, however, to see any tigers.

This was, however, the prelude to a much more alarming experience. After dinner in the lodge dining room and attending a lecture on the wildlife in Chitwan National Park, we retired for the night to our cabin. We heard a lot of noise and went out onto the front landing of our cabin. There were staff from the lodge brandishing burning tree branches. At first, we had not appreciated what was going on, but one of the staff told us to stay inside our cabin, as the wild bull elephant had come into the campsite. We noticed, barely 10m away, the wild bull elephant was looking in our direction.

Although we heeded the staff request to go back inside and continued to watch proceedings through the window, we were concerned as the elephant was so close, he could well choose to charge at our cabin. Despite how nicely built the cabin was, we didn't think it stood much of a chance against an enraged, charging bull elephant. After some anxious minutes, we saw the staff had managed to use the burning branches to scare the elephant away from our cabin. Being so close to a wild rogue bull elephant was quite scary.

The next morning, we were told a bit more about the rogue bull elephant. While they had succeeded in driving him away the previous night, they had to remain vigilant in case he should return. I don't know if it was fact or an urban myth that had developed, but it was said this elephant had trampled a woman to death in a village not far away. At the elephant corral where we were headed later that morning, there were a number of female elephants who would have been the object of the rogue elephant's intentions. Apparently, he wanted some 'heavy action'.

At the corral we were given a lecture on the physiology and habits of elephants. It was an obvious comment, but one of the handlers noted that each elephant had two fore-feet and two hind-feet. Towards the end of the lecture and to test how alert we had been, one of the handlers asked, *if there were 'twenty-four (fore) feet', how many elephants were there?* Most people said six, but there were all sorts of other ingenious answers; all wrong of course. I remembered the handler's initial comments and said there were ten as each elephant had two fore-feet. The handler congratulated me, but my hopes of getting a special prize, like a free pass to see an actual tiger, did not eventuate.

From the corral we walked down to the pond to watch the elephants bathing. In the hot weather, this was obviously a great time for the elephants, and they splashed water everywhere. Some of us were invited to help, but as I was not appropriately dressed in old and scruffy clothes, I declined.

One evening we accompanied our guide on a jungle walk. In the past, such groups had encountered a tiger. We were told what to do if we did; *stay calm and don't move abruptly*. Easier said than done, but fortunately in one sense, we did not have to put this advice into practice. In another, our count of endangered rhinos was going up every time we left the lodge. This jungle walk was no exception. We saw a couple of rhino in the distance by a river-bed. We were still yet to sight a tiger.

By the end of the day, our rhino count had gone up to just over thirty. Admittedly, some of these may have been duplications. However, as we were taking new routes most of the time, I think the number of duplicates was probably small.

What we learned on this walk was more about the bird life and the practical uses of the sal tree and leaves. The sal trees were abundant. The other thing we found was a recently used bear's lair. Unfortunately, Mr Bear was not at home, although, according to our guide, given the signs that the lair had recently been used, the bear was probably not far away.

The next morning, we went on our final early morning elephant safari ride. We took a completely different route and found a large number of rhinos drinking, washing or just gossiping with their friends by a waterhole. That morning alone we saw at least thirteen rhinos.

Seeing many rhinos was nice, and it was reassuring to see there were decent numbers in the park, which hopefully were free from the ravages of poachers. However, Odette told me she would *give anything* to see a tiger rather than another rhino.

Our experience reminded me of a story told by Jim Edwards, who was one of those larger-than-life Englishmen you meet from time to time. Jim had established another resort within Chitwan National Park. This was Tiger Tops. He told one unforgettable story about Tiger Tops.

In its early days, a fourteen-year-old boy had kept pleading with Jim to give him a job at Tiger Tops. The boy was so persistent that Jim eventually relented. He told the boy to report to Tiger Tops and that his job would be to don a tiger suit. Jim told the boy that American tourists, in particular, expected to see a tiger. His job, therefore, was that when he saw American tourists, he should flash a bit of tiger tail or a tiger leg so that looking through the long grass the tourists were convinced they were seeing a tiger.

The boy only lasted a couple of weeks in the job. One day he was out in the jungle and happened to look behind to see a rhino chasing after him. The boy was petrified and, according to Jim, began taking off his tiger head, racing towards the hotel administration office. As he did so, he heard a voice calling out from the 'rhino' behind asking how much they were paying him for pretending to be a tiger.

After breakfast, on our last day at Temple Tiger, we joined some other hotel guests in Jeeps and drove through the jungle to the Narayani and Rapti Rivers. On the way, we passed a group of monkeys up to morning hijinx at the top of a tree. One of the monkeys peed and succeeded in spraying one of the women in one of the other Jeeps. The woman was not impressed, but for the monkeys it was probably part of a usual game.

A Diplomatic Life

At the river, we boarded a long dug-out canoe for our relaxing trip down the river. The principal objective was to see mugger crocodiles and gharials. All crocodiles look pretty mean to me, the muggers particularly so. The gharials were more numerous and not as threatening looking, with their long thin jaws. The guide reassured us that the gharials preferred their main diet of fish and seldom ate other forms of meat. They were not known to go for humans. Nonetheless their long jaw and sharp teeth did look intimidating.

The other nice thing about the river trip was being able to see villages along the way and to watch people going about their daily chores. Perhaps heeding the advice about the gharials, this included women doing their washing along the riverbank. Still, it must be a bit risky. Like other crocodiles, the mugger seemed very adept at disguising itself as a log floating in the water, or a tree trunk lying on the shore.

It was now time to say goodbye to Temple Tiger Jungle Lodge and first take the boat across the Narayani River and then the drive back to Bharatpur. On the way back, we made a short detour in Bharatpur and visited the home of Rexona and her family. We met both her parents and her two sisters. After a light snack, a cup of tea and taking of photos, it was back to the airport for our flight back to Kathmandu.

It had been an enjoyable excursion to Temple Tiger Jungle Lodge. We saw plenty of rhino and other more common wildlife. We enjoyed the incredible variety of the bird life. Unfortunately, our prayer to see a tiger had not been answered. Maybe given the abundance of wildlife we observed, the tigers were well-fed and did not need to lie in stealth to catch prey. I know tigers are shy, but Odette and I are sociable people and all we wanted to do was say hello and take a couple of photos. Perhaps this is telling us that we need to go back another time to Chitwan National Park, just to be able to extend our greetings to the tigers. If we do go back, I certainly hope the effort is worth it and we can see some tigers. Even just one would do.

I felt a bit envious of my French colleague. Within a couple of weeks of taking up his assignment in Kathmandu, he accompanied some people on a visit to Chitwan. Not only did he see a tiger, he saw two of them. It just didn't seem fair.

As a post-script to our visit to Chitwan, during our stay in Nepal, progress was being made in reducing poaching activities and the rhino and leopard populations were on the increase, although the snow leopard remained endangered. In a recent visit to Nepal in October 2019, I saw a report following a recent census of tiger populations in both Chitwan and Bardiya National Parks that there had been a small increase in tiger numbers. In Bardiya, there were now just over eighty tigers and in Chitwan just over ninety.

Apart from these travel experiences, there were some other experiences from my time in Nepal that are worth mentioning.

Despite the tumultuous political developments in the first half of 2006 and the moves to side-line the king, King Gyanendra was still in the palace when the major Dassain religious holiday took place in October 2006. He was therefore still able to maintain some of the rituals that had been associated with the palace at the time of Dassain.

In one sense Dassain is a bit like Christmas for us. It is a religious festival, bringing together families to celebrate. However, unlike Christmas, it is a very bloody festival. *Tens of thousands* of animals and birds are ritually slaughtered at Hindu altars in the name of religion. Just as in the the United States at Thanksgiving, when it is not a good time to be a turkey, in Nepal during Dassain, it is definitely not a good time to be a goat.

I had sent my Nepalese domestic staff home so they could enjoy the Dassain festivities with their families. I asked Ganga, my cook, to ensure my fridge was well-stocked, but otherwise I'd been expecting a

A Diplomatic Life

few quiet days at home. Many of my diplomatic colleagues saw Dassain as a good time to take a short overseas holiday, as practically everything in Kathmandu closed down for a few days.

One morning, I had taken advantage of the quiet to go into the garden and play with Orsa, the German shepherd dog, that had been bequeathed to me by my predecessor, who in turn, had been bequeathed it by his predecessor. Orsa was an unusual dog, in liking to chase after small rocks. After playing chase the rocks with Orsa for a while, she had shown her pleasure and excitement by jumping up at my chest and smudging my T-shirt with dirty, muddy, long paw marks. This was what I was wearing when I went back into the house.

Barely had I got inside when the doorbell rang. There was one of the Embassy security guards saying that two gentlemen from the Palace had come to the embassy and wanted to see me. I wanted to change my shirt, so asked the security guard if he could ask them to wait, however, before I could finish my request, the two palace officials had already come to the door. I was embarrassed being dressed as I was, but this didn't seem to faze them; they just carried out their courtly duties.

Between them they were carrying a tray covered with a white linen cloth. They explained that

it was a gift from the king to mark Dassain, but they needed to take back the tray and the cloth. I lifted the cloth and my reaction was, 'Oh my God!' On the tray were two pheasants, fully feathered but with their throats slit. They were quite colourful birds and I'm sure I would have been more impressed to see them alive. I accepted the birds with some trepidation, although realising the two Palace officials were only doing their duty. I do recall asking them to convey my sincere gratitude to the King.

However, now what to do? I had never de-feathered a bird for cooking and I certainly had never tried cooking pheasant. I'm also pretty sure I have never eaten pheasant. What's more, my fridge was fully stocked and there was nowhere I could put the pheasants for a few days before Ganga returned to work.

After the palace officials had gone, I turned to the security guard and explained the situation. I told him I didn't wish the pheasants to go to waste and asked if he would like them. He was overjoyed and reacted as if all his Christmases – pardon, Dassains – had come at once. I'm sure being able to take home a gift from the king would have made him very popular at home, regardless of the politics of the day.

It was a memorable experience, but one that, thank goodness to the subsequent political changes in Nepal, I did not have to experience again.

Another memorable experience in Kathmandu was my participation in the opening ceremony for the annual food festival organised by the *Himalayan Times* newspaper group. A number of ambassadors from countries represented in the festival's international food stalls had been invited to participate in the formal opening of the festival. We were each presented with a white dove to hold. On a given signal, we were to release our doves.

I was standing next to the Indian ambassador; someone I liked and greatly respected. However, on this day, I could see he was anxious for the ceremony to be completed quickly and that he wished to release his dove. I saw he was holding his dove quite tightly and the bird seemed to be fretting every bit as much as he was. I did not wish for my dove to feel anxious, so I gently stroked its back feathers and talked quietly to it. My dove did seem quite relaxed.

When the signal came to release our doves, the dove of the Indian ambassador was off like a rocket. However, I had clearly overdone things and my dove was so relaxed, it didn't want to leave. Eventually, I had to thrust my hands sharply upwards several times before my dove got the message that it was time to fly. I wondered afterwards whether my dove, perhaps, as a result was as much traumatised as the dove of the Indian ambassador.

Some Memorable People

With Dr Ruit and team at Tilganga.

There must be something about the Himalayan Mountain air, as I met quite a number of inspirational people in my three years in Nepal and during a visit to Bhutan. The one who I got to know best, was Dr Sanduk Ruit.

Dr Ruit's life has been written about extensively in two readable and insightful biographies. One is *Second Suns* by David Oliver Relin. The other is *The Barefoot Surgeon* by Ali Gripper. I offer below my personal impressions.

Dr Ruit grew up in a poor mountain village in Eastern Nepal and

A Diplomatic Life

initially studied medicine in India. He showed promise as a surgeon and studied ophthalmology. Following an earlier meeting in Nepal and development of a blossoming friendship, Dr Ruit was invited in 1988 by the legendary Australian ophthalmologist, Professor Fred Hollows, to study for a year under his tutelage at the University of New South Wales in Sydney.

Not only did Dr Ruit study with Fred Hollows, but he and his wife Nanda also lived with Fred and Gabi Hollows in their family home. Theirs became a deep and lasting friendship which extended beyond Fred Hollow's untimely death from cancer in 1993. The memories of the lessons and experiences of their time together remain with Dr Ruit to this day. I think another legacy of their friendship manifested itself when I first got to know Dr Ruit after arriving in Kathmandu in early 2006. Dr Ruit returned to Nepal a connoisseur of fine Scotch whiskey. Perhaps age and wisdom have caught up with Dr Ruit, as he no longer drinks whiskey or other alcohol.

Soon after my arrival in Kathmandu, Dr Ruit invited me and other embassy staff to a welcome gathering with himself and other staff at Tilganga Eye Centre (now the Tilganga Institute of Ophthalmology). This is the hospital established in Kathmandu in 1994, initially with the support of then Australian Ambassador to Nepal, Les Douglas, and with funding assistance from AusAID. Right from the start, I was made to feel that Dr Ruit and the Tilganga team were like extended family. This feeling was reinforced when I later came to know Dr Ruit's wife, Nanda, and their three children, Sagar, Serabla and Satenla.

I've been back to Nepal several times following completion of my tour of duty, and every time Dr Ruit and his team at Tilganga have continued to welcome me and Odette as members of their extended family. The family included not just Dr Ruit's close associates at the hospital – Dr Reeta Gurung, his quiet and always smiling, but very capable deputy, Rex Shore who sadly passed away in late 2017, Nabin Rai and Kedar Acharya – but also the members of the Tilganga Board.

When Odette first visited Nepal, she was made to feel welcome at a dinner organised by Dr Ruit and hosted by Suhrid Ghimire. Suhrid was an interesting man in his own right. Not only was he a senior Tilganga Board member, but he was an active and successful businessman. He was also an avid golfer and quite successful at it, winning many prizes. Suhrid and his wife had a young daughter, Aditi, who quickly took to Odette, and they became good friends.

At Australia Day receptions, we would invite members of the Tilganga Board and Nepalese guests would often comment how impressed they were that Hari Bansha Acharya and Madan Krishna Shrestha attended. Together they formed Nepal's most successful comedy duo, but their work was not restricted just to satire of Nepalese politics and society. They also played an invaluable role in raising awareness about health issues in Nepalese society. It was in this role that they were valued members of the Tilganga Board. And it was again, through the Tilganga connection, that I became very friendly with them.

Under Dr Ruit as director, Tilganga has grown from modest beginnings into a world-class facility. Dr Ruit still maintains close links with Australia and the Fred Hollows Foundation and Fred's widow, Gabi. AusAID continues to provide some support to Tilganga, but given its growing and glowing reputation, Tilganga now attracts funding support from many other international governments and organisations. Tilganga and both Dr Ruit and Dr Reeta Gurung have taken on an important regional leadership role in training ophthalmologists from neighbouring countries, including China, Pakistan, North Korea, Cambodia and Bhutan.

The Fred Hollows Foundation continues to support the Intraocular Lens Factory at Tilganga. When I first arrived in Nepal, this was the only International Standards Organisation-accredited medical facility in Nepal. It is an impressive operation which I visited a number of times. It produces high-quality but inexpensive intraocular lenses under the strictest hygiene and quality controls. It now exports most of its product, with China, Pakistan and Turkey amongst its biggest customers.

Part of Dr Ruit's success undoubtedly rests in his love of his work, but what he has done that inspires me most was that he has built on what he learnt under Fred Hollows. He has adapted and improved the surgical techniques so that they can be delivered in developing countries by trained ophthalmologists without needing the more sophisticated and expensive equipment available in developed countries.

Dr Ruit and Dr Reeta have refined their techniques, so that when they travel to cataract surgery camps in remote areas of Nepal, they can deliver one to two hundred surgeries a day. Dr Ruit has also developed some specific tools that assist in delivering surgery in developing countries. This has brought eyesight back to many people in isolated and mountainous rural communities, who might not otherwise have had the chance to visit a hospital in the city.

I have watched CCTV a number of times, to see Dr Ruit perform cataract surgery. The standard operation, if there are no complications, only takes five to seven minutes. I understand in developed countries it is usually twenty to thirty minutes. The next patient is backed up on a second bed and is rolled in for surgery as soon as the previous one is finished. Dr Ruit makes it look easy and straightforward, but I know that it requires considerable care and skill.

Dr Ruit has justly been acknowledged for the pioneering role he has played in making cataract surgery more widely and safely available in Nepal and other developing countries. He has received the Magsaysay Award from the Philippines (2006), which is often described as the

Asian Nobel Prize. He also received the Prince Mahidol award from Thailand, and he has been named *Readers' Digest* Asian Man of the Year. However, given his close connections with Australia, I was concerned that he had not received any Australian recognition for his work.

Accordingly, I was very pleased, that together with the support of Brian Doolan, the chief executive officer of the Fred Hollows Foundation, Rex Shore, representing both Tilganga and the Fred Hollows Foundation, Les Douglas, former Australian ambassador to Nepal, and Professor Hugh Taylor, then professor of ophthalmology at Melbourne University, we were successful in recommending Dr Ruit to become an Honorary Member of the Order of Australia in 2007.

It was a proud moment for me that, having been authorised to hold an awards ceremony in Kathmandu, I was able to personally hand over the Order Medallion and certificate to Dr Ruit. Apart from Les Douglas, all the others who had supported his nomination for the Order of Australia were able to attend. Dr Geoff Tabin, a long-time colleague of Dr Ruit's, from the Himalayan Cataract Project based in the United States, was also able to join us. Geoff's association with Dr Ruit and his involvement in Nepal flowed from his successful ascent of Mount Everest and his wish to give something back to Nepal. In 1994, he and Dr Ruit established the Himalayan Cataract Project. (Geoff is the other ophthalmologist celebrated in David Relin's book.)

I have also to thank Dr Ruit for one of my most memorable experiences in Nepal. Dr Ruit asked me in my role as ambassador to officiate at the opening of the Hetauda Community Eye Hospital, which was set up as part of Tilganga's outreach activities. Much of the funding for the new hospital had been donated by an Australian Hong Kong Chinese lady, Mrs Leung, who had raised much of the money in both Hong Kong and Australia through her All for Charity organisation.

The opening was not to be your usual cutting of a ribbon type affair, but something more appropriate for a hospital devoted to providing cataract surgery for disadvantaged communities. Dr Ruit asked me to remove the bandages from an elderly lady who'd had both eyes operated on.

The first bandage came off relatively easily. However, the second one was another matter. I could see the skin of her cheek stretching and stretching more when I tried to pull off the bandage. I was genuinely concerned I was hurting the lady even though I was keen to be as gentle as I could. Eventually the bandage came off.

If I had caused the lady pain in removing the bandages, it was clearly quickly forgotten. After fifteen to twenty seconds, she realised she could not only see, but she could see members of her family in the audience. She was so excited. I became caught up in her excitement and was pleased to see how happy she was.

A major focus of my work in Kathmandu became the need to address the sudden upsurge of interest amongst Nepalese young people in going to study in Australia. I was keen to encourage Nepalese students to come back and contribute to the development of their own country. There was no better role model I could draw on, than Dr Ruit.

I referred to his example many times. I noted that he had come back to Nepal, and not only had he put his training in Australia to good use, but had built on and further fine-tuned what he had learned to adapt it to local circumstances. I said that Dr Ruit had become a legend in Nepal, as well as many other countries, and someone that all Nepalese could be proud of.

I hoped that other Nepalese would be inspired by his example. I hope I had some impact in inspiring at least some students to be motivated by Dr Ruit's example.

We had personal experience of Dr Ruit's surgical skills. We knew that Odette's mother had cataracts, but she had been so spooked by negative stories that she had heard in the Philippines about the dangers of cataract surgery, or how the surgery was carried out. One such story was that your eyeballs had to be removed! When she came to Nepal, we introduced her to Dr Ruit, and he calmly and reassuringly persuaded her that she needed surgery.

Odette's mother duly underwent surgery, first on one eye, and then a few weeks later on the other. When she recovered from the surgery, she was excited that she could see the colours of the birds, the butterflies and the flowers, all of which were abundant in our garden in Kathmandu. However, one morning we heard her mother screaming. She had made one other discovery … horror of horrors … she could also now see her wrinkles.

Dr Ruit refused to accept payment for her surgery. I could not let this pass and so made a donation to Tilganga that would cover the cost of surgery for a handful of other needy patients.

As a final comment, I consider Dr Ruit to be a great and remarkable man. He has done so much to help so many people recover their eyesight and return to a productive and healthy life. Yet what impresses me most about him, perhaps like other truly great men, is that he is a modest and humble man. Conscious of his own background in a poor rural community, he is committed to giving back to such communities, some of the good fortune and benefits of the experience he has achieved.

Dr Ruit is also a very caring person, and I saw, many times, his gentle manner in dealing with patients. He is also a devoted father. But most of all, he is someone whose company I enjoy, as he has a good sense of humour and some wonderful insights into life in Nepal. Both Odette and I feel honoured to be part of his extended family.

Odette's mother said she had two favourite people in Nepal – Dr Ruit and Ganga, my cook, who looked after her so well during her

A Diplomatic Life

visit.

Another inspiring person I came to know reasonably well in Kathmandu was Mrs Anuradha Koirala. Mrs Koirala is a social activist who founded Maiti Nepal in order to assist women and girls who have been trafficked across the border to India.

Mrs Koirala's efforts involved trying to rescue or intercept women and girls who were being trafficked, provide medical care and attention to them, often young girls also, when they returned with sexually transmitted diseases, especially HIV AIDS. She provides an orphanage and schooling for children who had lost their mothers, often to AIDS, and seeks to identify and prosecute people involved in human trafficking. Perhaps most difficult, she helps women who have been victims of trafficking to re-enter normal society, even though there remains social stigmatism attached to such women.

In 2010, Mrs Koirala was named as a CNN Hero of the Year, but her work has been recognised through a number of other awards. One of her principal benefactors was a German family who had lost their only daughter to illness. This largely assisted Mrs Koirala in being able to build living quarters for the women and girls, separate quarters for the orphans, a school for the children and a hospice for women and girls who are seen as having incurable AIDS or other diseases.

I visited Mrs Koirala at both the main Maiti Nepal headquarters and at the hospice. Both places were well and caringly run. What impressed me was that Mrs Koirala seemed to know every woman and child by name – and was obviously greatly respected by all of them. She had a very direct personal involvement with all the Maiti Nepal activities and lived at the headquarters, where she was constantly on call.

The visit to the hospice was a very moving experience for me. The people there knew their days were numbered, yet the positive spirit they seemed to have was most uplifting. Their conditions were comfortable, but basic. Those who were fit enough sought to keep themselves occupied with handicrafts, growing vegetables or other activities. It was a tribute to Mrs Koirala that the women at the hospice were able to calmly and peacefully wait for their inevitable death.

I also had the pleasure to officiate at a fund-raising benefit concert, organised to support the charitable work of Mrs Koirala's son in assisting Kathmandu street-children. Obviously, this was an endeavour that Mrs Koirala strongly encouraged and supported.

The concert was the launch of a new incarnation for a well-known and accomplished Nepalese musician, Bijaya Vaidya, with his 'Rock Sitar'. Originally, the French ambassador was going to officiate, but as he turned up late, I was asked to step in at the last minute and had the honour of presenting a cheque for the money raised by the concert. Bijaya and his family became close friends of both Odette and me, and so it was a double pleasure for me to be able to support Bijaya with his musical endeavours, as well as to show support for the worthwhile project of assisting the street children.

Like Dr Ruit, I found Mrs Koirala to be committed to her work and determined to achieve results. I know that sometimes, the work of rescuing women and girls or pursuing prosecution of traffickers involved personal risk to both Mrs Koirala and her staff. However, she was not deterred. The other quality she shared with Dr Ruit was great modesty and humility.

In 2008 while living in Nepal, Odette and I thought we should take advantage of its proximity and visit Bhutan. We planned to go as tourists, but thanks to the intervention of our good friend, Dr Ruit, the visit turned into something much more and provided the chance to meet with the then Queen Mother, but now Queen Grandmother, Ashi Kesang Choden Wangchuk.

It's a long story as to how this came about. In March 2008, I was involved in the launch of a trial vaccination program against cervical cancer in Nepal. I had agreed the Australian Cervical Cancer Foundation (ACCF), led by its chairman, Mike Wille, could use the grounds of the embassy residence in Kathmandu to conduct the launch. We got some media coverage of the event and amongst those who read about it and expressed direct interest, was Dr Ruit, wanting to know if it might be possible for his two teenage daughters to be vaccinated. This was duly arranged. Dr Ruit has continued to be an enthusiastic supporter of the vaccination program and more generally of ACCF's work in Nepal.

When Dr Ruit heard we were going to Bhutan in May that year, he was keen that we meet his good friend and ophthalmologist colleague, Dr Kunzang Getshen. Dr Ruit shared his enthusiasm for the cervical cancer vaccination launch with Dr Kunzang. When we arrived in Thimphu, the capital of Bhutan, Dr Kunzang and his brother were there to meet us.

Dr Kunzang, who also serves as a physician to Her Royal Highness, informed us he had arranged for us to meet with Her Royal Highness the Queen Mother at her residence in Dechencholing Palace on the outskirts of Thimphu. He told us he had informed the Queen Mother about the launch of the cervical cancer vaccination program in Nepal.

Odette and I were not experienced in having afternoon tea with royalty, so were quite daunted at the prospect of meeting with the Queen Mother, even though Dr Kunzang had sought to reassure us we had nothing to worry about. As it turned out, Dr Kunzang was right, and it was the start of a lasting relationship with both Bhutan and the then Queen Mother and now Royal Grandmother.

The afternoon tea took place in the Royal Highness' lounge room at her palace. The room was decorated with Buddhist thangka paintings, Buddhist bronzes and woven carpets. The room had a strong sense of Buddhist spirituality and made us feel at peace. We were treated to smoked salmon sandwiches, scones and marmalade, and some other tasty morsels. The Queen Mother made us quickly feel at ease and encouraged us to eat and chat.

The Queen Mother was interested to learn more about the cervical cancer program and asked lots of questions. She was also interested in what was happening in nearby Nepal and, again, asked lots of questions. The Queen Mother and Odette also struck up a close bond, perhaps because both were mothers and grandmothers.

At the end of our discussion, the Queen Mother asked me if it might be possible to launch a vaccination program in Bhutan as, like Nepal, cervical cancer was the major cancer killer of women aged between thirty and sixty. I said I could not make any promises, but I would contact Mike Wille to see if he was interested in pursuing such a possibility. Odette and I then posed for some photographs with the Queen Mother and her daughter Princess Pem-Pem. A striking feature of all the photos, which we only noticed afterwards, was that the Queen Mother was holding Odette's hand closely in hers.

Following our return from Bhutan, I contacted Mike Wille. Mike was indeed interested and, through the channel of Dr Kunzang, arrangements were made for Mike and his wife, Lenore, to visit Bhutan.

Almost two years to the day from that first meeting Odette and I had with the Queen Mother, now the Royal Grandmother, Mike and Lenore's contacts with Bhutan had blossomed. Odette and I were invited in early May 2010 to participate in the launch of a nationwide cervical cancer vaccination program in Bhutan; the first such program in a developing country. By this time, I had retired from government service and was now a member of the Australian Cervical Cancer Foundation Board.

The vaccination program was being run by the Bhutanese Ministry of Health with the strong support and patronage of the

A Diplomatic Life

Royal Grandmother and the joint support of the Australian Cervical Cancer Foundation and Merck, Sharp and Dohme, the manufacturer of the Gardasil vaccine. The support and enthusiasm of the Royal Grandmother and Mike and Lenore had helped this outcome to fruition, in a comparatively short time span. Implementation of the program to date has also proceeded smoothly and successfully.

At the time of our visit for the launch, Odette and I were able to renew our acquaintance with the Royal Grandmother and Princess Pem-Pem and to meet her daughter, Princess Kesang, who had studied in Australia. Our experiences with the Royal Grandmother have confirmed our view of her as a gracious, kind and caring lady. She was able to use her dynamism and commitment to achieve the launch of the vaccination program, yet in doing so, was also driven by a wish to look after and help the women of Bhutan.

Later in 2010, the Royal Grandmother celebrated her eightieth birthday. We had been impressed by how young and vigorous she was for a woman of her age. She certainly did not look eighty years old. In other respects, the Royal Grandmother did not conform to my impressions about royalty. We found her to be a down-to-earth and relaxed person. She was warm and genuine in her hospitality. She is truly a remarkable lady.

The Royal Grandmother continues to retain an interest in ACCF's work in Bhutan and usually hosts tea or lunch for ACCF VolunTour groups to Bhutan. For his part, Dr Kunzang continues his involvement and remains one of the principal points of contact for ACCF.

Given Up for Dead on Everest

Only a few months into my assignment in Kathmandu, I became involved in one of the most dramatic consular cases I had to deal with during my time in Nepal.

I had received a message that one of Australia's best-known climbers, Lincoln Hall, had perished near the summit of Mount Everest. Hall had been part of the ANU Mountaineering Club Expedition to climb Everest in 1984; the first Australian expedition to reach the summit. On that occasion, Hall had not been one of the successful summiteers and had been forced to turn back because of altitude sickness and frostbite.

In 2006, Hall was determined to give the summit another go and had joined a Russian-led expedition. Amongst them was a fifteen-year-old Australian schoolboy, Christopher Harris, who sought to become the youngest climber to reach the summit. His father was also in the expedition with Mike Dillon, an Australian cameraman, who was there to follow the attempt by Harris. Harris was forced to turn back because of altitude sickness and returned to Kathmandu.

On this occasion, 25 May, Hall made it to the summit, but, on the descent, he collapsed into unconsciousness. The Sherpas sought to revive him. They talked by satellite phone with the expedition leader back at base camp and told him they could detect no sign of a pulse or heartbeat. The expedition leader, Alexander Abramov, told them to return to base camp to ensure their own survival.

It was this message that was relayed to Hall's wife, Barbara, and their sons at their home in the Blue Mountains in Australia. Given Hall's standing in the Australian mountaineering community, I started receiving messages from some of Hall's colleagues in Australia, including Simon Balderstone and Christine Gee. At the time, she was the Honorary Consul for Nepal in Sydney.

Barely twelve hours later, I started receiving other messages that, 'No, Hall was in fact still alive.' By some miracle, Hall had survived the night in bitterly cold conditions at an altitude of over 8,500m. A team of climbers led by American Daniel Mazur, and including Canadian Andrew Brash, Brit Myles Osborne, and Nepalese Jangbu Sherpa, had found Lincoln.

The scene was perhaps best, and most dramatically, described by Osborne in a dispatch he wrote on 28 May:

'Sitting to our left, about two feet from a 10,000ft drop, was a man. Not dead, not sleeping, but sitting cross legged, in the process of changing his shirt. He had his down suit unzipped to the waist, his arms out of the sleeves, was wearing no hat, no gloves, no sunglasses, had no oxygen mask, regulator, ice axe, oxygen, no sleeping bag, no mattress, no food nor water bottle. "I imagine you're surprised to see me here," he said. Now, this was a moment of total disbelief to us all. Here was a gentleman, apparently lucid, who had spent the night without oxygen at 8,600m, without proper equipment and barely clothed. And ALIVE.'

(*'Update: Myles Osborne for SummitClimb Everest Tibet, Dispatch 28 May 2006'. everestnews.com. Retrieved 17 November 2017.*)

Dan Mazur and his team abandoned their attempt to summit Everest and opted to stay with Hall, until a team of Sherpas, dispatched by Abramov arrived to rescue and escort him down the mountain. Later, Hall told me that the Mazur team gave him hot tea and helped dress him more suitably.

Some months later, I was asked to lend my support to bravery commendations for Dan Mazur, Andrew Brash and Myles Osborne. I was happy to do so, but said I was sure that Hall would have liked the role of the Sherpas to be recognised. I never heard whether the awards were given but had no reason to think otherwise … apart, perhaps, for the Sherpas' commendations.

Knowing that Hall was alive, I knew it would be a big media story and, therefore, as ambassador, I should be directly involved in providing consular support. I had been contacted by Mike Dillon and agreed that he and I would travel together to the Nepal and Tibet border.

The trip to the border proved to be something of an adventure in itself. There had been some heavy rain and landslides along part of the road as we neared the final stretch to the border. In one section, the road was blocked by a semi-trailer and there was also another truck bogged in the slushy mud that was supposed be part of the highway connecting Kathmandu to the Tibetan border. We could not pass. There were a lot of people offering suggestions, but, for the best part of two hours, traffic was completely blocked.

Eventually, smaller, and mainly four-wheel drive vehicles like ours, were able to get around the impasse. We at last made it to the aptly named Last Resort. This was to be my first and only experience of glamping. However, to get to the resort, one other challenge awaited us.

A Diplomatic Life

We could not drive right up to the entrance. Access was by a narrow steel suspension bridge. Although well-built, the bridge still swayed noticeably as we and others sought to cross it. Midway along the bridge was what was said to be, at the time, the second highest bungee jump platform in the world. I did not feel in the least inclined to try it out. It was certainly a long way down to the swiftly-flowing Bhote Koshi River running through the canyon below – some 160m in fact. I did my best to look straight ahead.

After a light dinner, we checked in for the night into our 'luxury' tents. I could stand upright in the middle and there was a proper bed to sleep on. During the night, I could hear the sound of crashing water below. I learnt later that one of the other attractions of the Last Resort was white-water rafting.

Next morning, we had breakfast at the hotel and learned that at least one Australian TV team had stayed overnight as well. By the time we got to the Nepal-Tibet border, we found that there were three Australian TV crews in attendance. I was also aware by this stage, that Simon Balderstone, Chairman of the Australian Himalayan Foundation, together with Hall's wife, Barbara, were arriving that day, on the daily Thai flight from Bangkok. I had been asked to keep this a secret from Hall as they wished to surprise him.

Another piece of news I had been asked to keep secret from him was the death of leading Australian woman mountaineer, Sue Fear. I had been told that Fear and Hall were good friends, but not knowing the state of Hall's health, I was asked not to mention her death to him. He would be told about it when he got to Kathmandu.

Some weeks later, together with Kumudh, a consular support officer at the embassy, I met Bishnu Gurung, the Sherpa who had been accompanying Fear on the climb. Gurung told us that, as they were descending from the summit of the approximately 8,160m Mount

Manaslu, the weather took a turn for the worse and Fear asked him to take the lead for the descent. At one point, he felt a strong tug on the rope that joined them together and turned to see her fall into a crevasse. He tried to pull her, but to no avail. As the crevasse was getting wider, and as there was no sound coming from Fear, he assumed she was unconscious. He tied the rope to an ice axe as an anchor and cut himself free so that he would not fall.

Bishnu said he could not see how far Fear had fallen into the crevasse and that even if a rescue team had been available, it would be unlikely that they would find her body. As there was no body available, Bishnu's account formed the basis for issuing Fear's death certificate.

Back to the Nepal-Tibet border and waiting for Hall's arrival, I had spoken with the Nepalese police and immigration officials, and they were ready to smooth things over for processing Hall's arrival. The police encouraged me to walk partway across the bridge linking the two countries, to wait for Hall. I had barely reached a quarter of the way across when Chinese sentries moved threateningly towards me, gesturing me to get back. I did step back and did not have to wait long before I saw Hall moving towards me from the Tibeten side of the border.

My first impression was that he looked like walking death. I was aware that he was suffering from cerebral edema, but I could see he also had respiratory problems. He was coughing and spluttering as he made his way painfully towards me. Although I had not met Hall before, I assumed, as a mountaineer, he would have been in good physical condition. This was not what I saw. Hall had clearly lost a lot of weight. I also observed his hands. The tips of his fingers were blackened by frostbite – not a pretty sight.

Nonetheless, it was a relief for me, and I am sure also for Hall, that he was back in Nepal. Hall had been accompanied to the border by a

Russian doctor from the expedition, who then parted from us. After completing the Nepalese paperwork, Mike and I escorted Hall to the Australian embassy Land Rover.

Although Hall continued to nibble from his packets of dried fruit, he asked if it might be possible to get some bananas. I left him in the car for a few minutes to go and thank the Nepalese police and immigration officials for facilitating Hall's entry and I asked my driver, Rabi, to go and buy some bananas and some bottles of drinking water. I found the Nepalese officials to be helpful and friendly, so I later wrote a note to the police department commending them for their good service.

Once we started to move, Hall's spirits seemed to lift. He commented on the green vegetation and the occasional glimpses of the river that we saw as we drove. It seemed refreshing after the barren, rocky terrain of Tibet adjacent to the border with Nepal. Another factor was perhaps the medical care he was about to receive, indicating he was on the first part of his journey home. Perhaps it was the taste of bananas.

As Hall's spirits lifted, so did his wish to talk. Mike and I sought to encourage him not to overexert himself, but Hall was determined to continue.

Much of the detail was included in Hall's subsequent book about his experience; *Dead Lucky*. When I read the book, it seemed to me there were a few differences with what I recall Hall told us on our drive back to Kathmandu.

Perhaps not surprisingly, there were some differences in his account of the hallucinations he experienced while waiting on the icy ledge, some 8,500m above sea level.

The part of Hall's story he shared driving back to Kathmandu that had the most profound effect on me was his depth of feeling and love for his wife and two sons, and how this motivated him to maintain the will to survive. As Hall acknowledged, there were times during the night while on the icy ledge that he felt frozen and questioned his will to persevere. He said he kept coming back to the fact that he could not desert his family and that he had to stay alive for them.

Given this background, I was glad that Barbara would be in Kathmandu to meet Hall, but I kept the surprise a secret. The reunion took place at the Radisson Hotel where they were staying. The Radisson was probably the closest major hotel to the Australian Embassy and was close to the CIWEC Clinic.

When we got back to Kathmandu, a major priority was for Hall to be checked out medically. Manju, another consular support officer at the embassy, and Kumudh had arranged a number of appointments for him. These were with Dr Prativa Pandey, Medical Director at the CIWEC Clinic – one of the major clinics in Kathmandu tending to foreign patients – and the Nepal International Clinic, headed by my good friend Dr Buddha Basnyat who dealt with travellers and specialised in altitude sickness. The key priority was to ensure he was medically fit to take the return flight to Australia.

About a year later, I had the chance to meet Hall in Sydney at an event organised by the Australian Himalayan Foundation. By this stage, the tops of some of his fingers had been amputated.

It was good to catch up with Hall. He was looking in better health than when I had last seen him. He was keeping busy with writing, public speaking, and being active with the Australian Himalayan Foundation. We had a chance to reminisce.

In 2012, I was living in Hanoi, accompanying Odette on her assignment to the Philippine Embassy in Vietnam. I was deeply shocked to learn that, on 20 March, Hall had died of mesothelioma, a disease caused by exposure to asbestos. Apparently, in his younger days, Hall had assisted his father using asbestos in the construction of children's cubby houses. My initial reaction was how ironic and unfair this seemed after surviving what he'd been through on Mount Everest.

I wrote to Barbara and expressed my condolences. I had a chance, later, to see her again at a dinner in Manly, organised by Simon Balderstone, and coinciding with one of my visits back to Australia.

I feel honoured to have met Hall and to be associated with his inspirational story. While it was an incredible story of courage and survival, the time spent with him inspired me in another way while I was living in Nepal. His experience convinced me that I never wanted to climb Mount Everest, or other high and challenging mountains. The risk of attitude sickness, frostbite, the discomfort of camping in extremely cold places, and the deprivation of oxygen do not seem much fun to me.

Lincoln Hall, Rest in Peace.

Yeti Airline Crash in Lukla

Another complicated consular case involved the death of two Australians who were onboard the ill-fated Yeti Airline plane that crashed at Lukla Airport on 8 October 2008.

As usual, I had entered the Embassy about 8am on 8 October and picked up the latest read-out from our wire service printer. I saw an item referring to the plane crash at Lukla Airport, noting the plane had crashed as it was trying to land at about 7:30 that morning. It referred to foreign tourists being onboard. My initial reaction was that we needed to confirm whether there were Australians on board.

Apparently, the plane was the third Yeti plane that day to undertake the Kathmandu-Lukla route and visibility at time of landing was disrupted by fog. The plane tried to make a visual landing and clipped the top of a perimeter fence, causing the plane to crash and then catch fire.

Subsequent reports indicated the majority of the tourists were German, but there were two of other foreign nationality, reported either as Swiss or Austrian or Australian. To be doubly sure, we needed to check the passenger manifest. Manju and Kumudh, the embassy's consular staff, tried getting in touch with Yeti Airlines, but their phone lines were busy. Then Manju remembered she had a close relative working at Yeti Airlines and she had his mobile number. She was able to talk with him and he provided us with a copy of the passenger manifest.

It seemed there had been some confusion about the final list as there was some last-minute changes to the passengers onboard, in part to keep the German tourist group together. An earlier list had even referred to some of the passengers by their middle names instead of their family names.

While Manju was making her enquiries, I received a phone call from 2GB radio in Australia which Sanjana, my assistant, had put through to me. When I answered, a woman said she was ringing on behalf of her boss at 2GB and would I be prepared to go on air and speak to him about the Lukla plane crash. I said I would be willing to talk to him, although at that stage there would be very little I could tell him, as we were still trying, ourselves, to confirm whether any Australians had been onboard.

The radio talk-show host then came on the line and, from his comments, I was made aware I was already on air. I was not happy I had been duped in this way. His tone from the outset was quite aggressive. He asked me to confirm if there were Australians onboard. I replied that we were still trying to confirm this, as there had been some conflicting reports about the nationalities of the tourists onboard, besides the Germans.

The radio host tried a different tack and said he understood there were two Australians onboard and could I tell him their names. I repeated that we were still trying to confirm the details, but even if I knew their names, which at that stage I did not, he would appreciate that it would not be appropriate for me to provide them until we were certain next of kin had been notified, however, the radio host continued to press me to provide names.

I explained that we followed this procedure out of respect to the families and asked him how he would feel if a close relative had been killed and he first heard about it over the radio. Maybe this antagonised him, because he brought the call to an end by saying something to the effect of, 'Listeners, it is obvious that the Australian ambassador is of no use to us.'

I was upset by this call, not just because of the aggressive approach, but it had delayed me from following up on whether or not there were any Australians onboard. And, if there were, further delayed me from notifying the department so they could contact their families.

As we were able to confirm a short time later, there were indeed two Australians onboard. In total, eighteen people had died in the crash – the two Australians, twelve Germans, two Nepalese tourists and two air crew. The only survivor was the pilot, although badly injured.

The two Australians were Andrew Frick McLeod (his name was incorrectly recorded on the flight manifest and did not show his proper surname) and his girlfriend, Charlene Zamudio. Based on several Australian press articles, McLeod's father had said that his son had intended to ask Charlene to marry him when they got back to Australia and had enlisted some help in trying to find a suitable ring. It was also revealed in press articles that Andrew and Charlene should have flown to Lukla a few days earlier, but Charlene's luggage had gone astray. If not for this, they would not have been on the ill-fated flight. Their correspondence indicated they had enjoyed travels on the Annapurna trekking route and in the Chitwan National Park.

I also read one report which touched me, reflecting the importance of what I had said to the radio host. The first time Charlene's family had heard about her death was when the trekking company contacted them seeking details of her travel insurance. I was surprised the trekking company acted so quickly, before even DFAT could contact them.

Having confirmed two Australians were amongst the dead, Kumudh arranged for the two of us to meet with the coroner assigned to the case. It became apparent from talking with him that he had limited personnel support and inadequate equipment and facilities to undertake the task. He advised that the Germans were sending a Disaster Victim Identification (DVI) team, but he would welcome an Australian DVI team too. Any additional help would be welcome. I put the case for a DVI team to Canberra, and they agreed to send a team.

Next, the Nepalese Coroner's Office advised us that the recovered bodies were being air-lifted to Kathmandu and we were invited to be present. Kumudh and I both attended. The bodies arrived in a military helicopter at an out of the way part of the tarmac. Being present gave us another chance to meet with the coroner, as well as to meet and talk to some senior Nepalese aviation officials. It also helped us get a better feel for the accident investigation process. Some media representatives were present, but there was no-one from the German embassy.

When I reflect back on that day, I am still haunted by what we saw. A number of bodies were bundled together on a trolley. As the army and/or police had insufficient supplies of body bags, the bodies were covered by plastic or canvas sheets, and not everything was properly covered.

Prior to the arrival of our team, I attended a preliminary meeting with the German DVI team. They indicated that the Australian team would be welcome, but as the German team had arrived first, and because there were more German victims, they saw the Australian team as playing a strictly supporting role.

Kumudh and I met the Australian DVI team when they arrived at Tribhuvan International Airport. After dropping them off at their hotel, we proceeded to a meeting at the German embassy with the German team, where the Australian team acknowledged their supporting role.

This was not unfamiliar. They had similar experiences in other multinational disasters. The acknowledgement of the Germans having primary carriage of the investigation is reflected in the comments below, but it also demonstrated the added complications involved in working in a subordinate role to officials from another country.

I met regularly with the Australian team to be updated on the progress. They encountered a number of difficulties. The first, and in a sense, one of the most awkward, was that the German dental specialist had not brought adequate equipment with him and relied on the Australian dentist's equipment, including their portable x-ray device. The Australian dentist felt there was more he could do and that his skills were not being properly utilised.

Secondly, while the Australian team acknowledged they had to fit in with the German bureaucratic requirements, they found it tedious that every step had to be referred to their headquarters in Bonn, and results could only be confirmed and notified after Bonn's say-so.

Thirdly, there was an incident that surprised me in particular. The German team had been seeking to match the jaws of the victims with the dental records they had received from Bonn. In one case, they couldn't find a match and assumed it must have belonged to one of the Nepalese victims. The Australians looked at it and observed that there was one mandible missing and so, it was little wonder it didn't match.

The leader and one other member of the Australian team thought it would be useful to visit the crash site in Lukla and get a better appreciation of the accident. It also afforded them a chance to see if they could find the missing mandible. They didn't find the mandible, but they did find some personal property of the victims, either at the site or for sale at one of the local stalls near the airport. This included at least one passport.

When the bodies had been identified to the satisfaction of both

A Diplomatic Life

DVI teams, the bodies of the two Australians would need to be stored safely prior to finalising the paperwork required for entry of the remains into Australia. Although the German embassy had a large, refrigerated storeroom, we preferred to find somewhere that would allow us timely access. The American Club in Durbar Marg, Kathmandu agreed we could use their facility.

There was some property that Andrew and Charlene had left at their hotel in Kathmandu, and the embassy was given direct access to this by the hotel. This contained gifts they had bought for family and friends. The embassy made an inventory of these items, and they were to be included in the container with the bodies.

Kumudh, again, took the principal role for the paperwork. This included death certificates issued by the Nepalese coroner's office, quarantine clearance papers, and the inventory of personal items. Kumudh had to go to the American Club to certify that the bodies being transported, were indeed the ones in the container.

In accordance with departmental requirements, we sent a cable to Canberra confirming the paperwork had been completed. We received a message back from the Victorian coroner's office saying our list was incomplete. They also needed an autopsy report.

Knowing the difficulties of getting an official Nepalese autopsy report, and the fact that the bodies were badly burnt, I asked DFAT to go back to the coroner's office. I noted the family had already suffered enough grief, and to delay transmission of the bodies would only compound this. Secondly, I was not sure what an autopsy would prove, as both Andrew and Charlene had died as a result of the aircraft crash. I am glad that DFAT successfully argued the case.

It was a tragedy that their young lives should end so sadly.

I was also involved with another aviation tragedy while I was in Nepal. On 23 September 2006, a helicopter arranged by the World

Wildlife Fund crashed soon after take-off in Taplejung. Twenty-four people died in that accident, including one Australian, Dr Jill Bowling Schlaepfer, and several other people I was acquainted with, including Forestry Minister Gopal Rai and his wife, and Nepalese WWF advocates Chandra Gurung and Harka Gurung, and good friend Pauli Mustonen, charge d'affaires at the Finnish embassy. Pauli often joined my friend Abraham and I for dinner get-togethers.

The wreckage was later located, and bodies were recovered and released for burial or transportation, after identification.

Jill Bowling had formerly worked for a while at the department of the prime minister and cabinet and, at the time of the accident, was working for WWF UK. She was married to a Swiss and had dual nationality.

The Australian embassy got involved in paperwork relating to processing her Australian death registry requirements. Her husband, Herr Schlaepfer, came to see us at the embassy where he said he was not getting all the help he wanted from Swiss officials. At the time, Switzerland had an Aid Office in Kathmandu, but not a formal embassy.

We undertook to provide him with duplicates or copies of the Australian paperwork to assist him in finalising Swiss requirements. This could not be done until we had obtained the Nepalese death certificate. We offered to send the relevant papers through the diplomatic bag to the Australian Mission in Switzerland, asking them to contact him when they had arrived.

Herr Schlaepfer was obviously pleased with the service we provided, as he wrote a letter thanking us for our help and commenting that, *although he was not Australian, we had treated him as if he was.*

Looking to the Future and Moving On

Before starting my assignment in Kathmandu, I had decided I would retire when I finished the posting. I wanted to find something productive and creative to do, like helping people in need, while I was still young and fit. I hoped I could find something through the auspices of a non-government organisation.

As it turned out, two opportunities presented themselves during my work in Nepal. Odette had joined me at the beginning of 2008, having completed her assignment in Canberra in mid-2007 and then taking a year's leave after her return to Manila. This meant that whatever I did, would have to be something I could do from Manila.

During the course of my dealings with Dr Sanduk Ruit of Tilganga Institute of Ophthalmology, I had come to know Brian Doolan, the CEO of the Fred Hollows Foundation (FHF). Brian was a regular visitor to Nepal because of the ongoing FHF support for Tilganga and, in particular, its intraocular lens factory.

One evening, not long before my assignment was due to finish, I was attending a dinner with Brian and Sanduk Ruit and the idea of working as a volunteer for FHF when I moved to the Philippines came up. Sanduk mentioned that Philippines ophthalmologists had asked him to try and assist with extending cataract surgery cooperation for indigent communities in the Philippines. This request had been made in the context of Sanduk's visit to Manila to receive his 2006 Magsaysay Award presentation.

As progress on the Philippine proposal seemed to have stalled, this was something I could follow up from Manila.

When I got to Manila, I contacted Dr Noel Chua, who was chairman of the Philippine National Committee for Sight Preservation and a prominent ophthalmologist. Noel was a lively and helpful companion. I learned he had a secret passion he reserved for his Friday afternoons – ballroom dancing, especially Latin-style dance.

The other person I contacted was Dr Bel Ambrosio. Bel was a sincere person, with a strong humanitarian outlook, who voluntarily sought to provide pro-bono cataract surgery for needy people in her hometown of Naga. I learned she was a deeply religious person. Bel had been the principal author of a proposal to provide cataract surgery to indigent people in Masbate Province.

It seemed like the project had fallen between a crack. Noel and Bel thought it was under consideration by FHF, and FHF indicated they were still waiting to receive the proposal. My discussions were useful in clarifying things. I was then contacted by Ross Hardy of FHF and, during his visits to Manila, we made progress in fine-tuning the project proposal.

This involved several visits to Masbate. Masbate, at the time of our visit, was among the poorest provinces in the Philippines, but it was also a place of contradictions. It was known as Cowboy Country and had an annual cowboy rodeo. It was one of the main cattle producing provinces in the Philippines and had pasture land with rugged, densely

A Diplomatic Life

forested areas. I learned that much of the original cattle breeding stock had come from Australia. The coastal waters were rich in fisheries and some of the nearby islands were said to have good tourist potential for scuba diving.

Masbate is also said to sit on a rich vein of gold. For a long time, traditional gold mining techniques had been used, and these relied on using mercury and cyanide as flushes. There is now a major commercial gold mining operation which is required to adhere to international environmental practice. At the time of our visits, the mine was under the management of an Australian company.

The first visit to Masbate proved memorable for reasons unrelated to the project proposal. At the time, there were no direct air services to Masbate. Our plan was to fly to Legazpi and then drive to Pilar in Sorsagon Province to take the ferry for Masbate, which departed at about 4am. We boarded our flight to Legazpi, but because of extreme fog, were unable to land and had to return to Manila.

As we had an appointment the following morning with the then governor of Masbate, we decided to rent a microbus to drive us to Legazpi. The driver said he had travelled the route once before and it should take between eleven to twelve hours. We figured that should get us to Legazpi in time for a late meal, and probably four to five hours of sleep, before heading to Pilar.

We got to Naga in reasonable time, but from Naga, several of us suspected the driver had missed the turn and questioned him. The driver was adamant we were on the right track. We progressed for another hour or so and insisted the driver stop, so we could check. Sure enough, the driver had missed the turn and we had to retrace our route. We eventually reached our hotel in Legazpi after 11pm. We had to be on the road by about 2am.

One benefit of arriving so late and departing so early was we were treated to a spectacular sight. Against the night sky, nature presented a fireworks display for us. Mount Mayon volcano is renowned for its almost perfect conical shape and it serves as a landmark for Legazpi. A few weeks before our journey, Mayon had been showing signs of volcanic activity. Appearing scarlet against the sky, we witnessed hot lava spewing from its crater. Even though we had been deprived of sleep, we were treated to a rare sight and felt privileged.

I found the Masbate experience to be instructive. As with other poorer provinces, it was dominated by political dynasties, and violence between these groups was common. It seemed to me, the city hospital in Masbate was mismanaged and underfunded. The pharmacy shelves were stocked with band-aids, a few aspirin and not much else. Patients had to share beds and often these were placed in the corridors, as there was no space in the wards. There was no linen on the beds; apparently families had to provide their own. It was not an encouraging impression for our project to support cataract surgery.

In Cataingan, about 77km south-east of Masbate City, we also visited the district hospital. This was a marked contrast to the Masbate City Hospital and seemed to be quite well-managed and better equipped. Apparently, rabies was a common problem within the district.

However, in Cataingan, we were treated to a lesson in provincial politics. We met the local mayor and he wished us to see a tourist resort he was developing along the coast. He asked us to follow his car. We had to stop while he changed cars. He told us he had six identical cars, all without number plates. He said that when he was out driving, he changed cars regularly as this would help confound any political enemies who were trying to stalk him. I now know that such fear is common at the provincial level.

Mobo is another coastal municipality, about 27km from Masbate City. At the time of our visit, many of its inhabitants were involved in

A Diplomatic Life

the fishing industry, and we were pleasantly surprised during our visit to the municipal office. A round-table meeting had been organised with key stakeholders, predominantly health workers. The meeting was well run and well-attended.

We also visited the Filminera Gold Mine in Aroroy Municipality, about 50km from Masbate City. We had not been able to arrange a visit inside but were able to drive around and get an impression of the site. We had met with the company in Manila, and they had provided information on the corporate social responsibility activities of the mine, the environmental impact assessments that had been undertaken, and plans to rehabilitate the site at the end of mining activity. They had also discussed action taken to contribute to the local community, including paved roads around the mine site, schools for children, medical clinics and a significant number of jobs for local people.

On the way to the mine, we drove past some small-scale traditional mining operations. These were not required to rehabilitate the damage they did to the environment, and their use of mercury and cyanide caused leaching of the soil and contamination of the water table. Long-term exposure to cyanide and mercury also represents a health risk, including poisoning.

We held a stakeholder meeting in Masbate city, and this highlighted important issues. One related to the fact that there was no resident ophthalmologist. There were only periodic visits by ophthalmologists from Manila or the Bicol region. One doctor operated on a strictly commercial basis, and it was apparent to me he would not welcome a service being introduced that would undercut his income earning visits, even if the focus was largely on indigent communities who could not afford to pay for his services anyway. Another major topic of discussion was how to encourage young ophthalmologists to spend time in Masbate when they had secured their qualifications. It was also pointed out that we needed to ensure the Catholic Church was onside, and that what we planned complemented their own plans to build a private hospital in Masbate City.

On a subsequent visit, we spent some time in Legazpi meeting with the regional office of the Department of Health and the bishop of Legazpi, both of which had oversight of Masbate Province for their organisations.

The meeting with the Bishop of Legazpi took place at the historic Cathedral of Saint Gregory the Great. We informed the bishop of our basic objective, to provide cataract surgery to people who were unable to afford it. We mentioned our wish to ensure all potential stakeholders, including the Catholic Church, were onboard. We also discussed the possibility of linking up with the proposed Catholic Hospital when it was built.

I cannot recall if we raised the subject or if it was the bishop, but he outlined the Church's staunch opposition to mining in the Philippines. The bishop inferred that if we had any dealings with the mine, he would ensure that there was no local support for our proposed project. For various other reasons related to the overall viability of the proposed project, we did not follow up with Filminera.

From my investigations via the internet, it seems that the gold mine has developed considerably since our visits to Masbate in 2009 and 2010. The mine is owned by a Canadian company, B2Gold, and Filminera are still involved as managers in the Philippines. According to the Filminera report of November 2018, 1881 people were employed by the mine of whom 67% were from the local Aroroy District. Almost P$450 million was spent under social development and management programs, the majority in the eight host barangays, but also including about P$63 million in other neighbouring areas.

One successful project, mentioned in other documents, was training local people to grow vegetables, initially for use in the mine kitchens, but later as a source of income for their communities.

Despite considerable time and effort invested in trying to develop a workable project for Masbate, the project ended up being shelved for a combination of reasons. Political changes, as it seems often happen in the Philippines, led to changes in support and priorities. Trying to develop a system to ensure ophthalmologists would be prepared to come to Masbate proved too difficult. Guaranteeing anything other than moral support proved an impediment to ensuring involvement by the Department of Health. At the Australian end, staff changes at FHF led to a change in their priorities.

For me, the Masbate project offered many insights into the complexities involved in ensuring successful projects in the Philippines. This was useful knowledge.

The second opportunity to contribute something useful through an NGO came about very differently.

One day in 2007, my assistant Sanjana told me there was a man ringing from Brisbane. I was greeted on the other end of the phone by a booming American accent. Mike Wille introduced himself as chairman of the Australian Cervical Cancer Foundation. Mike told me he wished to introduce the human papilloma virus vaccine developed by Professor Ian Frazer in Nepal to combat cervical cancer and asked if he could come and see me when he visited Kathmandu in October. I, of course, said yes.

Come October, I was meeting face-to-face with Mike in the embassy's conference room. He told me he had been a successful businessman in Brisbane and, in retirement, his wife Lenore was concerned he would get bored. She suggested Mike might like to combine his love of Nepal, derived from his days as a successful mountaineer, including Everest and Cho-Oyu, and his friendship with 2006 Australian of the Year Ian

Frazer – inventor of the HPV vaccine.

I had had a number of Australians call on me previously saying they had been so warmly received in Nepal, they would like to do something in return to repay this hospitality.

I'd had two Australian groups wanting to assist in providing micro-hydro projects so that remote villages could get electricity. This was not something easily undertaken. One group sought to persevere and did get to the stage of trying to raise the required funds, but in the end, they gave up as it proved too difficult.

Returning to Mike, I could tell he was different. He clearly had a lot of drive and I was sure he could make things happen. Sometime later, when I had gotten to know him better, I told Mike about my impression of him.

Mike had been doing his homework and identified two possible Nepalese partners and sought my views. I had dealings with both but agreed with Mike that Dr Surendra Bade Shrestha seemed a good choice. Our choice was vindicated as Surendra proved to be an asset for ACCF in Nepal.

Surendra and I both sought a way with the Ministry of Health for vaccination to be possible. We were given the go-ahead, but as we found out when we wished to undertake the second round of vaccinations, no written record had been maintained by the Health Ministry, so we had to repeat the request for approval.

Accordingly, Mike and Lenore, who was a qualified nurse, arrived in Nepal carrying the precious cargo of twelve doses of the vaccine. On 9 March 2008, I hosted the first HPV vaccination ceremony in the gardens of the Australian embassy residence. Initially, five girls had been selected to be vaccinated, but one girl got stage fright and dropped out at the last minute. She was later vaccinated in the second round of vaccinations.

A Diplomatic Life

Thus began my association with Mike and Lenore Wille and the Australian Cervical Cancer Foundation.

In October 2008, Professor Ian Frazer visited Nepal. His visit coincided with the vaccination of the next one hundred girls. Ian gave a presentation to a group of doctors, academics and journalists at the Radisson Hotel in Kathmandu. Something he said that resonated with me was that, even if we could save the life of one woman, we were making a difference, but hopefully we could save the lives of many more women. This was what inspired me to support the work of ACCF, and still motivates me today.

When ACCF started out in Nepal; Mike thought that it would be an achievement if, within ten years, ACCF could vaccinate one thousand girls annually in Nepal. Eight years later, we had vaccinated over 31,000 girls. Our task had been made easier because of the availability of free vaccines provided under the Gardasil Access Program offered by Merck Sharp and Dohme through the Paris-based organisation, Axios. ACCF just had to support transport, storage and administration costs.

Working with the World Health Organization, ACCF sought to encourage Nepal to apply for a GAVI (Global Alliance for Vaccination and Immunization) demonstration project. Nepal did so, and the project was successfully conducted and resulted in Nepal deciding to introduce a national vaccination program from 2019-2020. This was a great outcome and way beyond our dreams of what might be possible within ten years of the first four girls being vaccinated at the Australian embassy.

Unfortunately, political changes and the Covid-19 pandemic in Nepal have resulted in the delayed introduction of the vaccination program, but the work continues, now with a new chair, Dr Sheela Verma, appointed after Dr Surendra Bade Shrestha passed in May of 2023. A memorial service was held for him in October 2023, reflecting the wonderful contribution he made to the health of so many women and girls across Nepal.

When I retired from the Department of Foreign Affairs and Trade in early 2009, Mike invited me to join the ACCF as a director. This is a voluntary position, but I was only too pleased to accept. In 2016, I succeeded Mike as chairman of ACCF.

As an organisation, ACCF now seeks to address cervical cancer in all its dimensions – raising awareness, vaccination, screening and, where feasible, treatment and counselling. Personally, I remain involved directly in ACCF programs in Nepal, Bhutan, Vietnam and the Philippines, but ACCF is involved in varying ways in Kiribati, Solomon Islands, Vanuatu and Papua New Guinea, as well as in Australia.

After finishing my assignment in Kathmandu, I returned to Canberra in early 2009 to complete the formal paperwork prior to retiring. About two months later, I joined Odette in Manila, where she had resumed working for the Philippines Department of Foreign Affairs. In November 2010, Odette was assigned to the Philippines embassy in Hanoi and then, in July 2013, to the Philippines embassy in Yangon.

When I first moved to Manila, Mike Wille had encouraged me to look at opportunities for ACCF to play some sort of role in the Philippines. Because of political changes, changes of key officials, changes in policy priorities, disruption caused by typhoons and other factors, it was not till September 2015 that we finally began preparatory training of health workers in Catarman, Northern Samar. Our counterpart in Catarman has proved excellent, and we are looking at continuing activity in the area.

Similarly, when we moved to Vietnam, Mike encouraged me to look at opportunities there. After consulting with relevant people and

A Diplomatic Life

completing the Vietnamese government requirement to obtain an NGO operating permit, ACCF commenced its first project in Thai Binh Province in Vietnam in November 2011, about a year after my arrival in Hanoi. In Vietnam (and the Philippines) ACCF support focuses on raising awareness of cervical cancer, screening women using the Visual Inspection with Acetic Acid method (VIA) and facilitating treatment for women who test positive.

Thai Binh has now progressed to trying to screen all women in the province, relying primarily on their own resources. Again, this is a better outcome than we could have hoped, but it is one consistent with our goal of encouraging greater local responsibility. We hope in the foreseeable future Can Tho may follow in Thai Binh's footsteps.

One particular experience in Hau Giang Province during a monitoring visit there stands out.

When I undertake monitoring visits to screening camps, I seek the help of whoever is acting as my translator to interview as many women as possible, who have tested VIA positive. On this particular day, Phu from the Research Center for Rural Population and Health was acting as my translator. The first woman we met with was clearly very anxious when she sat down to talk to us. She listened closely and attentively to what we had to say, the key points being always follow the doctor's advice and to ensure she goes for follow-up treatment when advised to do so. She asked some pertinent questions, and by the end of our discussion, she was notably more relaxed. As she got up to go, she expressed her sincere thanks that we had taken the time to explain everything clearly to her and asked if she could give me a hug. Of course, I said yes, as it was reassuring to have such a positive response to our discussion.

The last woman we spoke to that day was also anxious, less for what VIA+ meant and more for how she could find time to go for treatment.

She ran a small, street-side stall and barely eked out enough money each day to make a living. She could not afford to miss work. After checking with the staff from the Hau Giang Reproductive Health Center, we advised her she would need to allow a maximum of two hours. That would cover her travel time, registration, preliminary check and counselling, cryotherapy treatment, and the wait, after the procedure, to check she was fine. We also explained the procedure to her in some detail. We suggested that on the day she went for treatment, we hoped she had a friend or relative who could keep an eye on the stall for her. Again, this lady seemed more relaxed and less concerned about how to manage her time. As she got up to go, she too asked if she could give me a hug.

Two hugs in one day was unprecedented, and left me feeling that the time and effort we put into meeting with the VIA+ cases was worthwhile. That day, I left the clinic with a warm feeling of satisfaction. Even more reassuring was that, when we next visited Hau Giang, we were able to check that both women had indeed followed up and undergone cryotherapy.

I think my experience has shown that there is a worthwhile life to be had after retirement from the Department of Foreign Affairs and Trade.

Impressions of Hanoi

I first visited Hanoi in February 1983 when John McCarthy was the Australian ambassador. I returned on a short visit in 2004. I also accompanied Odette when she was assigned on posting to Hanoi in November 2010. However, it was only then after returning to Hanoi twenty-seven years after my first visit, that I started to appreciate the differences. The changes have been both positive and negative.

Hanoi Then

In 1983 there were no skyscrapers, let alone modern buildings, in Hanoi apart from the newly built Thang Loi Hotel and the Swedish aid compound. The Thang Loi Hotel was, in fact, considered to be too far out of town for us to consider staying there. There were no shopfronts with plate glass windows. I had to buy souvenirs at a government-run shop catering to foreign visitors. There were very few restaurants and only a handful considered suitable for foreigners. Traffic was light, probably with more bicycles than cars or motorbikes.

In 1983, you did not have to travel far before being out in the countryside, among rice fields and farmland. Hanoi still had the air of a quiet, slow-paced and charming city. The French had left their mark, with many wide tree-lined streets and stately French-colonial-style villas, although many in quite a run-down condition.

Although the war had ended some eight years earlier, there were few signs of Hanoi opening to the outside world. Japanese cars were starting to appear on the roads alongside the clunky and chunky cars from countries of the Soviet-bloc. In the market, I remember seeing unbranded jeans for sale, but with shopkeepers offering a choice of foreign brand labels to attach to your jeans.

Another thing that caught my attention, back then, were signboards advertising dentists and depicting oversize teeth. I wasn't sure if this indicated there were lots of dentists or whether there was a high demand for dental treatment.

In 1983, there were many obvious signs of poverty. We were told that even little things like discarded batteries or ballpoint pens were considered valuable and would be collected, with the remaining battery fluid or ink removed to make a working battery or a working pen. People scavenging in the streets and going through rubbish was quite a common sight, as people sought to salvage anything of value.

That first visit took place in February, still the Hanoi winter. I don't know if I was just lucky or if it was because the air quality was better, but I do recall seeing blue sky several times during my visit. In February nowadays, it is very rare to see blue sky.

In 2004, the changes I noticed after an absence of a bit over twenty years were dramatic, but my stay in Hanoi was short and I spent quite a lot of time outside the city. So, perhaps I did not appreciate the extent of the changes quite as much as I did when returning at the end of 2010. However, in part this may also be attributable to the rapid spurt in development that people have told us occurred in Hanoi from 2006 when Vietnam hosted the annual APEC meeting. Overall, we enjoyed living in Hanoi and I have enjoyed my regular visits back to Vietnam

A Diplomatic Life

for the monitoring of ACCF funded projects.

How has Hanoi changed?

The skyline has changed dramatically, as there are now many multi-storey high-rise buildings, and seemingly more being constructed every day. I don't know what the highest building in Hanoi is, but there are certainly many buildings twenty storeys or more. More generally, there has obviously been a major building boom, and many old houses have been torn down to make way for new four-, five- or six-storey houses, often on extremely narrow blocks of land. Houses only 3m wide are common; the house we rented during our stay in Hanoi had four storeys in a building that was only 3m wide.

Secondly, there are no longer rice fields and farmland close to the heart of the city. The Thang Loi Hotel is now in the inner city and connected by a good road to downtown Hanoi.

Our house in Hanoi, during our stay from late 2010 to mid-2013, was located in the Tay Ho (West Lake) District, about 4-5km from the Old Quarter and Hoan Kiem Lake. From our house, it was 26km by road to Noi Bai Airport. The 12km or so till we reached the bridge crossing the Red River (Song Hong) was almost completely built up with houses and commercial properties, although there was still some unoccupied land or bushland along the banks of the River.

During our time in Hanoi, once across the bridge over the Red River, itself a vast change to the narrow old bridge that spanned the river in 1983, we did encounter some rice fields and farmland, but also saw a growing number of factories or light industry sites. The road is also punctuated at frequent intervals with large advertising billboards, something that would have been unthinkable previously.

Since our time living in Hanoi, a modern new Japanese built bridge, with colourful light displays at night, has been completed. This has taken, maybe, 4-5km off the trip into the city from the airport and is probably fifteen minutes faster.

On the positive side, the modern development in Hanoi has largely not been at the expense of the charming legacy left by the French with wide tree-lined streets, plenty of parklands and stately French style villas. In fact, many of the old villas have been restored and put to practical use. Even some of the newer buildings have sought to replicate the grandeur of the old buildings. An example I was made aware of are the buildings on the Hanoi Medical University campus. These buildings built after the end of the war in 1975 have sought to blend in with the old architectural styles.

The charm of Hoan Kiem Lake largely remains unspoilt, although it too, has seen some changes. The shores of Ho Tay, however, have been sullied by some crass modern developments, as well as floating restaurants, and the fun-fair type pedal boats shaped like swans detract from the lake and its tree-lined shores and give a rather tawdry effect.

Of greater concern was that the embankments surrounding some of the smaller ponds close to where we lived, were being turned into rubbish dumps. I'm sure this was not officially sanctioned by the local government authorities. Rather, local people threw their rubbish there, probably because it was convenient, but were unmindful of the environmental consequences. We saw the waters becoming polluted, even though people still went fishing in these lakes or ponds. I was also concerned about the toxic nature of some of the waste being dumped in this way.

Motorbikes

One of the other really big changes in Hanoi has been the traffic. The motorbike revolution has taken control. There were signs of this when I visited Hanoi in 2004, but the motorbike was not quite as paramount as it is now. Nonetheless, even then, it was a challenge to cross the road in the Old Quarter areas of Hanoi.

When Odette had to visit Ho Chi Minh City for a work meeting in 2010, well before she knew she was going to be assigned to the Philippines embassy in Hanoi, we did a daytime trip to the Mekong Delta region. I remember our guide telling us that there were more motorbikes in Ho Chi Minh City than people. Without knowing the actual numbers, I could well believe the same now applies in Hanoi.

It was not just that the motorbike had become so numerous in Hanoi, nor was it the challenge that motorbikes presented in trying to cross roads by foot, rather it seemed more to be a case of the normally sensible and polite Vietnamese person transforming Dr Jekyll-like into a manic Mr Hyde once he or she got on their motorbike. Man or woman, the motorbike rider seemed to believe they were the king or queen of the road and they could do whatever they liked.

In terms of violent crime, Hanoi during our stay was a very safe city, especially for foreigners, and compared with probably many other major capital cities around the world, the incidence of crime was low. However, when it came to motorbike riders, there was little respect for rules and regulations and the motorbike riders followed their own rules.

Motorbikes did not obey traffic lights. It seemed it was better to risk an accident than stop at a traffic light for a while and rest your legs on the road. This, of course, also complicated things for pedestrians trying to cross the road. Green pedestrian traffic lights became meaningless, as you had to stop and wait for all the motorbikes going through red lights.

Neither did motorbikes heed the need to drive on the correct side of the road. If there was a bit of traffic congestion, why not ride on the wrong side of the road, even if there was a physical barrier dividing the lanes of traffic travelling in opposite directions? Failing that, if there was an adjacent footpath, that made a convenient extra lane for motorbikes to avoid congestion. Too bad for pedestrians who might be trying to use the footpath for the purpose it was intended.

Another complication for pedestrians wishing to use footpaths was that the footpaths were often used as parking lots for motorbikes and you had to navigate your way around them.

On one occasion, I was hit by a woman on a motorbike while I was walking on a footpath. She spoke some English and I asked if she realised that I was walking on a footpath which was intended for pedestrians. She said 'yes' but was looking for a parking space. Her clear implication was that I was in her way and too bad that she happened to hit me and badly bruise my arm. How can you argue with such logic?

Strictly designated one-way roads were, according to motorbike riders, one-way only for cars, trucks and other vehicles. Again, for pedestrians trying to cross the road, but also for other vehicular traffic, this represented an additional hazard that you needed to be alert to.

There was, apparently, a regulation that required motorbike riders and their passengers to wear helmets. This regulation was observed more in the breach than adherence. Even if a motorbike rider was wearing a helmet, in many cases it would not serve much use if they had an accident as they did not bother to strap it on properly. The helmets worn by many women did not seem very strong, as they had an indentation that allowed their ponytails to hang out neatly.

Of course, the inevitable happened when a motorbike rider had an accident and was not wearing a helmet. I witnessed one such accident. There was a collision between two motorbikes. The motorbike rider who caused the accident failed to stop and kept on going. The rider and passenger on the other bike both fell off. The rider was pinned under the bike. The passenger went flying. He landed awkwardly hurting his leg and badly scraping the skin off the side of his face; blood was pouring everywhere. He was definitely a hospital case.

Despite the undisciplined behaviour of motorbike riders, the motorbike has come to play a very important role in modern Vietnamese society. It served as the family car and it was not uncommon to see a family of four together on a motorbike, usually of course, without helmets. It had also become a major goods vehicle. Motorbikes were often seen carrying incredible loads, such as large water bottles, or a 2m-high porcelain vase on each side, or masses of fresh flowers or farm produce, or, in the lead up to Tet, the Vietnamese New Year, being loaded up with large cumquat or plum blossom trees.

Some of the riders of these motorbikes showed great dexterity. I remember driving behind a motorbike rider with two large flat-screen TVs on the back of his bike. They were not secured in any way and so one hand was used to hold the TVs and the other to navigate the motorbike. I hoped the TVs arrived safely at their destination.

This role of the motorbike did have one distinct advantage in a place like Hanoi, where many houses were situated down narrow lanes. A goods van would be unable to access these places, but a motorbike could. Hence, our bamboo furniture was all delivered on the back of a motorbike and our drinking water supply was delivered by a motorbike, usually three large bottles at a time.

A more common sight, and not one to be condoned, were motorbike riders busily talking or texting on their mobile phones, as they steered with one hand. They often were not paying proper attention to the road ahead and represented a major hazard for other drivers.

In case I have given the impression that crossing a road in Hanoi was impossible, take heart – it was not quite that bad. There was an unwritten protocol which I first read about in one of the guides to Hanoi. I found that generally this advice held good.

You, of course, had to wait till there was a slight lessening in the volume of motorbike traffic and then you should start to cross slowly and surely and, to your amazement, you would find that, as the guidebook said, the stream of motorbikes would separate and allow you to cross as if you were Moses parting the Red Sea. However, it was important you not hesitate, and that you continued to move slowly but resolutely forward. You would not succeed if, mid-stream, you tried stepping backwards.

This unwritten protocol was not completely fail-safe. I had one experience where two motorbikes were racing each other through a red light and one passed behind me. The other passed uncomfortably close in front of me. So close, in fact, I instinctively put up my elbow to protect myself and, sure enough, both the rider and his passenger hit my elbow. The rider turned back and gave me a rude look as if to say, how dare I seek to cross the road when he was coming. Fortunately, no one was hurt.

This sort of experience was just a reminder of the need to be ever-vigilant when crossing the road, but generally the unwritten protocol did seem to work.

Changing Fortunes

Another major change in Hanoi since 1983 had been the reduction in obvious signs of poverty, along with the manifestation of ostentatious wealth. When I visited previously, I often saw people scavenging and few signs of obvious wealth. Rather, people dressed modestly. There were no lavish shopwindow displays. There were more bicycles than other vehicles and cars were either mostly old Eastern European or Japanese imported models.

Today, living standards and expectations have increased dramatically, and the majority of people appear to be much better off. However, there are still occasional signs of poverty. Something we only noticed towards the end of our stay in Hanoi, perhaps because the weather was warmer, were small numbers of homeless people sleeping under overpasses. There were some other groups who clearly found it hard to make ends meet.

One day, I was riding in a taxi and, rarely, the driver spoke good English. I'd lived in Hanoi for around seven months and he was only the third driver I had met who spoke reasonable English. We had stopped to let through an elderly woman carrying a heavy load in two baskets balanced on each end of a pole across her shoulders. She represented a common image of women in other rural parts of northern Asia, carrying such loads and wearing a conical hat on her head.

The taxi driver mentioned there were many women, like her, who came in from the countryside with their produce as they were having trouble making a living in their local areas. Their loads often weighed 30-40kg. The driver said these women hoped to earn more money in the city than they could at home, but a problem was the women were not used to life in the city and could not adjust to the city hustle and bustle; they didn't know how to cross busy streets.

There continued to be a lot of building activity going on around Hanoi; a sign that landowners were prospering. However, on many of the building sites, the labourers lived in makeshift housing and fairly basic conditions. What struck me in particular was the number of women, many quite gaunt and frail-looking, undertaking heavy manual labour. Often it was a woman shovelling the gravel into the wheelbarrow or operating the pulley to raise a load of bricks. The working conditions were basic, as was the manner of construction. I was sure the people working on these sites received small wages, despite the hardship of their job.

After finishing our assignment in Vietnam, I continued to visit at least three times per year to monitor ACCF projects. In this time, I had come to characterise Hanoi as being in a constant state of destruction, construction or reconstruction. There seemed to be little sentimentality about knocking an old family home down. New boutique hotels and restaurants were mushrooming all over the city.

Something that would have been unthinkable in 1983 was that you now saw the occasional beggar around Hanoi. A couple of old men regularly used to show up outside the church we went to, seeking money in their upturned hats. Occasionally you ran into beggars in the Old Quarter, an area frequented by many foreign tourists.

More often in the Old Quarter, however, you were approached by touts selling photocopied books, T-shirts, cigarette lighters and the like. Most of the booksellers seemed to be students trying to supplement their income.

While some of these touts were quite persistent, they would generally accept 'no' for an answer. The same could not be said for the shoeshine boys. I suppose these boys should have been given credit for trying to do something productive to earn money and not sitting around idly, however, some of them were persistent to the extent of being annoying. They would even grab hold of your arm.

I had only encountered such behaviour in India before and never elsewhere in Southeast Asia. I did not appreciate my arm being held or being told I needed my shoes shined, even when I had just shined them myself or I was wearing shoes that would be damaged if they were polished.

Once, I was wearing a new pair of shoes, and the boy claimed there was a slit in my shoe. I had been standing at a traffic light waiting to cross the road. When I looked, sure enough there was a slit. I am sure the boy had slashed my shoe with a knife while I was watching the traffic to cross the road. Obviously, my shoe had to be stitched, and reluctantly I agreed to have it done. His stitching job was quite neat and it was cheaper than buying a new pair of shoes, but I let the boy know I wasn't happy and suspected him of cutting the shoe in the first place.

Economic data is not accurately reported in Vietnam, and I did not know what the true figure for unemployment was or the real rate of inflation. The CIA World Factbook was the only source I found that provided reasonably current estimates for both unemployment and inflation. Its estimates for 2010 for unemployment were 2.9%, and for inflation 11.8%.

While we lived in Hanoi, I saw press articles expressing concern about the need to keep inflation under control, but the articles studiously avoided referring to what the current rate of inflation was. One article referred to the need to keep inflation within the range of 15-17%. This still being quite high. During our time in Hanoi, we noticed an increase in many prices. Such price increases would clearly affect those groups who were struggling to make ends meet.

On unemployment, similarly I'm sure there is more unemployment than is acknowledged. What is clearly visible, is that there is a high level of under-employment. At almost every street corner, there were men, and the occasional woman, sitting around on their motorbikes offering their services as a motorbike taxi. I know they did pick up the occasional passenger each day, but much of the time they sat around chatting or drinking tea.

I walked past many shops and observed the staff also sitting around reading, smoking or drinking tea. There were many improvised streetside tea stalls and, again, I would see people sitting around for hours just chatting. Perhaps the most institutionalised sign of under-employment were the large numbers of men at almost any time of day sitting around drinking beer and eating light snacks at one of the many

Bia Hoi Hanoi shops. What was worrying were the number of men who having had their fill of beer, got unsteadily on their motorbikes to tackle the Hanoi traffic.

Reflections on Modernised Hanoi

For the majority of people, modern Hanoi is a vastly different place to what it was in 1983. Hanoi, like other modern cities around the world, has all the latest perks of consumerism. However, I have seldom encountered such ostentatious displays of wealth and consumerism elsewhere.

Particularly around Hoan Kiem and the Old Quarter, there were many fashionable shops and boutiques. Many shops offered real brand name ware or products from the top manufacturers and fashion houses of Europe, Japan and America. Many of the Vietnamese women sought to dress very fashionably, and I'm sure it was mainly them, rather than tourists, who visited these shops.

That said, alongside the shops selling the genuine articles, there were others selling imitations or perhaps in some cases production overruns or seconds from the factories licensed to produce such goods. Many girls and women who could not afford the genuine article, no doubt kept up with the fashions by going to these shops.

It was quite obvious that there was a lot of money in circulation and the Vietnamese were as much into consumerism as their counterparts in many other parts of the world.

I used to go to the branch of the ANZ Bank in Le Thay Tho Street, where I had my bank account. One afternoon when the bank was particularly busy, I watched several customers withdraw massive amounts of *dong*.

I recall one woman who was dressed in very modern fashion, wearing an expensive-looking watch and jewellery and had brought her own security guard. She had brought a briefcase, and it was filled completely with 500,000 *dong* (about US$25) notes. I had never before seen briefcases filled with money like this, except in the Hollywood movies. Admittedly, a briefcase full of US dollars would be worth more than one filled with *dong*. However, even in *dong*, there would have been several thousand dollars' worth, at least, inside.

Barely had the woman finished, a man accompanied by a woman, similarly withdrew large amounts of money. His briefcase was not big enough to fit it all in, so he and the woman stuffed equally large amounts of *dong* into shopping bags.

These two incidents drove home to me several lessons about Vietnamese society. While the money they were withdrawing may have been simply to pay staff salaries, it showed that Vietnam remained a largely cash dependent economy, and up to and during our stay in Hanoi in 2013, cheques or credit cards were not yet a preferred method of payment. However, on more recent visits, I noticed increasing acceptance of credit cards and people paying at the supermarket with bank debit cards. It also showed that Vietnam was a safe enough society that people could feel comfortable going out into the street with such large amounts of money, however, it did reinforce my impression about the amount of cash in circulation, much of it being used to support the consumer economy.

The growth in wealth among certain sectors of the Vietnamese economy and the increasingly ostentatious display of such wealth, was manifested in other ways. I have never been anywhere else where you would see so many luxury cars on the streets. Every day, I saw Bentleys, Rolls Royces, Porsches and Lexus cars, as well as, slightly less frequently, Ferraris and the occasional Lamborghini. Mercedes and BMWs were common but seemed did not have quite the same brand appeal.

In Hong Kong, I was used to seeing a lot of Rolls Royces. Some were owned by wealthy local businessmen, but I think the majority belonged to the Peninsula Hotel Group. In Sydney, I have seen many Porsches and the occasional Ferrari. However, neither came close to matching Hanoi. Even in Ho Chi Minh City, the main commercial centre in Vietnam, I didn't see such an abundance of luxury cars.

I asked some expatriates, who have had longer experience of Vietnam, about this. Their response was invariably that there was a link to corruption. They pointed out that one of the most lucrative avenues for official corruption, was government contracts, and notably, most of the senior government officials are located in Hanoi.

I might also say that, with one exception, I have not yet directly encountered corruption in Hanoi and hope this continues to be the case. The exception related to taxis. When I came to Hanoi in 2004, I was literally taken for a ride by a local taxi driver.

As I exited the airport, there were no clear signs as to where the taxi rank was located and no metered taxis in sight. A man approached, showing me ID, claiming he worked with the Vietnam tourism authorities and assisted me into a 'so-called' taxi.

I first realised something was amiss when the driver stopped at a cubicle before the toll gates and said I had to pay a toll fare. I cannot remember the exact amount, but it was quite expensive, maybe the equivalent of US$20-30. The next clear sign something was wrong was that he dropped me off at a hotel that was not the one on my pre-paid hotel voucher. At least the hotel staff were honest and helped me get a taxi to my actual hotel, but this was an additional fare I had to pay.

This scam must have been so common that there are large warning notices now posted in the airport arrival area.

Another common taxi scam related to use of unreliable meters, or meters that have been tampered with. Often, the taxis with such meters were in cars that were in similar colours or had similar names to some of the known reputable companies. This was a common problem in Hanoi, but from our brief visits to Ho Chi Minh City, we found such practice was even more widespread there, and the number of taxis imitating reputable taxi company cars were more numerous.

While there was much talk of corruption, this alone did not explain the wealth in Hanoi, or other parts of Vietnam for that matter. There were undoubtedly rising standards of living. Land was becoming scarcer in the downtown parts of the cities and had obviously become a major source of wealth for the landowners. The growing demand for office space and expatriate standard housing had certainly contributed to the rising land prices and the increasing wealth for the people who owned the land. Additionally, it was clear that many private businesses had been very successful and prospered.

I referred earlier to the English-speaking taxi driver I encountered. He had some other interesting observations on the economy. He said he had worked as a carpenter in Malaysia. The salary was sufficient to be able to buy a car and a house, if he had stayed on in Malaysia, but he missed his family in Hanoi and came back. He said in Hanoi on a similar salary he might be able to buy a car, but he did not think he would ever be able to buy a house, as the cost of land was so expensive.

Along with an improved quality of life, people's aspirations have also changed. Perhaps this was one of the more disappointing aspects

A Diplomatic Life

for me about modern Hanoi.

Changing Behaviour

When I came to Vietnam 1983, we did a Sunday trip out to a number of nearby pagodas. I cannot remember their names, and then, they seemed to be way out in the country. Probably today they are not so isolated. There were several memories about this day trip that have stuck with me, and which seemed to indicate that, compared to today, there have been some fundamental changes in the attitudes of the people.

I recall it was the first pagoda we visited where we encountered a fairly large group of young people out enjoying themselves for the day. The pagoda was surrounded by some grassy hills. About a dozen of the young people came and spoke to our group. Fortunately, we had a couple of Vietnamese speakers with us.

The conversation was not very deep or meaningful – such as where did we come from, what we were doing and the like. They were interested in our cameras as they did not have cameras themselves, and asked if we could take their photos. There was a lot of genuine friendly laughter, and they asked if we could send copies of the photos to them, giving us a couple of addresses. I promised to do so and did, in fact, post some photos to one of the given addresses. I hope they received them, but I never received an acknowledgement.

However, what really touched me was that as we were about to leave, one of the girls who seemed to be one of the leaders of the group disappeared. The others told us to wait awhile. When the girl returned, she presented me with two small plastic items which she had obviously just bought from a local souvenir store. It was an unexpected, but very nice gesture and probably represented quite an expense for the girl.

At another pagoda, we came across lots of families and groups of young people picnicking in the pagoda grounds. There was one group of young men in one section of the grounds who were trying to shoot birds with air-rifles. This was not a past-time I condone, but they were not annoying other people and obviously enjoying themselves. Thankfully, they also seemed to be lousy shots.

When they saw us, one of the young men came to us and asked the then Australian ambassador, John McCarthy, who was with us, if he would like to have a shot. John willingly agreed. Again, thankfully he was a lousy shot.

Perhaps having seen us with our picnic baskets, a group of Buddhist monks approached us and invited us to have our picnic lunch inside the monastery, as they were concerned we might not be left in peace to enjoy our lunch if we tried to eat outside. They implied curious people would come to see what we were eating and may pester us to give them some.

We accepted the monks' invitation and went inside the monastery. I remember sitting in a cosy courtyard at a long wooden table. As we ate, a couple of the monks and some visiting Buddhist nuns came to talk to us. We shared some of our food with them.

As at the previous pagoda, they were interested in our cameras and asked if we could take their photos. They too asked if we could send them copies. I know they did receive the photos I sent them. They were delivered by one of the staff in our embassy.

What was memorable about these experiences was that there was an innocence, as well as a genuine openness and friendliness, among the three different groups we met. Most of them were probably quite poor, but they seemed to find pleasure in enjoying simple things. For me, these unrestrained contacts helped make our day even more interesting and enjoyable.

In contrast, in the Hanoi of today, this innocence seems to have been lost, as has too, to a large extent, the spontaneous friendliness. People seem more pressured and more driven. They have grander expectations. They are certainly much more consumerist. In this respect, the modern Hanoian is probably not much different from people in many other parts of the world, however, for me this was a step backwards from what I experienced in 1983.

Despite these overall impressions, I feel privileged that I was able to make some very good, and lasting, friendships with a number of Vietnamese people, especially through my role supporting the Australian Cervical Cancer Foundation in Vietnam. I remain in touch with a group of such people, and we continue get-togethers via email or Zoom meetings, and I looked forward to catching up with them whenever I visit Vietnam.

Accompanying the increasing consumerist trends have been unwelcome signs of blatant greed. We had experienced quite a number of shops or businesses that seemed more interested in making money than offering good customer service. This prompted me to walk out of a number of shops where I sensed they were only interested in making a quick, or big sale, and not trying to help. At least two of the shops I visited when looking for a television set fell into this category.

The most extreme case I've heard of involved an Australian colleague. She was trying to get a replacement for an electrical appliance that did not work. The shopkeeper got out a new appliance, but she saw him attempt a sleight of hand and put the malfunctioning appliance back into the new box.

When the shopkeeper refused to provide a new appliance, my colleague went to the local police and showed the receipt. The police rang the shopkeeper and told him he had to provide a working replacement.

Despite this, when she went back to the shop, the shopkeeper continued to refuse to replace the appliance. Rather, he became aggressive and grabbed her shoulder bag and started pulling her. He badly bruised her arm and shoulder. He pushed her into the shop roller door and then punched her in the face. She needed medical treatment for a bad cut above her lip.

My colleague then went back to the police, and they brought the shopkeeper into the police station for questioning. The upshot was that the shopkeeper was required to reimburse the cost of the appliance, pay medical expenses and pay a fine of 1.5 million dong for assaulting a foreigner. I think the shopkeeper got off lightly. In Australia, he would have been charged with assault causing actual bodily harm and could well have been looking at a jail term.

While we had a couple of unpleasant experiences in Hanoi, our worst experience was in Ho Chi Minh City. We had gone to the night market at Ben Thanh Market looking for some T-shirts to take back as souvenirs to Manila. The first stall we went to seemed expensive, but it also did not have the sizes or colours we were looking for.

The woman stall owner became very abusive when Odette refused to buy something that we didn't want, calling Odette all sorts of names. Ignoring our statements that she did not have what we wanted, she claimed we had an obligation to buy something, as we were the first potential customers in her stall that night. The worst, however, was that the woman then physically tried to prevent Odette leaving the stall unless she bought something. Unfortunately, there were no police readily at hand for us to turn to for help.

By the way, a few stalls down the road, we found one with a much better selection of sizes and colours, better quality and much cheaper prices. We were happy to buy there.

Both these specific incidents indicated that commercial greed, rather than customer service, prevailed. This was a most concerning trend. If there was a wish to encourage greater tourism to Vietnam, it would be important to try and stamp out such practices.

Maybe Hanoi, and Vietnam more generally, should follow the lead of the Hong Kong Tourism Association (HKTA) about forty or more years ago, in response to tourist complaints about exploitative or dishonest shopkeepers. The HKTA developed a system of certifying shops that proved they met established standards and provided good service to tourists. If certified, shops could display prominently the HKTA certification and put a HKTA logo outside the shop. This helped provide tourists with greater assurance and protection.

Food

Finishing my impressions of Hanoi on a more positive note, the changes in the food availability, both in the markets and in restaurants, has improved dramatically. Hanoi now has some excellent world-class restaurants and an uncountable range of choices.

In 1983 there were not very many restaurants clearly identifiable, and there were very few considered suitable for foreigners for health reasons. In fact, during my visit to Hanoi, we were told there were only four restaurants considered suitable for foreigners. We checked them all out.

I recall there was one restaurant that specialised in pigeon and another in crab farcie (basically crab meat baked in its shell with cream and breadcrumbs). Both of these were quite reasonable. Another restaurant specialised in steak. I don't know how this restaurant got on the list. The steak was so tough, the toilet was crawling with maggots and the kitchen did not look much cleaner. I can't remember the fourth restaurant.

Our visit to the main market in Hanoi was also an eye-opener. I think it was probably Dong Xuan market that we visited. I know that Dong Xuan is the oldest market in Hanoi. What I do recall is that the meat on display did not look particularly healthy or appetising. Compared with the Hanoi markets of today, I remember there was certainly a much smaller array of fresh seafood, fruit and vegetables.

Fast-forward to today and what a contrast! The range and availability of Vietnamese food is enormous. Many fine dining restaurants have been established in beautiful old mansions. To date I have only had the pleasure of visiting a small selection of such restaurants, which offer a nice ambience and a good selection of food choices, as well as good-quality and tasty food. Obviously, you have to pay more for dining in such places. However, I understand there are even grander places as well as ones that are setting new dining trends and developing a modern Vietnamese cuisine.

There is a second tier of good-quality restaurants serving Vietnamese food. Some of them are also located in old mansions, some in new purpose-built buildings and one, in particular, I am aware of that has converted an old temple into an attractive courtyard restaurant. There are also a number of places set up with stalls offering street-style food but cooked under more hygienic conditions, offering the diner a more pleasant dining atmosphere. The food in these places is often just as tasty and usually considerably cheaper.

There is a third tier of restaurants that offer Vietnamese food at cheaper prices, directed more at the backpacker tourist. They tend to offer more comfort and, certainly in many places, more hygienic food than many street stalls. The Pho 24 chain was previously a case in point.

Finally, there are the street stalls. Some of them do look reasonably hygienic and seem very popular. However, there are many others where I have seen foreign tourists eating that worry me. There are some, I have seen, where you can look into the kitchen or cooking area and they don't provide much confidence about their hygiene and cleanliness standards.

A Diplomatic Life

I am used to eating street stall food in Malaysia, but what distinguishes the Malaysian street stalls, for the most part from those in Hanoi, is that you are segregated from the direct fumes of passing traffic. The closeness to passing traffic is one thing that has generally deterred me from sampling food at some of the better-looking street stalls.

As to the food in Hanoi itself, one thing both Odette and I really liked was the availability of different types of vegetables and fresh herbs. I have enjoyed sampling many of the different types of salads available in Vietnamese menus.

In Manila, you need to be very careful about eating fresh salads. However, in Hanoi, it is such an integral part of everyday dining, and there are so many hygienic-looking places around, that we have enjoyed many wonderful salads. Pomelo, green mango and banana heart salads are amongst my favourites.

Other favourites are the *nem,* or spring rolls, or the various types of wraps either in rice paper or fresh vegetable leaves. Whether you have the *nem* fried or fresh, the variety of fillings provide you with many tasty and interesting surprises.

Of course, there are the *pho* restaurants which are typical of Hanoi cuisine. A good *pho bo* (beef noodle soup) is determined by the quality and flavour of the soup. A good soup usually takes up to eight hours to prepare and needs to be clear of sediment when served.

Bun cha, which is a grilled pork dish served with rice vermicelli, herbs and a soup which acts as a dipping sauce, is another favourite Hanoi speciality.

There are many other wonderful and more complicated or sophisticated dishes available. I have enjoyed the subtle use of tamarind and lemon grass in a number of seafood or poultry dishes.

I was pleasantly surprised when we went to a restaurant serving food from the Hue region of Vietnam, and how different the food was in terms of taste and presentation, but also very enjoyable. We have sampled a few other regional specialities and, hopefully, we'll get the chance to travel more in Vietnam and try more.

Generally, the variety of dishes and the freshness of the ingredients made eating out a major pleasure for Odette and me, during our stay in Vietnam.

In Australia, there is no doubt that the growth of Vietnamese restaurants has broadened our dining choices and enriched our dining experiences. However, while there are some very good Vietnamese restaurants in Australia, coming to Hanoi has shown me how limited Australian choices are. We can only obtain a small and selective sampling. You really have to go to Vietnam to enjoy the best Vietnamese food.

Compared with 1983, the Vietnamese food scene has clearly blossomed. Back then, you would have been certified crazy if you had sought to eat the sort of salads and fresh rice paper wraps that are now readily available. Either the ingredients would not have been available, or the hygiene practices would have left very much to be desired.

However, it is not just the availability of Vietnamese food that has shown remarkable progress, but the availability of good quality Thai, Japanese and western food. There are also other international restaurants offering Middle Eastern, Indian, Korean or other foreign cuisines. Certainly, the availability of such restaurants in 1983 would have been unthinkable, apart from the small number of French-inspired dishes on offer.

Apart from the incredible range of fresh produce in the Hanoi markets of today, with so many different varieties of fresh fruit and vegetables, seafood, meat and dried goods for sale, but there has also been a growth in specialist bakeries, delicatessens, butcheries and other specialised food shops. There are numerous shops specialising in Japanese groceries and, much to my delight, I have also found one shop specialising in Thai ingredients.

While the physical changes in the appearance of Hanoi since my first visit have been dramatic, it is perhaps in the food scene where I have seen some of the most dramatic and pleasing changes. I look forward to continuing my culinary adventures during further visits, as well as broadening my knowledge and experience of Vietnam in more areas outside Hanoi.

A Sense of Place – Moving Back to Manila from Yangon

We returned to our current apartment in November 2016. Our apartment is located along Roxas Boulevard in Malate and has a long verandah overlooking Manila Bay. Odette and I often enjoy sitting out on the verandah with a glass of red wine, while we admire the fantastic sunsets that are a regular feature over Manila Bay.

We had been away almost six years. In that time, our apartment had been rented out to four different tenants. Settling back into our apartment and life in Manila, however, proved quite a challenge.

Despite providing notes that advised if there were any basic problems, such as blocked drains or electrical faults, they could seek the assistance of the engineering team maintained by the condominium office, the tenants obviously had not done so. We were therefore appalled to return to the mess that confronted us.

Some of the problems we encountered would not have been as bad if they had been attended to when they first occurred. It took us the best part of six months to get everything properly repaired. However, now we are happy with our apartment and its location, although I still have trouble coming to grips with Manila traffic.

Immediately prior to returning to Manila, we had spent just over three years living in Yangon. We enjoyed our time in Myanmar and departed with many happy memories.

However, settling into life in Yangon presented many challenges at first. Many simple things we take for granted in other countries were not readily available in Yangon.

As a private individual, I could not open a bank account. Because the Myanmar Military-controlled government had twice, in the not-so-distant past, demonetised the currency, local people had been reluctant to put their money into banks.

At the time we arrived in Yangon, banks were only just starting to regain public trust and become an established part of daily life. By the time we left Myanmar, there had been a profusion of new banks opening, and licences had been granted for a limited number of foreign banks to establish representative offices and support financing for commercial activities. However, I still could not open an account.

Telephone use was problematic. Theoretically foreigners could not purchase SIM cards. At the time we arrived, a limited number of SIM cards were allotted through a lottery system to local people. Some people obtained multiple SIM cards and would place the spare ones on the open market. This was how Odette and I obtained our SIM cards, at the bargain price of about US$150. As attested by our next-door neighbour, this was cheap, as a year or so earlier she had paid US$3,000 for her SIM card.

Even with a SIM card, phone and internet services were unreliable and expensive. Both were under the control of the Ministry of Posts and Telecommunications.

Our apartment was supposedly wired for a landline phone. Although several times phone company representatives came to check the phone connection, they were unable to get it to function.

Fortunately, these problems began to lessen within six months of our arrival following the approval of telecommunication licences for the Qatari company Ooredoo and the Norwegian company Telenor. As these two companies built more communications towers throughout the country and expanded their networks, services became more readily available, efficient and, importantly, cheaper. The Government Ministry also linked up with the Japanese firm KDD and their services also became more competitive. Often SIM cards were given out freely, but even if you had to purchase one, it was likely to cost about US$1.

As Myanmar gradually began to open up to the outside world shortly before and after our arrival in mid-2013, we were conscious of more foreign businesses and international organisations wishing to set up in Myanmar. This had a number of positive effects. There was a wider availability of food products, and more and more restaurants began to open. It also sparked a construction boom, as new shopping complexes, hotels and apartments were built.

On the other hand, it also had a major negative impact. Decent quality and affordable housing became more hotly contested. When we arrived the standard expression for accommodation was, 'Manhattan prices, but not Manhattan quality.' We ended up finding a 'reasonable' apartment in a convenient location for just under US$2,000 per month. Our apartment was a decent size by Yangon standards, but we had plumbing problems and, like the rest of the city, had to put up with frequent extended power disruptions.

Towards the end of our stay in Yangon, there was a minor downwards adjustment in rental prices, as more properties became available. Our landlord slightly reduced our rental for our last year in Yangon.

The biggest issue for us in Myanmar remained money. Myanmar continued to insist on mint condition US bank notes, and in return we often received grotty Kyat notes in exchange.

Thanks to ongoing US sanctions, there were limits and controls on currency transactions. For much of our time in Myanmar, the amount of US dollars you could bring into the country was fixed at US$10,000, although when we first arrived it was US$5,000. As we were required to pay rent one year in advance, this meant at least two trips back to Australia to purchase mint condition US dollars. The Philippines government only provided three months rental advance to Odette. As she received these payments, she would reimburse me.

I had tried to purchase mint condition notes in the Philippines. It was difficult to obtain more than US$1,000 at a time. One officer at the ANZ Bank in Makati told me that each bank in the Philippines would check US dollars as they received them, to ensure the notes were genuine, and then put their own mark on them, usually a bank stamp. She said she heard of one bank that used a Hello Kitty stamp. Definitely unacceptable in Myanmar! In fact, anything other than an erasable pencil marking on a note was unacceptable.

However, the money difficulties did not stop there. One other issue I encountered was when I tried to purchase air tickets for family in the Philippines to come and visit. The tickets were being purchased for travel on Singapore Airlines through a Manila-based and Philippine-operated travel agent. However, because the documentation referred to Yangon as the travel destination, my attempt to transfer funds to the travel agent in Manila was rejected. When I checked with the bank in Australia, I was advised that all international transactions in US dollars were vetted in New York and, because of US sanctions, would be disallowed. I thought this ridiculous, as none of the money would have been going to Myanmar, but rather to Manila and Singapore.

Money transactions did not show any improvement during our time in Yangon. I believe US sanctions on financial transactions remain in place, although some relaxation has been allowed for commercial transactions not in violation of other sanctions. For example, trade in rubies and jade remain prohibited into the United States, as they are linked to the Myanmar military.

Despite the challenges of life in Yangon, we enjoyed our stay. We made many good friends. Yangon is a safe city with a low crime rate and foreigners are very seldom targeted. Apart from poor lighting and potholes in the pavements, it was otherwise a safe city for walking at night.

We sampled many local dishes. I enjoyed goat curries and tea-leaf salads. We had a particularly tasty fish noodle dish which was a specialty in Myeik. Mohinga, which is often referred to as the national dish, I sometimes enjoyed, but often found it quite bland and uninteresting. I certainly never acclimatised to the taste and smell of fermented bamboo, which I seemed to encounter almost everywhere.

We enjoyed the chance to travel widely and learn more about Myanmar's unique and rich history and culture. The golden and bejeweled Shwedagon Pagoda in Yangon was spectacular, no matter how often we saw it. Bagan, an ancient centre of Burmese civilization, was a magical and inspiring place where the landscape was dotted with several thousand centuries-old temples and pagodas. Viewing sunset along the banks of the Ayeryarwady River (formerly Irrawaddy) against the backdrop of the silhouettes of the temples and pagodas was truly memorable. However, places like Myitkina, Dawei, Mawlamine and Hpa'an were all impressive for their scenery or historic buildings.

We also happened to be in Myanmar at a politically and historically interesting time. We witnessed the first free general elections in over fifty years, which saw Aung San Suu Kyi obtain a majority of votes, but still subject to a parliament controlled by the military. Immediately after the elections, there was a strong mood of optimism that change was on the way. However, given the military's controlling stake in parliament, the hoped-for atmosphere for change did not materialise.

Even when we were leaving Yangon, we had still been hopeful, but now viewed from afar in Manila, the lack of progress is sad and disappointing. I believe the people of Myanmar deserve much better, as they have been subjected to years of military rule.

During our stay in Yangon from late July 2013 to November 2016, Odette and I were present for the short-lived halcyon days when there was some attempt at relaxation of restrictions, promotion of major construction projects and an opening up to some extent of the economy. There still remained problems – the military still had a controlling share of parliamentary seats; and there were continuing ethnic tensions throughout the country.

The repressive nature of the 2021 military coup provided fertile ground for strong-man tactics. Aung San Suu Kyi was arrested and if the political situation remains unchanged, I believe, could see her in prison for the rest of her life. Thousands of opponents of military rule were killed, injured, arrested or locked up in jail. Among these were the Australian academic Sean Turnell, whose crime was seeking to advise Aung San Suu Kyi on ways to strengthen the economy, but which translated to breaches of official secrets. Fortunately, he has now been released, but he spent almost two years in prison.

It saddens me that a majority of Myanmar people continue to suffer under tight military rule. I sincerely hope there might be some positive changes in the future.

A final reason for my pessimism about the future is that one day I was talking to Odette's colleague at the Indian embassy, and it occurred to me as we talked that 'Myanmar' is an anagram for 'Armyman'. Thus, as long as the country continues to be Myanmar, it is likely to be dominated by the military. In part, this seems enshrined in the constitution, which provides that at least 25% of seats are reserved for the army, yet at least 75% support is required to make substantive legislative changes.

As we were able to see in our travels, Myanmar is a beautiful country. It has a unique and interesting culture and history, which we were impressed to see and learn about. Being a predominantly Buddhist country, the people are largely kind, friendly and generous, mostly interested in living peaceful and productive lives.

And Finally ...

At the end of November 2020, Odette and I moved to Melbourne, as Odette was taking up the position of Philippines Consul General to Melbourne.

For my part, I have continued my volunteer involvement with the Australian Cervical Cancer Foundation and continue to hope I can contribute to achieving the elimination of cervical cancer by at least 2035, as presently planned. This should be achievable if we can continue to encourage women to be screened regularly and to ensure the continuation by the Australian government of the school-based HPV vaccination program. Working to support these objectives will be a major priority for me.

After retiring from DFAT, this helps affirm my view that it's possible to do something useful in life after a lengthy and largely fulfilling career.

www.ingramcontent.com/pod-product-compliance
Lightning Source LLC
Chambersburg PA
CBHW030542080526
44585CB00012B/232